World Religions and World Community

LECTURES ON THE HISTORY OF RELIGIONS
SPONSORED BY THE
AMERICAN COUNCIL OF LEARNED SOCIETIES
NEW SERIES, NUMBER SIX

World Religions
and World Community

by ROBERT LAWSON SLATER

New York and London 1963

COLUMBIA UNIVERSITY PRESS

COPYRIGHT © 1963 BY COLUMBIA UNIVERSITY PRESS
LIBRARY OF CONGRESS CATALOG CARD NUMBER: 63-9805
MANUFACTURED IN THE UNITED STATES OF AMERICA

In Memory of C. F. ANDREWS

THIS VOLUME is the sixth to be published in the series of Lectures on the History of Religions for which the American Council of Learned Societies, through its Committee on the History of Religions, assumed responsibility in 1936.

Under the program the Committee from time to time enlists the services of scholars to lecture in colleges, universities, and seminaries on topics in need of expert elucidation. Subsequently, when possible and appropriate, the Committee arranges for the publication of the lectures. Other volumes in the series are Martin P. Nilsson, *Greek Popular Religion* (1940), Henri Frankfort, *Ancient Egyptian Religion* (1948), Wing-tsit Chan, *Religious Trends in Modern China* (1953), Joachim Wach, *The Comparative Study of Religions*, edited by Joseph M. Kitagawa (1958), and R. M. Grant, *Gnosticism and Early Christianity* (1959).

Contents

Acknowledgments

THE NATURE of my subject extends the list of my acknowledgments. No writer on religions in general can pretend a special knowledge of every part of the wide field with which he deals and his dependence on others is perhaps even greater if he is dealing with living religions and contemporary situations. What is more, there is ground for the view expressed by my former colleague at McGill University, Professor Wilfred Cantwell Smith, that at this time of day any statements about religions other than one's own should be submitted to critics who themselves profess adherence to the religion in question. In these respects I have been especially privileged.

First there was the opportunity provided by the invitation of the American Council of Learned Societies through its Committee on the History of Religions and its chairman, Professor Erwin Goodenough, to give the lectures which are here presented in book form. One of the attractive features of the invitation was that it meant visiting other universities and discussing questions raised in the lectures with colleagues in the field of the History of Religions: Professors Mircea Eliade, Joseph M. Kitagawa, Philip Ashby, Norvin Hein, Richard Gard. To my friend and esteemed mentor, Professor Horace Friess, I am especially grateful. It was his advice which led me to develop the particular theme of *World Religions and World Community* when it came to preparing the lectures for publication. (The original title was *Unity and Diversity in Reli-*

gion.) To all my hosts at Chicago, Columbia, Princeton, Yale, and Wellesley I am indeed grateful not only for their most kind hospitality but for some very helpful comments.

Next there was the fact that when it came to the revision of the lectures for publication I was resident Director of Harvard's new Center for the Study of World Religions. This meant a very special opportunity indeed to discuss my chapters with visiting and resident scholars representative of various religions and countries. When Dr. Radhakrishnan, now President of India, gave his inaugural lecture at the opening of the Center he observed that its function might be related to the need to convert a world which is now a "neighborhood bound by political ties and economic arrangements" into a world community, since one of the things needed for such community was a better understanding of the religious standpoint of the different peoples. My book has been written with this aim in mind and I think that those connected with the Center who have so generously helped me by their comments and corrections have viewed it in that light. I am particularly grateful to the following for their advice:

On Hinduism: Professor T. R. V. Murti, Banaras Hindu University; Professor A. N. Pandeya, Delhi University; Professor T. K. Venkateswaran, Presidency College, Madras; Dr. S. C. Roy, New York.

On Buddhism: The Venerable U Thittila, Burma; Professor Fumio Masutani, Japan; Sao Htun Hmat Win, Burma; Bhikkhu Vinita, Ceylon; Dr. Clarence H. Hamilton, Oberlin College; and my colleague, Professor M. Nagatomi.

On Islam: Dr. Mohammad Anas, Afghanistan; Professor D. R. al Faruqi, Karachi; Professor Wilfred Cantwell Smith; Professor Seyyed Hossein Nasr, Tehran; and Dr. Kenneth Cragg.

If I have any understanding of contemporary Judaism, this is largely due to my friend Rabbi Harry Stern of Temple

Emmanu-el Montreal and the very helpful comments of Professor Emilio Goldschmidt, University of Chile, and Mr. Charles Krahmalkov.

For comments and criticism of the book in general I am very greatly indebted to the friend and teacher who first introduced me to this study of religions, Dr. A. C. Bouquet, Cambridge University, England; to Professor R. B. Y. Scott, Princeton University; to Mr. Peter Pardue, and to my son, the Reverend C. P. R. L. Slater, who has not spared the rod of filial criticism.

It is, I know, already a long list, but I should be singularly ungrateful if I did not express how much I owe to those who have helped so loyally with the preparation of the manuscript: Miss Joyce Heissenbutel, Mrs. Richard W. Swanson, Mrs. Peter F. Krogh, and Mr. and Mrs. David Miller. Nor must I fail to express my gratitude to the Director and staff of the Columbia University Press and, in particular, to Miss Elisabeth L. Shoemaker for her most valuable editorial assistance.

As to my wife, without her help there would have been neither ending nor beginning of this book, and I think that perhaps my best thanks to her would be to promise never to write another book.

ROBERT LAWSON SLATER

Center for the Study of World Religions
Harvard Divinity School
Harvard University
December, 1962

World Religions and World Community

CHAPTER I

Religious Diversity and World Community

A PRIMARY REASON for selecting this subject of unity and diversity in religion is that I am a member of the human race and jealous of my membership. As such I share the present concern for the survival of the race. At the same time, together with a good many others, I see new prospects of world community which offer hope of something more than survival.[1] In this situation what are significantly called the forces of religion—forces manifestly resurgent today—cannot be ignored. Here, however, we encounter two opposite opinions. There are those who look to religion, dynamic, unifying, drawing men together, holding them together, for a contribution, an indispensable contribution, towards the making of world community. Others demur. If anything, they see the forces of religion standing in the way of such community as they observe how frequently religion has spelt diversity pressed to the point of division. In either view, need may be seen for some survey of the present religious situation which looks beyond the more familiar Western scene, takes account of new developments in religious life and thought in various parts of this changing modern world, and poses some new questions prompted by contemporary studies and discussion. Such is the nature and purpose of the survey attempted in these chapters.

Interest in the subject of unity and diversity in religion is of course no new thing. Nor is it an interest solely related to world community. It pertains to almost any study of religion and to almost any practice of religion. It was central in the minds of Max Müller and others when they advocated the comparative study of religions some ninety years ago.[2] As they saw it, it was a study which would demonstrate a basic unity in the world of religions behind all appearances of diversity, by exhibiting certain "radical elements" common to all religious traditions and thus promoting the unity of mankind.[3]

But that was ninety years ago. Much has been written on this subject since that day, much that goes to show that the issues presented by the phenomena of unity and diversity are not quite so easily resolved as then appeared. Few, however, would question that there is, if anything, a more urgent interest in these issues, especially when they are seen in relation to prospects of world peace. Along with a growing sense of world community there is a new scrutiny of all that may promote or disturb this sense of community. And religion certainly comes under this scrutiny.

A striking testimony to both this sense of world community and the new scrutiny it involves is contained in a comment by Dr. Paul Devanandan on what is happening in contemporary India. Hindus today, he remarks, are undoubtedly "self-conscious"; they are "strangely alive as Hindus." Together with the new nationalism, there is a new affirmation of distinctively Hindu culture. At the same time it is also recognized that all such respect for local interests—national, cultural, religious—comes "under judgment of the desire for world unity [which is] characteristic of the modern temper." This is true not only of India, but of Asia generally. "There is a widespread interest in the felt need for realizing a true sense of human solidarity so that the basic unity of the world of nations may not be jeopardized by unnecessary conflicts." [4]

Religion comes under this judgment because its role in respect to political solidarity is manifestly ambiguous. Thus national leaders in India are said to be of two minds about resurgent Hinduism. They are both thankful for it and wary of it; thankful because the recovery of faith meant the dynamic required for the nationalist movement; wary of it because certain expressions of Hinduism may mean evils like the murder of Mahatma Gandhi. It depends on *what* is reanimated in the variegated pattern of Hinduism—the temper, tolerant and comprehensive, manifest in the *Bhagavad Gita* or the divisive spirit promoted by communal, sectarian Hinduism. In short, Hinduism is seen as both a unifying and a divisive power and its possible contribution to national community is estimated accordingly.

Much the same may be said of attitudes taken by political leaders towards religion the world over. For it is not only in Hindu India that what are significantly called "the forces of religion" are very much in evidence. Besides resurgent Hinduism there is resurgent Buddhism. Nor is it only Hindus and Buddhists who are "strangely alive" [5] today. The faith of Islam is still a missionary faith, notably in Africa; Judaism is still amazingly resilient, and there are more signs of new purpose and resolution in the Christian world than are sometimes recognized.

In the face of this situation it is not surprising that statesmen and others concerned for world peace are more alert to the role of religion than was perhaps the case a few decades ago. Whatever else may be said about religion, it has meant in the past and still means a dynamic motivation. Time and again, men and women inspired by religious conviction have shown persistence, fortitude and determination beyond what seemed credible. Their faith has moved mountains. It is this same dynamic which many today would enlist in the cause of world community.[6]

Some indeed would go as far as to say that without this support from religion there is little or no hope of world community: "Religious community . . . spins the web of a potential world society." [7] Those who hold this view (greatly encouraged, maybe, by the signs of vitality which they observe in the religious world today) are in the tradition of the Emperor Constantine who, observing in religion that which draws men together and holds them together, made alliance with this power and even sought to control it.

But there are others of contrary opinion. Their tradition is that of the Japanese Emperor Shirakawa who quipped wryly that the only things he could not control were the flow of the Kamo river, the fall of the dice, and the armies of the rival Buddhist sects.[8] For such as these, the spectacle of resurgent religion is cause for dismay rather than encouragement. Religion as they see it is more frequently a disturber of the peace than a means to peace.

Others, perhaps the majority, are torn between these two opinions. They know their history well enough to know that the role of religion in respect to community is indeed ambiguous. If the page of history shows men in the name of religion burning each other's churches, stoning each other's prophets and waging fanatical war, it also presents the Justin Martyrs affirming, in this same name, without fear of contradiction: "We who once . . . hated and destroyed one another and . . . would not share the same hearth with men of another tribe, now, since the coming of Christ, live on intimate terms with them, and pray for our enemies." [9]

Fully aware, then, of this ambiguous history and persuaded that in any case the forces of religion cannot be ignored, a good many may also be persuaded that something more is indicated than sweeping conclusions based on a swift glance at the page of history. If the page of history is to be consulted, time must be taken to read all that is written on that page. Neither the wars of religion nor the concords achieved in the name of religion constitute the full story, a fact which is perhaps more clearly perceived when this history is read backward in the light of what is happening today, and also in the light of new considerations, new directions taken, and new issues which have been raised in the course of modern studies dealing with religion. Need may therefore be seen for fresh inquiry which, allowing at the outset for the ambiguous role of religion, will expect neither too much nor too little from the "forces of religion" in regard to world community.

Instead of impatient political demands that religion should do this or do that or impatient impulses to dismiss religion from view, there may be the more realistic attitude that religion has to be accepted, so to speak, on its own terms, as an undeniable aspect of the human situation with which statesmen and others have to deal. Inquiry may then be directed to ascertaining these terms. There is some evidence that this is how an increasing number of the Constantines and Shirakawas of today are approaching the subject.

As for religious leaders, it is not perhaps claiming too much to say that there are signs of a new conscience in regard to religious differences. There are significant ecumenical movements designed to promote religious unity in both the Christian and the Buddhist world. And an increasing number of religious leaders are sensitive to the criticism that in a world which so urgently needs to be one world it is intolerable that religion should promote the "unnecessary conflicts" to which Dr. Devanandan refers. At the same time they may raise uneasy questions in regard to what may be considered *unnecessary* conflicts.

They may also be critical of a good many popular opinions expressed on this subject, opinions which may be mischievous if they fail to take account of the realities of the religious situation. It is all very well to say, for example, that religious people should "forget their differences" and come together in the interests of world peace. But what if such a forgetting of differences should mean a forgetting of religion itself? What if the dynamic motivation expected from religion cannot be given on such terms? And what, precisely, are the "differences" which should be "forgotten"? What is meant by such a "forgetting"?

Generally speaking, religious leaders the world over are critical of any proposals which seem to ride roughshod over the phenomena of religious diversity. Few among them, for example, are sympathetic to the idea that one world should mean one religion, unless the one religion contemplated is, in some form or other, their own religion. Such an opinion may be suspect. The layman is perhaps disposed to dismiss it as no more than the reflection of a clerical conservatism which is concerned to maintain traditional standpoints and traditional boundaries at all costs. There are indeed stout bastions of such conservatism throughout the religious world today. They constitute one of the realities of the situation which have to be taken into account. It may, however, also be observed (and this is significant) that even among religious conservatives today there are those who are looking beyond traditional boundaries. There is, for example, the Christian bishop, Stephen Neill, whose orthodoxy would be generally regarded as unimpeachable. In one breath he affirms that Christians cannot compromise on their claim that all men everywhere need the Christian Gospel. But in the next breath he affirms that the Christian must not only respect other religions; he must also "expose himself to the full force of these other faiths . . . he must rejoice in everything that they possess of beauty and high aspiration. He must put himself to school with them, in readiness to believe that they may have something to teach him that he has not yet learned." [10]

He points, moreover, to the earnest efforts of other religions today to relate themselves to the needs of men in the modern world. He may have in mind, for example, some Buddhist teachers in southeast Asia, a stronghold of religious conservatism, Buddhist teachers who are very much aware of new horizons. Together with a new resolve to derive a "social ethic" from Buddhist principles, they have, very definitely, a world outlook and a new interest in what other religions have to say. At the same time it is not an interest which leads them to blunt the edge of religious differences. They are, if anything, more "strangely alive" as Buddhists, just as Bishop Stephen Neill is "strangely alive" as a Christian.

Generally speaking indeed, religious leaders, whether conservative or not, are more alert than others to the challenge of religious diversity. They are aware of a zeal for diversity which appears to be as deeply rooted in genuine religious concern as any zeal for unity. In other quarters it is frequently implied that where there is diversity, especially diversity leading to conflict, there is departure not only from religious profession but from genuine religious motivation; that religious differences have no right to be there; that they necessarily betoken something less than true religion. Hence some of the exhortations to believers to "forget" their differences, ignore them, or obliterate them. Zeal for unity, yes. That is what may be expected. Religion means community; it is that which "makes a people," that which draws men together; religion means integration. But zeal which results in the breaking of community or sets a man apart from his fellows, no! There is no genuine religious motivation here, but only that which masquerades in the name of religion: distorted or demonic religion. This view is often advocated.

A good many religious leaders, however, would demur. Such a view, they would say, takes little account of the constrained, reluctant Luthers of history who have cried, "Here stand I; I can no other." Nor does it take sufficient account of the declared conditions of what John Oman once called "honest religion": the demand for freedom from any coercion of faith, freedom for criticism, prophecy and new intellectual adventure, freedom meaning diversity even at the risk of division. Nor again does it allow sufficiently for that tenderness towards religious diversity which may be observed on the Hindu scene. It is nearer the truth to assume that diversity no less than the quest for unity is rooted in religious concern. Religious differences have a right to be there. The resolution of some religious leaders to affirm this right derives from something more than a regard for vested interests.

Turning to the world of scholarship, we find much to support this view. By and large, scholars engaged in the study of world religions take religious differences no less seriously than do religious leaders. Their fundamental emphasis is on the rich diversity of the total, complex pattern of religious life and thought. Whereas pioneers in this field a century ago were convinced that further study would demonstrate the fundamental agreement of apparently dissimilar statements, a good many today are more disposed to draw precisely the opposite conclusion from this same further study: apparently similar statements, they affirm, when interpreted in the light of their own particular contexts, are seen to be essentially dissimilar.[11] Besides this regard for particular contexts, there is a regard for what is special or singular. One example of this modern approach is Dr. Scholem's statement that "there is no such thing as mysticism in the abstract . . . there is no mysticism, as such, there is only the mysticism of a particular religious system, Christian, Islamic, Jewish mysticism, and so on." [12]

Some, indeed, would still maintain that believers the world over have more in common than might at first be evident. Evidence, however, would generally be sought today at other levels than that of intellectual statement. Fuller account is taken of the many and various ways in which men may indicate the faith they live by.

Fuller account is also taken of what may lie beneath the surface of speech and practice. When Max Müller proposed comparative studies in this field a century ago, he was certainly not unaware of the need for something more than a surface view. He reminded his readers that in dealing with religion they were dealing with "the most intimate convictions" lying deep in the very heart of man.[13] But he nevertheless followed the fashion of his age in giving priority to that which came from the conscious mind of man; he emphasized the new knowledge of Oriental texts and "articles of faith" and what he mainly contemplated was a comparative study of basic terms of belief or fundamental ideas. In some quarters today the pendulum has swung so far in the opposite direction that almost everything and anything which have to do with religion *except* these more explicit terms of belief are taken into consideration.

Yet the opinion that the study of religion is principally or solely the study of texts and ideas dies hard. It may, however, be qualified, as we have remarked, by the recognition that these same ideas must first be studied in their own particular contexts. We are then led beyond the literary context to all the life and practice enfolding it. If this means a greater sensitivity to religious differences at the intellectual level, it may also mean the recognition of affinities (as well as differences) at other levels. In brief, the fuller report on the religious situation which comes from the world of scholarship today is a report which leads us to look in more than one direction for that which may hold men apart or draw them together in the realm of religion. It is a report which may persuade statesmen and others concerned for world community, if they need to be persuaded, that they certainly cannot ignore religion. But it may leave them wondering just *what* to expect.

As, then, we approach the survey of different religious traditions which will be pursued in the following chapters we may conceive it as a study which will mean, in the first place, a wider view, a world view, a view which will supplement and perhaps correct impressions formed from our better acquaintance with our own Western situation and the Judaeo-Christian tradition, a view which will take some account of movements of religious life and thought elsewhere which may affect prospects of world community.

But we may also conceive it, in the second place, as a study "in depth," to use a much overworked phrase, a study in which we shall be concerned to observe something of the "depth" of each particular situation. We shall look in various directions for what may influence religious behavior. We shall be concerned not only with religious beliefs and practices but with attitudes towards beliefs and practices, as well as with attitudes towards tradition and community, especially with such attitudes as induce a Yes or a No to proposals for religious cooperation in the interest of world community.

Our inquiry will gather around three great living religions: Hinduism, Buddhism, and Islam. In each case we shall be confronted by a challenging diversity, a diversity most obvious and bewildering in the case of Hinduism, not at first so obvious, perhaps, in the case of Islam, but nevertheless there. We shall note different attitudes taken towards this diversity and different conditions promoting it within each religion. In each case we shall also find an affirmation of unity or a sense of community—Hindu community, Buddhist community, Islamic community—affirmed despite internal differences which may seem to break such community or to come near to breaking it.

Our first concern will be with description, description of what may be seen to make for diversity and what may be seen to make for the sense of community in each particular case. While this description will inevitably involve selection, with emphasis on what we ourselves may consider most significant, it will, we trust, be sufficiently broad and free from prejudice to include evidence from which the reader may draw his own conclusions, conclusions which may differ from those which we may suggest.

The questions considered in each successive chapter will not be quite the same. For as we pass from one scene to another, new, though related, issues will be presented, as each particular tradition is seen to pose, so to speak, its own questions. Thus there will be a gradual build-up of questions, related questions, which are relevant to the discussion of religion and world community, with the earlier questions carried forward as our inquiry proceeds.

We shall begin by remarking opposite attitudes which may be taken towards statements of belief as we observe how the Hindu relativist attitude challenges dogmatic attitudes prevalent in the West. We shall ask what lies behind this Hindu relativism, an inquiry which will call in question some Western views on the subject. In the next chapter it will be seen that while this same relativism is reflected in the Buddhist outlook it is here qualified by what amounts to a confessional allegiance. To be aware of this confessional allegiance, however, is at the same time to take a further step and see the issue of relativism in relation to questions concerning forms and conceptions of religious community.

The theme of community is continued in our next chapter, which deals with Islam. But here again another issue comes into view. Comparison between Buddhist and Islamic forms and conceptions of community leads us to question the sharp line which is sometimes drawn between East and West. Such a line is drawn when Islam is grouped with Judaism and Christianity as a Western religion on grounds which emphasize that in all three there is a confessional allegiance which is said to be lacking in the case of Oriental religion. Our presentation of Buddhism, however, raises new questions here, questions which are enlarged by what may be observed not only in Islam but in Judaism.

What is observed in regard to Islam and Judaism also leads to further inquiry when we come to Christianity. For while the Christian Western world may still be seen by Oriental critics as the home of dogmatism, there are today in the West itself new movements of thought which go a long way towards disarming such criticism. There are movements, too, which prompt new questions, questions of interest to East and West alike. What, for example, may be concluded from contemporary Western studies of religious symbolism? Or from the discussion of what may be termed "depth religion"?

We have, then, all told, to deal with a total pattern of challenging diversity. But threading this diversity we may find that which makes for similar attitudes towards certain issues on the part of men of different faiths, as we may also find new grounds for diversity within each particular tradition. What happens when men of different religions meet in conference, as they do more frequently today, may be compared with what happens when Christian theologians representing different churches meet for ecumenical discussions. An issue is raised and we have alignments which we might not expect. There together, in one corner, are all the Barthians (Presbyterians, Lutherans, Anglicans, and others) speaking with one accord against an opposite group similarly composed of Presbyterians, Lutherans, Anglicans, and others. Some of the prophets of today have a wide audience not confined to their own traditions. It is said, for example, that Martin Buber has greater influence outside Jewry than within Jewry. Much depends on the nature of the issue raised. The issues of religion and world community also produce unexpected alignments. At the same time we may look for attitudes which may be influenced by particular conditions in particular traditions.

One major issue which comes more and more into focus as we move from scene to scene is the confessional issue. This is the issue which appears when it is remarked that there is nothing in Hindu India which quite corresponds to the confessional church pattern of religious community with which we are familiar in the West—so familiar that a good many assume it to be the only possible form of religious community. "You believe what I believe; therefore, we are together in one and the same household of faith." That, by and large, is our Western conception. Allegiance to some one particular confession of faith may be "pinned down" (to use Toynbee's phrase) to a specific propositional statement, to which all within the community are required to subscribe.[14] Accredited teachers are expected to toe the line of this statement and prospective members of the community are schooled in it before they are admitted to membership.

Along with this conception of community we have the attitude to statements of belief which is popularly called "dogmatic," firmly distinguishing between statements, regarding some as authoritative, adequate, final and regulative. Certain pronouncements are given, as it were, a higher status than others. They may be held to come from God, not man, or they may be regarded as demonstrably true, beyond reasonable question. Men will go to the stake for them or put others to the stake for them. They are taken with "desperate seriousness." [15] They betoken the quest for certainty which is characteristic of the West.[16] They breed fanatics, martyrs, and tyrants, ecclesiastical and political.

Turning from the Christian West to Hindu India we find conceptions of community and related attitudes which are diametrically opposite, so opposite that the Western observer often wonders how there can here be any sense of community at all. He looks in vain for most of the things he associates with church community in the West. There is here no central ecclesiastical authority, no Rome, no Canterbury, no Geneva, nothing indeed which quite resembles our Western patterns of church organization and certainly no demand for subscription to any one elaborated statement of belief. Instead there are castes and sects and schools of thought constituting so complex a pattern that the Hindu scholar is the first to acknowledge that the pattern is bewildering.[17] There are at least six different systems of interpretation, all of them considered "orthodox." Even if it is allowed that Hindus share certain basic assumptions such as the operation of the law of karma, these scarcely amount to a "confessional statement of faith" after the Western pattern. In brief, instead of community on a basis of "I believe what you believe," we have the Hindu saying in effect, "Because you see what I do not see and I see what you do not see, there is all the more reason for being together in the same household of faith."

Associated with this view we have Hindu relativism: the appraisal of all statements of religious belief as, at best, no more than approximately or relatively true. The attitude here stands in sharp contrast to Western "dogmatic" attitudes.[18] Far from there being any disposition to regard any formulation of belief as "the last word" or a word sufficiently certain to determine the lines of community, all such formulations, including the believer's own word, are regarded as deficient; they express no more than glimpses of different aspects of the Truth; the final word can only be Not this, not this (*neti, neti*).

Confronted, then, by this relativist attitude and by patterns of religious community so different from his own, a Christian observer from the West may very well feel strongly challenged as he stands on the soil of India and looks around him. And he may hear vigorous criticism of dogmatic attitudes and exclusive ideas of religious community. Professor Murti of Banaras Hindu University, for example, is outspoken. "Denominational religions with their dogmas," he protests, "[tend] to create vested interests and to breed corruption." They stifle freedom of expression, they coerce conformity, they promote religious conflicts.[19]

But is not Western man, it may be asked, more than half prepared for such challenge? Prepared, and indeed disposed to welcome it? Prepared by the remarkable growth of relativism today in his own Western world? Does he need any Hindu pundit to tell him that one way is as good as another, that it does not matter what a man believes provided "he does the right thing"?

On closer scrutiny, however, it may appear that this is *not* what the Hindu is seeking to tell him. It may be what our western relativism, or at least some version of it, is telling him. But our Western relativism is largely our own making, and the temper of it and the conclusions drawn from it may prove to be anything but a good preparation for the Hindu challenge. For Western relativism is largely the fruit of Western science, which leads us to question any and every belief, however venerated or venerable, so that we are never sure when today's medicine may become tomorrow's poison, today's truth tomorrow's fiction, today's assurance tomorrow's dismay; never sure of anything. There is indeed another relativism, differently rooted, a relativism known to those theologians who see all theological prose as under the judgment of biblical poetry.[20] There is, again, a relativism associated, as we shall later remark, with a growing interest in what we have termed "depth religion" together with a growing interest in mysticism which leads some to avow that "it is better to be vaguely right than precisely wrong." [21] Taken together, these various expressions of the relativist attitude result indeed, in the West itself, in a mounting criticism of "dogmatic positions" with new searchings of heart when Karl Marx is found in the company of the dogmatists, responsible for what has been described by a Catholic theologian as "an empire controlled by a dogma." [22]

Nevertheless the mood of this criticism is not quite the mood of Hindu India. Generally speaking, our Western relativism is cold, as cold as the science which sponsors it. It is dispassionate. But the mood of Hindu relativism is different. The breath of it is hot and scorching. It is passionately religious. It is affirmative rather than negative. The context of Professor Murti's criticism of dogmatism, for instance, is a call for "spiritual regeneration," for "the realization of the spiritual which is the bed-rock of all our endeavour," for the kind of religion which "can hope to unite the world."

The confessional issue is raised first, then, by a *contrast*—a contrast as between Christian and Hindu patterns of religious life, thought, attitudes and community.

The confessional issue is raised in the second place, however, when we turn to Buddhist Asia, by grounds for *comparison*. And they may be unexpected grounds, for they are grounds for comparison as between the Buddhist East and the Christian West, whereas what might be expected and what is more generally affirmed is the comparison between Buddhism and Hinduism, a comparison which may be expected because the founder of Buddhism was born, lived, taught and died in India and established his religion there. And there are indeed several ways in which Buddhist Asia continues the pattern of Hindu India. The Buddhist shares with his Hindu cousin certain fundamental beliefs such as the belief in rebirth. He reflects, too, the Hindu tolerance towards other faiths, the Hindu aversion to dogmatism and the Hindu relativist attitude to statements of belief. But there is also a difference here, a difference which is not always recognized. It is a difference which arises from something which is present in Buddhism and absent in Hinduism: a central confessional allegiance.[23]

It is this same element of confessional allegiance which invites comparison with the Christian West. Consequently the Western observer may feel more at home, less bewildered though none the less challenged, by what he observes in Buddhist Asia. To begin with, he finds the Buddhist world divided in much the same way as his Christian world, with a Mahayana version of the Buddhist faith expounded in China and Japan over against the Theravada or Hinayana version maintained in southeast Asia. But next he may remark today a pan-Buddhist movement which may be compared with ecumenical movements in the Christian world.

If it is then inquired what may best serve this Buddhist movement towards unity, the answer may be found in a certain central loyalty: to the Buddha, or, more strictly perhaps, to the ideal presented by the character of the Buddha. The Buddha may be variously named. Some Mahayana Buddhists, for example, may have the name of Amida more in mind than the name of Gautama. But even in Mahayana Buddhism, with its elaborated Buddhology, there is still the Buddha who says "Go" and points the Path: Gautama.[24] And whatever the name, the character presented is essentially the same. Thus just as Christians of all denominations may be described as those who seek to have the mind of Christ so Buddhists of all sects may be described as those who seek to have the mind of Buddha. We have, then, in Buddhism, what is present in Christianity and absent in Hinduism: a unifying confessional allegiance. While, therefore, Buddhism reflects the Hindu relativism, it is in Buddhism a restrained relativism, restrained by this confessional reference, not a roam-as-you-will relativism.

With this confessional loyalty we have also in Buddhism a confessional pattern of community. But is it quite the same as our Western, Christian form? Here we may hesitate. We may fail to find in Buddhism anything quite similar to the subscription to some formulation of belief required in our confessional churches. As we hesitate, however, we may be led to question whether this confessional church pattern is, after all, the only pattern of confessional community presented by Christianity or by the West.

Much the same question regarding Christian forms of community may be prompted by what is observed, first in the Muslim tradition, second in the Judaic tradition. In both cases there is clearly a confessional allegiance. Moreover it is fundamentally an allegiance which Muslims and Jews may be seen to share with Christians. From the Christian standpoint the Muslim faith may be regarded as a Christian heresy, while Judaism may be regarded as the parent faith of both the Muslim faith and Christianity. Yet when we ask *how* this confession of faith is maintained, we observe in both the Muslim and Jewish traditions an emphasis on right practice rather than an emphasis on right doctrine. While it cannot be said that Muslims have no creed, there is nothing in either the Muslim or the Jewish tradition which quite corresponds to the confessional church pattern in the Christian tradition. In this respect, it might seem at first that Muslims and Jews have more in common with Buddhists than with Christians. Be this as it may, we are now led to remark that there are at least three traditions, Buddhist, Muslim and Jewish, presenting a pattern or patterns of confessional community which may be distinguished from the pattern of the confessional church.

Our question thus gathers momentum: is the confessional church pattern the only pattern of confessional community presented in the Christian tradition? Our answer must be "No." At the same time it may be acknowledged that it is not a "No" which is clearly apparent on every page of Christian history. On the contrary, for long periods of this history, the intolerant, dogmatic attitude which arouses Oriental criticism has certainly been prevalent. Associated with this attitude there has been a tendency to define Christian community in rigid terms of "You believe what I believe." Nevertheless, there have also been Christian mystics—and others—who have transcended this dogmatic rigidity. They have been bold to say, "Babble not of God." [25] The story of the Anglican bishop who said that he did not believe in the Salvation Army but he thought that God did may be apocryphal but it is significant that it is told, and told by churchmen. It is also significant that this story belongs to the twentieth century. For while the seed of resistance to dogmatic rigidity may be discerned within the Christian tradition from the beginning of its history, the present climate of opinion has been especially kind to this seed: its growth is encouraged by contemporary relativism, including biblical relativism.

It is certainly apparent today that forms and conceptions of religious community vary from church to church. Ecumenical conversations designed to promote unity have made this plain. In the light of these same conversations we may discern at least two patterns of confessional community, a pattern in which the members are wedded to some definite, elaborated statement of their belief and a pattern in which such subscription is absent or muted. Representatives of different denominations ask each other: "What do you stand for?" Some expect an answer in terms of defined belief. But Anglicans, for example, might perhaps better reply that they stand for a common worship rather than for any elaborated definition of belief, since they no longer emphasize adherence to their own Thirty-nine Articles. The Lutherans of Sweden when they discussed intercommunion with Anglicans some years ago had good reason to inquire whether Anglicans really toed the same confessional line.[26] Other Christian communities such as the Society of Friends would find it even more difficult to state their position in any terms of agreed belief. At the same time they would expect to be included within the Christian fold. They would affirm a confession of Christian loyalty. What they would call in question is the desirability or even the possibility of narrowly identifying this confession with any subscription to any propositional statement. They might say (as Dr. Munz suggests they ought to say) that their loyalty is to "symbols," not to sentences—loyalty to symbols so open to further interpretation that they forbid any rigid definition either of faith or community.[27] Here appears what I have called the confessional issue. Briefly stated, it is the issue whether confession means subscription.

Full discussion of this issue raises vexed questions for it has been argued that in the very nature of things—or in the very nature of religious faith—confession cannot be tied to subscription without despite to faith. I shall refer to this argument in a later chapter. Meanwhile it is sufficient to observe how this confessional issue is becoming urgent in the Christian world today, how it is raised in more than one way, and how it points to more than one Christian form and conception of confessional community. The issue is raised, as we have remarked, in conversations between members of confessional churches who take it for granted that confession indeed means subscription and members of other churches who dissent from this view. But it is also raised *within* the confessional churches themselves, when it is proposed to substitute a broad assent for a rigid subscription to the confessional statement of belief which is still maintained. Here, too, we have a departure from earlier dogmatism and a consequent change in the conception of community.

It cannot be said, then, that there is only one Christian pattern of confessional community. On the contrary, we have, side by side with a subscriptionist pattern, a form and conception of community which in some respects may be compared with that of the Buddhists. We are thus led, step by step, to observe a pattern which comes in between the Hindu pattern and the opposite pattern which Hindus may identify with Christianity. Instead of two main types of community in terms of confessional allegiance we name (rather clumsily) three: subscriptionist, confessional, and nonconfessional.

In coming to this conclusion we may come to three other conclusions which have a bearing on what religious believers may be expected to do—and not to do—in regard to world community, which will be the subject of our final chapter.

The first of these is related to what may be generally expected of the forces of religion. As we have seen, there is here, so to speak, a twofold demand. There is a demand for a coming together in the name of religion, for religion as a unifying influence. But there is also a demand for the strength of religion, for the dynamic motivation attributed to religion. Now it is sometimes suggested that we cannot expect both. Religious people are dynamic, it is held, insofar as they are inspired by a *particular* loyalty, loyalty to their own faith as against others. As such they are generally intolerant; they are more disposed to maintain differences than to forget them. It is then suggested that we have to choose between the amiable but ineffective tolerance which is identified with Hinduism and the Orient and the intolerant but effective dogmatic zeal which is identified with Christianity and the West.

Our description, however, points to something which seems to avoid this choice. It points to a form and conception of religious community which presents a confessional allegiance combined with a relativist attitude to statements of belief, such as would make for tolerance. There is here, then, an outlook which mediates between the two extremes, reflecting something of the virtues of both.

Second, our description suggests that this mediating outlook is what may be expected of a great many people, East and West. It is shared by Buddhists, Muslims, Jews, and an increasing number of Christians.

Third, the fact that this very prevalent outlook exhibits confessional allegiance means that while it may be tolerant it is only tolerant within limits. The relativism here which makes for tolerance is restrained by a particular loyalty. Is it realistic, then, to think in terms of one world, one religion? The answer

is not necessarily "No," but at least this confessional allegiance
has to be taken into account as a possible obstacle in the way
of such a goal. And we may then consider more closely whether
prospects of world community depend as much on prospects
of one world religion as is sometimes assumed. Our question
becomes even more pointed if we allow what some would
maintain: that even in Hinduism there is a confessional element.

Finally, our description implicitly challenges any sharp separation of East from West. It is often maintained that when it
comes to religion we have, in effect, to deal with two worlds,
not one: the world of oriental religion, and the world of occi-
dental religion. If this is true, here we have an obvious and
formidable barrier in the way of any coming together in the
interests of world community. And *if* this is true, it is one of
the realities of the situation which has to be accepted.

The argument presented in support of such a sharp distinction between East and West is certainly plausible. Hindu India
is first taken as typical of the Orient in general, the source of
a main stream of fundamental beliefs and attitudes. Next we
have Judaism, Islam, and Christianity grouped together and
named the "three western religions," [28] with Palestine as the
source of another main stream of dominant beliefs and attitudes. A sharp contrast is then drawn between these two worlds
in terms of their fundamental approaches, goals, beliefs and
attitudes. Between these two worlds, it may be concluded, an
immense gulf is fixed.[29] To recognize this gulf, it may further
be claimed, is in line with the respect for differences which is
characteristic of contemporary studies of religion as against an
earlier disposition to discount religious differences.

Plausible as this argument may seem, however, it is open to
question. Is it altogether faithful to the principle of differentiation which is avowed? Does it take sufficient account of differences *within* the oriental realm as well as within the occi-
dental realm? [30] Our own description emphasizes this objection

by distinguishing between Hindu and Buddhist patterns, between different patterns in the West and between different patterns within the Christian tradition. There is the more reason to do this if we reflect that we are dealing with *living* religions, responding to new challenges in the changeful world of today and responding to these challenges in different ways.

Further, as we distinguish between Hindu and Buddhist patterns, so also we observe some aspects of the Buddhist pattern which invite comparison with what is observed in the West. Thus even if it is still argued that there is ground for a broad distinction between East and West and something in the nature of a gulf between the two, the gulf is seen to be bridged. It is bridged by a form and conception of religious community and a consequent outlook confined neither to the East nor the West.

It is of interest to consider how this bridge comes into view and how it differs from other bridges which might be conceived. It is not a bridge of similar ideas or similar beliefs. It is not a *bridge term* of the kind which has led some Christian writers to see in the Logos (the Word which "was in the beginning") a communicating term between Christian and Greek thought. It is not a bridge which comes into view as the result of any attempt to show that fundamental beliefs in different contexts are "essentially the same." It is, indeed, a bridge of a kind which may never come into view at all if interest is confied to religious systems of thought and belief. It comes into view when we look in other directions and take more into account than such ideas and beliefs, similar and dissimilar, may suggest.

In this respect there has been a significant change in the whole approach to the study of religions, one which leads us to look in these other directions and one which prompts new questions and raises new issues. How this change has come about will be the subject of the next chapter.

CHAPTER II

The "Science" of Religions

THERE ARE SEVERAL reasons for including in this inquiry some account of what Joachim Wach called "the *modern* comparative study of the science of religions." [1]

To begin with, there is the fact that advocates of this study have conceived it as constituting in itself something which might very well be described as "a force of religion" designed to promote world community. They have not only studied the subject and taught it: they have preached it.[2] They have recommended it with religious fervor, convinced that they were dealing with a subject which was vital to the welfare, progress, and peace of all mankind.

Second, there is the fact that despite the fervor which has attended it—some might say, because of this fervor!—the modern comparative study of religions has been beset with ambiguities from its inception. Is it properly named a *science?* The answer is far from clear or unanimous. Whether we can resolve the attendant ambiguity is questionable. But acquaintance with some of the issues raised, this at least may be seen as relevant to a study of religion and world community.

Third, whatever may have been the attendant ambiguity, progress in this study of religions during the last hundred years has certainly resulted in new insights, new directions, and new questions which are significant for our present inquiry.

Addressing the Ninth International Congress for the History of Religions held in Tokyo in 1958, Dr. Friedrich Heiler said that it was "one of the finest hopes of the scientific study of religion" to contribute towards a new era of religious tolerance and cooperation and thereby to "the realization of humanity and world peace." Such study contributed more towards this goal than "all the noteworthy efforts of politics." [3]

In saying this, Dr. Heiler could claim that he was speaking in the grand tradition. Max Müller, "one of the greatest pioneers," concluded an address to a congress of Orientalists by quoting, as Dr. Heiler himself now did, nearly a hundred years later, the ancient Vedic hymn:

United come, united speak, let our spirits agree! . . .
Let your efforts united be, united your hearts! . . .
Let your spirit united be, by which you are firmly bound. . . .
Peace, peace, peace.[4]

Together with others of his day, Max Müller certainly had great expectations. Advocating the comparative study of religions, he said that it might be the last of the sciences, but when it was elaborated it would "change the aspect of the world." [5] It would show the Divine education of all mankind.[6] It would exhibit what was essential in all religions and thereby promote a new spirit of charity both at home and abroad.[7]

In France, Emile Burnouf, writing for the *Revue des deux mondes*, announced the new "science of religions" with the same fervor. He, too, had great expectations. The age of science had come! Science found the religions of the world separated and antagonistic, "breaking the unity of the human race"; but this same science, introduced in the study of religions, would promote truth, freedom, and concord. To show the fundamental unity of all religions and bring them together might well be "the supreme object" of this new science. Was this too much to be hoped for? He did not hesitate to answer, "No," it was *not* too much to be hoped for.[8]

But it must be science! Both Max Müller and Burnouf were emphatic that their hopes were dependent on the kind of approach to the subject which they proposed, a *scientific* approach. Remarking all the knowledge of oriental religions which was coming to the West, Max Müller exclaimed that the field must not be left to "mere babblers." It must not be left to those who would exploit such knowledge either to debase the Christian faith or to exalt it in order to deprecate others. No, the new territory *must* be occupied in the name of science.[9]

It was this emphasis on a *scientific* study which was new in the situation. There was no novelty in the opinion that what was essential in religion was to be found in all the great traditions. This had already been said in the name of enlightened philosophy. What was new was the conviction that this essential unity could now be *proved* by enlightening science.

But was it the *same* science, the science which Burnouf had in mind when he spoke of "the age of science," acclaimed its products, and summoned it to the side of religion? This is questionable. Looking back, we can see considerable ambiguity. It is an ambiguity which has attended the whole subsequent discussion of this subject.

As far as *negative* definition went, there was indeed a firm opinion: the new approach was to be free from prejudgment. It was *not* to be determined in the light of premises formed in advance and decided outside the field itself. It was *not* to be dominated by Christian theology.[10] It was *not* to be subservient to contemporary Positivism.[11] Neither philosophers nor theologians were to be allowed to impose their preconceptions. A basic cultural outlook would doubtless influence every man's approach, but this was a different thing from deliberate prejudgment.[12]

When it came, however, to what was to follow such freedom from prejudgment, the view was not so clear. One reason for this was the ambiguity of the term "science." Then as now there were two models which might influence conceptions of scientific procedure.[13] They were both there, in the background of thought, the one new, dazzling, and clearly attractive, the other inherited from the past.

The new model was the model of the natural sciences, indicating an empirical approach, with an emphasis on preliminary observation and no more than tentative hypotheses until the field had been searched and the facts assembled and examined. The process of reasoning here was inductive, moving from particular instances to general statements which might embrace them. It was associated with an attitude of mind frequently, though questionably, described as "objective." What it chiefly presented was the need to ascertain the data. This was the model indicated when Max Müller met objections by referring not only to what had been accomplished in the science of languages, but also to what had been achieved in chemistry and astronomy,[14] when he emphasized that scholars must deal with the facts as they found them [15] and also, perhaps, when he made the cryptic remark that he held "the right tests of truth" dearer than the truth itself.[16] It was again indicated when he drew a line between description and interpretation, distinguishing between "comparative theology" and "theoretic theology." [17]

Burnouf, when he said that the science of religions, while it would involve more than just the collection of facts, would be a far remove from studies determined by a priori theories, had this same model of the natural sciences in view.[18]

The second, older model had wider reference. It was the model of coherent statement following deductive procedures from clearly stated premises. In this sense theology was named "the queen of the sciences." The emphasis here was on a comprehensive, systematic, consistent presentation. Scientific knowledge thus conceived was not a knowledge of bits and pieces presented in bits and pieces. The facts were seen as related facts. What this model chiefly promoted was regard for rational order. When Max Müller talked of gathering together the results of particular inquiries to provide a view of the whole field which would exhibit the "radical elements" of religion he was thinking in terms of this second model.[19] He was thinking of it again when he addressed a congress of orientalists and deplored a "tendency to extreme specialization"; he contrasted this tendency with "the spirit of a former age"—the spirit of men who "could trace the vast outlines of the Kosmos of nature or the Kosmos of the mind."[20] In pleading for a science of "many religions," the only science of religions possible, Max Müller was convinced, that it should mean not only a wider view but a coherent view. Observation, as he saw it, led to comparison and comparison was essential to science. When this method was applied to the study of religion it would show, among all religions, "the same intention, the same striving, the same stammering, the same faith."[21]

Looking back, we can see how the different ways of thinking pertinent to these two models meant a confused counsel. We can see how enthusiasm for a "scientific" approach to the subject arose largely from a more explicit reference to the empirical procedures of the new model and the results attained thereby. At the same time, the rationalism of the older, traditional view of science expressed itself in the conviction that the more the world of religions was explored the more it would be seen to be one world; the new approach would mean not only a more extensive view but a *coherent* view.

We can also see a certain tension resulting from insistence on freedom from prejudgment on the one hand, and on the other hand the opinion that something more than a mere collection of facts was needed. We observe this tension mounting as the two models continue to haunt the debate which persists through the century. In the excitement of the chase for new data the pattern of the natural sciences comes more and more into view. There is increasing zeal for "objectivity," and increasing regard for the methods employed in the natural sciences. Demand was made that the study of religions should be pursued in precisely the same way as the studies of other sciences.

A *scientific* approach, it was held, meant adherence to the same methods whatever might be the subject. Now we might attribute this opinion to the spell of the "natural" scientists and the results achieved by their methods. But it might also be attributed to the persistent spell of that "rationalism" which derived from the older model of Scientia. When, however, the objection was made that methods of study might vary, depending on what method was most appropriate to the particular subject studied, the preference was again for the new model with its emphasis on adequate observation.

Whether we see it in terms of these two models or not, there was certainly ambiguity in the use of the term "science." This ambiguity haunted and confused the debate which persisted as the new science of religions was accepted, pursued, discussed, commended, opposed, and qualified in the decades which followed. Was such a science desirable? Was it possible? Was it sufficient?

Discussion was focused on two subjects: on the scientist himself, the observer of religions, his condition and qualifications, and on what he observes, his field of study, religion and religions.

In regard to the observer, the discussion might be presented in terms of the camel's head of prejudice or prior opinion. Some might say that during the century the discussion has come full circle from a vote for the camel's exclusion to a vote for its admission. The earlier vote for exclusion (directed largely against theologians and philosophers as disqualified by their beliefs or preconceptions) was zealously upheld by mid-century scholars who maintained that "objectivity" and an "open mind" were essential conditions of scientific inquiry in the field of religion as in other fields. Renan's remark has been quoted as an instance of this zeal for objectivity: "To give a good account of a religion one must have believed in it and then have rejected it." But his remark might also be quoted in support of a contrary opinion; that it takes a believer to see a believer; faith is not blinding but illuminating, and even a rejected faith is better than none. With this contrary opinion, the camel is back again.

Back again, and with right of entry fully acknowledged! There are various arguments in favor of this entry. There is the general argument that whatever may be said about an open mind there is no such thing as an empty mind. Better, then, the man who knows and admits that the camel's head of prejudice is at the door of his tent of science and is on the lookout against further intrusion, prepared to allow the camel's head but no more than the head; better such a man than one who is unaware of the intrusion or pretends to be unaware or, being aware, ignores it.

The uneasy reply may be made that yes, it is possibly better to see the situation in this way provided there is no more than the camel's *head* at the entry. Allowance for unavoidable prejudgment should not be made an excuse for complete surrender to prejudice, with all attempts at a scientific approach abandoned on the ground that no pure scientists are available or the ground that none can enter this field and remain pure. Granted that there is no such thing as complete objectivity, room may yet remain for avowed impartiality. A line may still be drawn between description as pure as it can be and frank interpretation as explicit as it ought to be.[22]

As to what is observed, namely the field of religions and the possibilities of its scientific survey, objections here came originally from two quarters: from churchmen and from skeptics. It was too sacred a field for such profane treatment, said the churchmen; Christianity, at any rate, could not be included in it, for Christianity was based on a unique Divine Revelation not subject to such scrutiny. The skeptics said that it was a field beneath serious consideration, a field exhibiting nothing but vain speculation and outworn superstition.

Echoes of these objections remain, but discussion today has moved to other grounds. There is, for example, the ground indicated by the opinion, already cited, that it takes a believer to understand a believer. Whether or not it is only the believer who is qualified to study this field, it is certainly true that, without believers, there would be no such field to study. The study of religions is the study of people. But if we follow the implications of this reference to people we encounter all the objections to a scientific approach in this field which have been raised in respect to related fields such as psychology and other "social sciences" where people are also under observation. It is to question whether empirical procedures and principles of verification devised for the study of *things* can be applied or adapted to the study of people. Can there possibly be and should there be the same objectivity? And if not, is there any virtue in pretending a scientific approach in such fields? Has the pretension of scientific method not meant, in fact, a curtain of abstractions, decorated by jargon, veiling the obstinate vitality of what is actually presented?

The whole argument, however, takes a new turn with the advent of the "phenomenologist." It might indeed be said that the subject of debate is changed. For there is here, it would seem, no question of looking first at the observer and next at what he observes. Both are here joined together, for better or for worse. Wherever he turns, whatever he sees, the phenomenologist sees with it his own shadow. He sees subject-object, not separated, but joined; not two worlds but one—the one world in which he lives and which lives in him, which he himself is all the time helping, but only helping, to make as he

himself is also partly made by it. It is not a question of any
avoidable camel's head of prejudice intruding, coming into the
tent from outside; it is rather a question of his own unavoidable shadow falling on what is seen. Nor can the view be described as *outside* the tent. Strictly speaking, there is no outside, no object away from the subject, no scene which can
be sharply distinguished from what the observer puts into it.
So perhaps, in clumsy imagery—though no imagery quite suffices—we may put the situation as the phenomenologist presents it. A distinction should be drawn, maybe, between "philosophical" phenomenology and what is broadly termed "the
phenomenology of religion" or the method of approach which
is described as "phenomenological." But if the classic presentation of Gerardus van der Leeuw is taken as a fair indication of
the latter, our image may be allowed.[23] In which case, we may
say goodbye to the camel's head of prejudice and put in its
place the phenomenologist's head of "empathy." But the question remains: *Is it science?*

Van der Leeuw compares the phenomenologist with a landscape painter.[24] He paints what he paints because of what he
is. He must have existential concern and "poetic originality"
to paint anything worth painting when it comes to religion.[25]
With sympathetic imagination (empathy) he must try to see
the other man's religion from the inside. At the same time he
acknowledges restraints to his imagination. His goal is "pure
objectivity," [26] he is anything but fancy free, and if his canvas
exhibits rhyme and reason, types and structures, it is because
reality itself is structured and presents "perceptible relationships." [27]

If not an empiricist, Van der Leeuw might have claimed that
he *was* nevertheless a scientist. Indeed, he said as much when
he remarked that what he himself understood by the phenomenology of religion had been called "the general science of religions." [28]

His statement, however, may only sharpen our question. Have we here a movement which has given new life to the "science of religions," or one which means a virtual abandonment of any attempt at such a science? The answer depends in part on where we find this movement and against which backcloth it is seen. Perceived against the background of European "rationalism" the phenomenology of religion may be regarded as a renewal of scientific purpose, insofar as it proposes a suspense of judgment in the approach to religious phenomena and is pursued by scholars who look with suspicion on theologians and metaphysicians who might disturb such "suspense." But seen against the backcloth of Anglo-Saxon empiricism, it may be regarded as opening the door to the camel's head of rationalism, insofar as it posits an observer who does a good deal more than describe what he sees; he must apparently project a great deal of himself and his own ideas in his effort to add "understanding" to description.

Nevertheless, the gulf between the phenomenologist (after this pattern) and the empiricist is not perhaps so yawning as some suggest. The "empathy" or imaginative entry into another man's religion which the phenomenologist advocates is not entirely absent from the empirical approach. Nor is the emphasis on this empathy a novelty. Max Müller came very near to saying all that the phenomenologist says about it when he rebuked Mr. Hardwick for his failure to "enter into the . . . atmosphere of the ancient world," adding, "We must become ancients ourselves, otherwise we shall never understand." [29]

Whether or not the phenomenologist is regarded as one who brings new life to the scientific study of religions depends in the long run, of course, on how broadly or narrowly science is defined. This indeed has been the central issue throughout the whole century-long debate. The debate continues. But so does the practice of science, or of what is believed to be science, in varied fields and new fields, with new and varied pro-

cedures. With respect to procedure there is increasing agreement that the definition of science must be sufficiently flexible
to allow for variation, since what is possible in one field is not
possible in another. On this showing, then, the scientific approach to the study of religions need not, and should not mean,
a slavish adherence to procedures proper to the natural sciences.

A good many, however, would agree that science at least
means, as Professor Goodenough puts it in a lively phrase, a
"shuttling back and forth between data and hypotheses." [30]
That perhaps is as far as we can expect agreement in regard to
procedure and as far as we need go. If it means no more than
agreement to differ, this at least would be preferable to the
acrimonious schism which prompts the remark that it is often
easier to get together scholars of different faiths than it is to
get together scholars of different schools. Sound procedure
in itself does not make a scientist. Something more is required.
This "something more" may appear if we turn to another question presented by our debate and ask "What's in a name?"
For, just as remarkable as the persistence of the "modern"
approach to the study of religions is the persistence of the
demand that it should be *named* "scientific." Does it matter
what the inquiry is named provided it is honestly pursued?
What value is attached to this name of science?

The glamour of the name, "science," shines through the pages
of Emile Burnouf and we can see why. He acclaimed the Age
of Science, an age (said another writer) "illumined by hope." [31]
This hope was the hope of progress aroused by this same science. With the passing of the years and the unexpected wars
of our own twentieth century the hope of progress has somewhat declined and perhaps, too, has something of the glamour
of this name of science. But there is still a persistent if more
sober allegiance to the name, and we may well ask why.

A first answer is that what is primarily valued is not any

particular method or procedure but what is sometimes called the *spirit* of science. This was the point made in another statement in the paper by Professor Goodenough to which we have referred, and he made it in a way which produced a good deal of discussion at the time. Modern science, he said, was itself a religion—one of the religions to be studied by future historians of religion, and he proceeded to plead that it should be a study informed by the "spirit" of this same "new religion."

Preeminently the spirit of science is the spirit of adventure, and all that goes with adventure: the readiness to accept trial and risk error, to take new bearings. In scientific study this means not only a continued search for data; it also means a readiness to revise and even abandon theory in the light of new data. But no *method* will, of itself, ensure this spirit. On the contrary, it is possible to become so wedded to a particular method or a particular hypothesis accepted as promising, that one may fail to observe that the promise is not being fulfilled. This has happened, says Dr. Peyton Rous in the field of cancer research. "The hypothesis of somatic mutation," he remarks, "has acted like a tranquilizer." [32] Much the same might be said of religious attitudes. In the past they have often acted like tranquilizers. Hence, in part, the conflicts between science and traditional religion.[33] Hence, too, maybe, the attempts to exclude theologians and philosophers from the field of the new science of religions unless they were willing to forget for the time being that they were theologians and philosophers.

A second answer to our question is an answer which points to what has been achieved by allegiance to this "spirit of science" in the study of religions. At the least, such allegiance has meant new communication. The scientific study of religions has meant the acceptance of common ground on which scholars of different faiths may meet together (as was demonstrated by the symposium sponsored by UNESCO which followed the International Congress for the History of Religions held recently in Tokyo). It is common ground not so much in regard to conclusions reached, but in regard to how they may be reached; how they may be supported, and by what evidence, evidence patent to all; and how they may be tested, in ways accepted by all who join in the discussion. There is no pretense, or there should be no pretense, that religion can be reduced to what may be publicly attested and scrutinized in this way. Nevertheless, the communication thus established, even if it is limited in its range, has resulted not only in new insights within the world of scholarship but in better understanding between men of different faiths thus engaged.

The question has been raised whether agreement of this kind might also be achieved, if not in the religious world as a whole, then at least among religious teachers. It is generally claimed, for example, that faith may be confirmed or verified by experience. But what, it is asked, is the principle of verification? Could there not be some established and agreed-upon answer here? Only so, it is urged, can the modern tide of skepticism which challenges all faiths be met.[34] While this particular suggestion comes from philosophers interested in the analysis of religious language, it might be claimed that it is the work of historians of religion which has exhibited the possibility of such agreement. They have not only advanced their own research in this way; they have set an example of fruitful conference and have thus done something to bring men and women of different faiths closer to each other and promote world community; they have, in effect, become one of the "forces of religion" to be taken into account. Such, in fact, was the substance of Dr. Heiler's claim at Tokyo. If this claim is allowed, it might further be claimed that whatever has thus been achieved has been achieved as the result of an avowed fidelity to scientific disciplines.

And what is the alternative, some may ask, if such discipline is abandoned? A babel of crass assertions, a mere appeal to the brute force of noisy opinions, a sheltering behind private authorities, a contempt for all rules of evidence because in some cases it is hard to apply the rules, a confusion of tongues without hope of communication, exchange, or understanding? It may well be that there are limits to our science. But science within limits is better than none and partial exchange on this basis is better than the complete absence of it.

What's in a name: this name of science? Too much, it may be replied, for all the aims and disciplines which go with this name of science to be lightly abandoned.

When it comes to asking just *what* has been achieved by the scientific approach to the study of religions we find both agreement and disagreement. There is agreement concerning the better, more comprehensive view of the field: there is disagreement concerning conclusions to be drawn from this view.

As to the latter, some might say that the great expectations of the pioneers have been largely fulfilled. In terms of our present discussion, Max Müller, for example, looked forward to a convincing demonstration of fundamental unity. He was convinced that the further the science of religions was pursued the more evident it would become that "the truths on which all religions agree far exceed those on which they differ." [35] Some would say confidently that achievements in this field have proved him right: what he expected has come to be. Dr. Heiler, for example, said as much at Tokyo. He was emphatic and lyrical about it:

This study [the science of religions] in which scholars of greatest stature participated, men like Fredrick Max Müller, Nathan Söderblom, Rudolf Otto, Tor Andrae, Alfred Loisy, Gerardus van der Leeuw, Raffael Pettazoni, has given us a host of insights by which century-old prejudices have been removed. . . . Scientific inquiry into religion has discovered more and more of the close relationship existing among outwardly differing religions. . . . Within the great unity spanning all religious forms and levels, the higher religions represent a closer unity.[36]

There might be, he acknowledged, "important differences," but they were "overarched by an ultimate unity," "a most profound unity," and he proceeded to name "seven principal areas of unity" manifested by the higher religions: (1) the reality of the transcendent, the holy, the divine, (2) the immanence of this transcendent reality in human hearts, (3) the identification of this reality with "the highest good" for man, (4) its identification with "ultimate love," (5) "the way of man to God as a way of sacrifice . . . renunciation . . . resignation . . . prayer, (6) the way of love, uniting man to man, and (7) the way of love as "a most superior way to God." [37]

One of the most important tasks of the science of religion, he added, was to bring to light this unity of all religions.

But there are scholars in this field who might say sadly—and some maybe not so sadly!—that Dr. Heiler is the last of the prophets in this grand tradition, or at least, the last of the Western prophets, the last to be so confident that the final word of the science of religions is, or will be, Unity. To judge from much that is being written today the final word is rather seen by a good many to be the same as the first word: Diversity. At least there is a revised emphasis, as we remarked in our previous chapter, on what is particular and special in each of the great traditions.

On one point, however, there might well be general agreement with Dr. Heiler: that such unity as may be established is to be established not "artificially," but "lifted up out of the deep." And on a second point there would certainly be general agreement with Dr. Heiler: that (whatever conclusions may be drawn from it) there has developed in the last century "a more comprehensive and profound view of religion and reli-

gions." There would also be further agreement with Dr.
Heiler's statement that this "more comprehensive view" has
resulted, not merely from studies in the history of religion
but "through the corporate efforts of various modern scientific
disciplines such as philology, ethnology, pre-history and history, archaeology, psychology, sociology, and philosophy." [38]

One way of appreciating the enlarged view that has developed during the century is to remark how some of these related disciplines have promoted it, each in turn and sometimes
together, providing new searchlights which have brought into
clearer view significant aspects of the field.

What is observed at the beginning of the century is a *horizontal* extension of Western knowledge as one oriental text
after another is studied and translated. Attention is very largely
concentrated on the ideas expressed in these texts and there
is high confidence that, given time, they can all be set down
on one broad map. It will be a map showing similar mountain
ranges everywhere rising above the plains, with here and
there a peak which is higher than others and different in shape.
It will be a map of the surface, of ideas on the surface. The
kind of question asked is: Do Hindus believe in God? or,
What is their conception of the Divine? Attention is very
largely focused on the more explicit *statements* of belief. The
religions of the world are classified accordingly.

There is also, it is true, at least a hint of some regard for
what may lie beneath the surface. Max Müller glances in this
direction when he remarks that "religion escapes our firm
grasp till we can trace it to its real habitat, the heart of one
true believer." [39] He knows very well that there is more in the
heart of man than in the speech of man. He mentions primitive
man unable to give full name or shape to his "vague yearning,"
his "spirit willing, but his language weak." [40]

With the advent of modern anthropology, however, there
is very much more than a glance in this direction. A sounding

of the depths begins as account is taken of the significance of primitive myths and rites. There is greater regard for the several ways in which men may indicate the faith by which they live. Beside the prose of credal statements there is set the poetry of mythical story. And time comes when this mythical expression is no longer dismissed as mere nursery speech. With fuller respect for such poetic expression there is growing respect for other ways in which men express, maintain, and communicate their faith in the form of story.

Second, there is regard for the significance of what men *do* in the name of religion, and, in particular, for the significance of their rites and ceremonies. From the view that "savage religion is something not so much thought out as danced out," [41] we come to the view that even under the canopy of the higher religions a great deal of it is still danced out.

In a cogent paragraph, Professor Werblowski has shown how this regard for the significance of religious *practice* has influenced our modern approach to the study of religions:

Even when authentic statements of faith are available in liturgy and creed, it would be wrong to say that religious practice merely "expresses" them. *We might equally well have it the other way round* by saying that theological statements are merely abstract, semi-intellectualized or conceptualized expressions of the *true fullness of the religious life of worship and practice.* One may get nearer to the heart of Catholicism by attending the Mass than reading theological manuals.[42]

Anthropology sires sociology as attention is drawn to the *function* of religion. There is a certain irony here. For the anthropologist was largely encouraged by the notion that to see primitive religion was to see religion simplified.[43] The diagrams of the sociologist may reflect a similar purpose but before drawing them he certainly presents a view which is anything but simple. His wood is very full of trees and his analysis has to be searching. We are a far cry now from any

presentations of the world of religions focused solely on ideas
or beliefs.

How far a cry it is becomes evident when we turn to one
of the classics of this sociological approach and follow the
subtle analysis by which Max Weber seeks to show the relation between religion (in this case Calvinism) and the capital-
istic system.[44] Incidentally, Max Weber is still very frequently
caricatured and the significance of his analysis obscured, as
when he is credited (or debited) with the view that Calvinism
promoted capitalism by conveniently providing doctrines
which permitted merchants to invest capital with an easy conscience. Medieval churchmen, it is said, frowned on such
"usury"; Calvinism approved it. A premise and an inference:
just that. To put his account in terms of such intellectual
reduction is indeed to miss the "far cry" of it.

For Max Weber has a great deal more on his canvas, much
more. John Calvin and his teachings are certainly there in the
background. So, too, in the foreground is modern capitalism.
And there *is* a connection between the two. But it is anything
but a single link of logical inference. What lies in between the
two on Max Weber's canvas is a whole complex structure of
motive, emotion and purpose, social and private—a tangle of
thicket, forest, marsh, and stream, as it were, teeming with life,
anything but a straight highway. And what establishes the
relation of the background to the foreground is a penetrating
analysis of this intervening complexity, not a straight line of
deduction from premise to conclusion.

Nor is the starting point, in the background, any such one
implicating premise. Calvinism here is not just John Calvin or
his teaching. It is not an ism. It is a whole context of life as
well as thought. At the heart of this context there is not just
a precept about usury but a massive doctrine of Divine Election
and all the purposes and motives and practices with which the
doctrine is associated. Out of this complex step not just argu-

ments but *people*—Calvinists in their privacy, seeking the assurance that they are indeed among the elect, Calvinists in society, changing society as they find this assurance in a rational, successful ordering of the workaday tasks to which they are "called." And Max Weber's conception of the capitalism thus produced is similarly complex, and similarly analyzed with an emphasis on its rationalized order and the attitudes and outlook of its votaries. There is psychology here as well as sociology. Indeed, insights from these two fields converge.

The psychology of religion, with its emphasis on the varieties of religious experience, has made so evident an impact on the whole approach to the study of religions that it scarcely needs comment. But it is especially relevant to our discussion of unity and diversity to remark how the definition of types of religious experience tends to discover in the depths what has disappeared from the surface. I refer here to the view that apparently similar statements of belief are seen to be essentially dissimilar when they are properly related to the particular contexts of separate systems of thought and life to which they belong.[45] When this is associated with the present disposition to emphasize the particularity of these contexts, accentuating a vertical line of division between Hinduism and Christianity, the conclusion might be drawn that there is nothing at all in common between Hindu and Christian, no possible grounds of religious affinity, that they belong to entirely separate worlds. But this conclusion may well be held questionable when we observe how the horizontal line distinguishing one type of experience from another crosses the border and cuts through the vertical lines drawn between the different systems. How this is so is shown by Rudolf Otto in his account of three "religions of grace," Hindu, Buddhist, and Christian.[46] At the intellectual level, his word is cautionary: the beliefs expressed are not as similar as they might seem to be: Hindu theism is *not* Christian theism. But when he sets the Hindu Ramanuja alongside the Christian Martin Luther and plumbs the depths of their experience he places them together. At *this* level, in the depths, there *is* affinity.

The same depths are certainly sounded in the latest word from psychology, that word which sets before us the fascinating, invasive realm of the unconscious—so fascinating and so invasive that there is a temptation to identify the whole realm of "depth religion" with what takes place in the unconscious: a temptation which will be discussed in a later chapter.

All in all, there emerges from this century of research an account which emphasizes the *complexity* of the religious situation. It is certainly a far remove from any simplified account in terms of conspicuous beliefs or surface ideas. Strictly speaking, there is not one account, but several, as religious life and thought are observed not only in different contexts or cultural environments (as when we refer to Hindu India) and at different times (as when we refer to *modern* Hinduism) but in various aspects, from different standpoints (as when we study the psychology of religion).

But all of these accounts are interrelated. There is need for constant cross reference. To give, for example, a sufficient account of both the significance and function of religious beliefs we have first to see them in their own particular contexts (Hindu or Muslim or Christian), then in relation to the total, assembled view of all such contexts, then in relation to other aspects. This obtains even when our interest is a specialized interest, centered in some one locality, tradition, or aspect of the subject. The earlier dictum that a knowledge of one religion only is a knowledge of none has to be supplemented by the dictum that a knowledge of one aspect of the situation is a knowledge of none: the sociologist needs the psychologist at his elbow and vice versa.

But who is sufficient for these things? Who can pretend to attain and marshal a knowledge of such a field in all its width and all its bewildering complexity? The captious critic might well say that what we have set before us today in this field of religions is a view so much more "comprehensive" that it is not only beyond full comprehension but beyond description.

In this situation the student of the science of religions is exposed to at least two temptations.

First, his very zeal for science may lead him to disregard the audacity of his abstractions and his generalizations. For whether we believe or not that order is heaven's first law it is the scientist's first demand. He must have his patterns, his diagrams, his maps, his structures, his types, his grounds for comparison and grounds for prediction. The temptation here, as Professor Cantwell Smith has recently observed [47] is to turn away from the encounter with man—man, the obstinate "variable"—which the sufficient study of religion demands. It is the temptation to present religion as we might present a temple empty of worshipers or as if it were never intended for worship or used for worship. Such a presentation of what is external has its place in the study of religion. But the study of externals is no substitute for the very personal encounter of man with man which any full inquiry concerning religion demands. Unless we allow for the *people* who build the temples and use them, for the *people* who write the bibles and read them, and for the *people* who compose the rites and perform them, we are studying something less than religion. We cannot ignore what Professor Smith calls "the essentially human quality of our subject matter." To allow for this human quality, however, is to recognize that we have here a subject which is not easily "called to order"; that we have to allow for the exception which may break the rule as well as for the exception which makes the rule; that our descriptions are only true as far as they go and that most of them do not go nearly far enough. Is it because he is dedicated to science or simply because he is human that the scientist in this field is tempted to forget or ignore the need for such qualification? It may be because he is both.

The second temptation is to hide out in some one particular area of the field. That indeed is what the situation demands. Specialized research limited to one area or one aspect of the situation is all that is possible in the name of science: it is simply a question of honest and realistic recognition of all that has to be taken into account in each particular area if there is to be anything which can be properly called scholarly, informed opinion. When we consider the languages which have to be studied, the texts to be compared, the historical inquiries to be pursued, and so on, it is obvious that no single man can hope to have such a knowledge of the whole field.

Nevertheless the question may be raised whether there is not here a "hiding out" from some of the questions which may arise. For any science depends on what questions are posed, and some of the questions raised cannot be answered without reference to the whole, wider field: "La religion étant un fait universel, elle pose des problèmes qui le sont aussi." [48] There are also specific issues which involve a world view. Our present subject is a case in point. Unless it is assumed that "religion is the same everywhere"—a large and possibly misleading assumption—we cannot properly or realistically conclude from a view of religion confined to one area or one aspect of religion, what the "forces of religion" may contribute to world community. Indeed it might be said that much of the opinion on the subject is due to conclusions so formed. Christians in North America are disposed, for example, to read their own pattern of church and state into other religious situations. Hence they misinterpret the association of religious revival with nationalism in Asia.

Difficult as such an approach may be, there is no escaping the need for a comprehensive approach when "universal" questions are raised.

There is, however, the further consideration that the same contemporary conditions which enlarge our difficulties present new opportunity—opportunity for the kind of teamwork which has been done in other sciences. We may have teamwork by scholars representative of different faiths who, today, can more easily come together. As I see it, however, this will mean something more than sporadic conferences and exchanges; it will mean sustained research by a team of specialists gathered in one place for a term of years, scholars representative not only of different faiths but of different disciplines.[49] As yet, we are only on the threshold of such opportunity. In the meantime, by individual adventures such as this present inquiry, we can at least help to prepare the agenda.

Our reference in this chapter has been a confined reference. The science of religions was proposed by Western scholars and the century of discussion we have had in review has been, for the most part, a Western discussion. But insofar as this has shown greater regard for the *depth* of the religious situation, it may better prepare us for what confronts us as we turn, in the next chapter, to the world of oriental thought and life.

CHAPTER III

The Challenge of Hindu Relativism

IF THE ACCENT on deep complexity is comparatively
new in the Western scholar's account of the realm of religion
as he has come to see it, it is certainly not new in the Hindu
scholar's account of it as he has always seen it. Indeed a good
many introductions to the life and thought of Hindu India
begin with precisely this emphasis, as does, for example, the
contemporary statement of D. S. Sarma prepared for Western
readers. Remarking "the great complexity of worship and
belief within the Hindu fold," he adds

Therefore . . . one is apt to miss the wood for the trees . . . amid
the bewildering variety of castes and sub-castes with their own customs and manners, and of sects and sub-sects with their own cults
and symbols and forms of worship . . . and many schools . . .
with their different texts and scriptures. . . .[1]

Nevertheless, the final word in his account is not diversity,
not "bewildering variety." It is unity: "Unity within Diversity"; the "One Reality, variously named Indra, Mitra, Varuna,
Agni";[2] the One Summit attained by the many roads. Asked
if religious leaders could work together for world community
despite their diverse beliefs, the instructed Hindu, impressed
by this vision of unity in diversity, would immediately reply,
Why not? His whole outlook challenges arguments to the
contrary which he finds in the West.

But what may first be observed is how this Hindu challenge
begins today at home. For the resurgent Hinduism which is

reported to be "strangely alive" in the towns and villages of
modern India [3] is a Hinduism quickened by a new vision of
Unity within Diversity in relation to the national interest, and
the movement towards religious unity in contemporary India
is largely motivated by a concern for national unity. "The
Hindus are a nation," cries the hero in one of Rabindranath
Tagore's novels.[4] By many in India today this is construed to
mean "The Hindus are a nation because they are Hindus."

Yet their outlook is not confined to home. What is also
observed, along with this national concern, is a wider concern,
a wider outlook, a world outlook, "a felt need for realizing
a true sense of human solidarity so that the basic unity of the
world of nations may not be jeopardized by unnecessary conflicts." [5] For Hinduism today is no longer a stay-at-home faith.
It has joined the ranks of the great missionary religions, and
the challenge implicit in a Hinduism discerned from a distance
by European scholars has been brought to our shores and
voiced by Hindu spokesmen such as Dr. Radhakrishnan and
the Ramakrishna missionaries.[6]

It is a challenge which is very relevant to our discussion of
unity and diversity, especially as it brings into high relief
what I have called the confessional issue when it flings down
the gauntlet against all who would divide and marshal mankind in terms of their professed systems of belief or ideologies.
"There is undoubtedly a Truth one and eternal which we are
seeking, from which all other truth derives," says Sri Aurobindo. "But precisely for that reason it cannot be shut up in
a single trenchant formula. . . . Nor has it been wholly found
by us if our view of it necessitates the intolerant exclusion of
the truth underlying other systems." It is, he says, the merit
of the Bhagavad Gita that "it does not cleave asunder, but
reconciles and unifies. . . . It maps out, but it does not cut
up or build walls or bridges to confine our vision." [7]

The view thus affirmed, sometimes described as Hindu relativism, has made a profound impression on our contemporary Western culture. The dictum of the many roads or streams leading to the one goal or ocean is almost as well known in the West today as it is in its own homeland. If it is vigorously repudiated by many religious teachers as a confusing obscurantism, a crying of peace where there is no peace, it is quoted and repeated by other Western thinkers as expressing the one idea most needed to resolve our discords, a challenge as salutary as it is timely, relevant to both our contemporary Western insights and our Western concerns, and not least to our concern for world peace.

The nature of this challenge, however, is often obscured and misrepresented. This happens when it is identified with patterns of thought home-grown in the West itself and reduced to the view that one belief is as good (or as vain) as another or the view that religious beliefs are of no consequence: "It doesn't matter what a man believes provided he does the right thing." This is *not* Hindu relativism. It is not what is intended by the doctrine of the many streams. Again, the challenge may be misrepresented when Hinduism is narrowly identified with one particular school of Hindu thought, Vedantist monism, an identification which may mean that the challenge of Hindu thought is brushed aside and any insights it may promote are refused entry. Dr. Hendrick Kraemer, for example, comes near to dismissing Hindu relativism in this way in his critique of Dr. Radhakrishnan's position, although Kraemer questions whether Radhakrishnan in his zeal to present the Hindu view of life, both as a challenge and a contribution to the Western world, is typical of the Indian mind. Hinduism, says Dr. Kraemer, attributes to all religions a relative value but no more; it holds that they only provide guesses at truth. While Hinduism "enunciates many deep and revealing half-truths" and is professed by many sincere and devout believers, it is as a system "religiously insincere," and for this reason its relativism is fundamentally life-weakening rather than life-liberating.[8] It really leads to agnosticism or even to atheism. True, there is mention of God, but in the Hindu context the term "God" is deprived of real significance.[9] Man is put in the place of God and all forms of religious endeavor are man-made instruments of human self-realization.[10] Thus Hinduism is tolerant of them all without discrimination,[11] though in Dr. Radhakrishnan's case this toleration scarcely extends to Christianity which he criticizes for its "emphasis on definite creeds and absolutist dogmatism."[12]

Kraemer's criticism is based on the view that Hindu relativism and all particular Hindu statements must be interpreted in the light of the total context of Hindu religious life and thought, a context with a long history behind it. "Notwithstanding many shades of expression different from the Hindu life-pattern in former ages, the present face and attitudes go back into the past and are in organic continuity with it."[13] Offering a "succinct sketch" of this Hinduism, Dr. Kraemer presents it as infected, nay dominated, by an "absolute monistic Idealism."[14] At the heart of this "absolute monistic Idealism," as taught by the great medieval scholar, Sankara, who is very much in fashion today, there is an interpretation of the equation presented in the doctrinal dialogue called the Upanishads, the central scriptural authority for all Hindu schools of thought. This is the equation of Brahman with Atman, the equation of the absolute unknowable cosmic reality with the soul of man: "the same reality expressed in different ways"; the *only* Reality, for the apparent plurality of the universe is due to the operation of maya which means that man lives in ignorance of his identity with Brahman. For man to discover and experience this identity means self-release, and Hinduism exhibits a gigantic enterprise for this self-release, "an all-pervading, all-energizing quest" for liberation (moksha).[15] In this system "God" is in principle, a means; man is the center and meaning of the whole process. There are indeed so-called monotheistic forms of religion and schools of thought in a monotheistic direction, including that of the great critic of Sankara's absolute monism, the sincere, religious soul, Rama-nuja. But to the detriment of India's spiritual health, Ramanuja's cry of the religious conscience has been suppressed by India. Thus Kraemer acknowledges the presence of a theistic tradi-tion in the Hindu context, but regards it as of small account besides the dominating tradition of monistic idealism.

I have referred to Dr. Kraemer's statement at some length because it presents a view which a good many in the West hold today, a view he himself has done much to form. It also serves to introduce what will follow in this chapter.

Much of what Dr. Kraemer says can be accepted. Dr. Radhakrishnan and other Hindu spokesmen certainly chal-lenge what they regard as the overemphasis on definite creeds and the "dogmatism" which they observe in Christianity. They do so as a result of a relativism which is tolerant of everything except intolerance. And a good many would take this to mean that all religious views are regarded as relatively true, although no more than that. Dr. Kraemer is right in saying that this opinion must be interpreted in the light of the full Hindu context. He is also right in saying that in this context we have to allow for the influence of Hindu absolutism, although his description of Sankara's system as "absolute monistic idealism" is open to criticism; it is more properly named non-dualism (advaita).[16]

But this is not the whole truth. What Dr. Kraemer fails to allow for is the corresponding impact of the persistent theistic tradition in Hindu life and thought. His conclusion that this influence has been swamped by the monistic emphasis is in-deed questionable. Against such a view may be set, for example, Dr. Basham's contrary observation: "the devotional theism of Ramanuja and his successors has been far more influential in the long run than the intellectual monism of Sankara. . . . It is theism which has been the real inspiration of most of the great Hindu reformers and continues to inspire them." [17] Besides the influence of the particular school of thought associated with Ramanuja, there are other ways in which theistic thought makes a profound impact on the Hindu outlook. To allow for this impact may mean a new reading of the challenge to Western thought implicit in Hindu relativism. It is the main purpose of this chapter to show how this may be so.

Glancing first at the general context of Hindu life and thought, then at the particular scriptural context from which the doctrine promoting Hindu relativism is derived, I shall try to show that alongside a qualifying monism there is a qualifying theism. Interpreted in the light of the resultant tension, Hindu relativism may then be seen to present insights and challenges which are very relevant to our discussion of unity and diversity as well as to our appraisal of religious forces in Asia.

Our contextual thinking, however, must, as we saw in our last chapter, range beyond texts and propositions to arrive at the intention or intentions of religious thought; it must include the history, the observances, institutions, attitudes, and all the many other ways in which a fundamental outlook may be indicated. In the present case, however, I must begin with a warning. Not only is Hinduism difficult to define, but any brief account may be very misleading since the selection and emphasis involved may suggest far more of a pattern than Hinduism, this most venerable, most tenacious and most flexible tradition, presents.

There is not only the possibility of missing the Hindu wood for the trees but also the difficulty of seeing where this wood begins and where it ends, and how it may be said to be different from other woods (though once we enter it we are well

aware of the difference). One reason for these difficulties is
the fact that we fail to find here the clues to definition accentu-
ated in our own Christian and other traditions. Hinduism, for
example, has no Christ, no Muhammad, no one single founder
whose teaching might provide a central reference. Instead,
there is reference to a great number of "seers" who in the
far-away past announced their vision in terms now recorded
in what is accepted by all orthodox Hindus as inspired scripture.

While this indeed means a scriptural authority, the full
reference is to such a vast corpus of scripture, so variously
presented by different schools of interpretation regarded as
orthodox, that it is little help to definition.

It is true that Hindu schoolmen refer especially to the
Upanishads. It is also true that a great many Hindus regard
the instruction given to the bewildered Arjuna in the Bhagavad
Gita by the god Krishna as a sufficient synthesis of essential
Hindu teaching, and special efforts are being made in India
today to promote the reading of the Bhagavad Gita for this
reason. But the Upanishads are unknown to a great many, and
the value of the Bhagavad Gita, while it is widely read, is variously estimated.[18]

Nor is there any one Hindu creed or confession. There are
indeed certain basic assumptions shared by all Hindus which
may be said to constitute a "hidden creed." All Hindus believe
in a time process (samsara) in which man is subject to a round
of rebirths from one existence to another (transmigration)
governed by the law of moral causation (karma), which
means that a man is bound to reap whatever he has sown in
this continued round of existences from which he hopes for
release (moksha). These conceptions are certainly fundamental.[19] We do not begin to understand the Hindu outlook
until we have felt within ourselves something of that sense of
a vast time process in a vast universe rimmed by the vast

Infinitude of Supreme Brahman which is indicated by these Hindu terms, an outlook far different from that pertaining to our Western conception of a comparatively short and urgent human history, with each man's destiny decided in a span of three score years and ten. The conceptions of the round of rebirth and karma indeed mean a boundary line. But these beliefs are held by Buddhists as well as Hindus. While they may prepare the way for definition, they are not by themselves sufficient to provide it.

Disregarding such setbacks to definition, a good many writers have presented the Hindu religion in a way which virtually defines it in terms of two traditions, existing side by side. They speak first of "popular Hinduism," with its worship of many gods, and second of a "philosophic Hinduism," which is described as pantheistic or monistic. Such a view is both inadequate and misleading. For any real understanding of the Hindu context, we must rid our minds of any such tidy reduction.

No, all that we can properly offer by way of definition is a line drawn around the whole subcontinent of India and the observation that Hinduism is the faith and practice of the majority of the inhabitants of this subcontinent, a faith and practice which has developed during a long history of four thousand years and more.

We can next observe how that tradition has been long in the making, is still in the making, and includes a good deal more than is sometimes realized.

Earlier accounts began with the Nordic "Aryan" invaders who came through the Himalayan mountain passes in the second millennium B.C. and came to stay, introducing a nature worship, naming Indra, god of storm and war; Varuna, god of the "wide expanse," ruler of the universe; Agni, god of fire; Surya, who every day drove his seven-horsed chariot across the sky; and other gods. These are among the gods whose praises are sung in the Rig Vedas, the first books in a great canon of sacred scriptures written over a period of two thousand years. They were gods worshiped with great sacrifices, at which the inebriating soma juice was drunk. "We have drunk soma; we have become immortal; we have gone to the light, we have found the gods"—gods forgotten by most Hindus today, though attitudes and aspirations prompted by their worship remain. The coming of the Aryans brought, too, the development of that distinctive feature of Hindu life, the caste system, a fourfold grouping of Brahmans (priestly intellectuals), Kshatriyas (warriors and rulers), Vaisyas (farmers and traders), and Sudras (laborers), today developed into a system of some three thousand castes and subcastes, with membership in each determined by birth.

This is how earlier accounts of Hinduism began. But modern scholars look further into the remote past. Recent excavations have brought to light the brick walls of houses equipped with bathrooms in the well-planned cities of a civilization firmly established in the Indus Valley before the Aryan invasions. Clay figurines and tablets suggest a fertility cult similar to that associated with a mother-goddess in other parts of the Ancient East, a cult surviving in Indian villages today. In one of these figures, a male deity sitting in cross-legged yogi fashion, thought to be a prototype of the god Siva, "the prince of yogis," Dr. Radhakrishnan has seen an early expression of the fundamental Hindu view of life: "This figure of Siva, the great Yogi, has been there from nearly 3250 B.C. (if not earlier) the date which archaeologists give to the Indus Valley civilization; calling upon all those who have ears to hear . . . to be kings not over others, but over themselves." [20]

The evidences are meager and not much can he said with full assurance about the religion of this early civilization, but phallic emblems and other indications have suggested religious observances which went underground when the Aryans arrived and reappeared later in Hindu history.

At the other extreme of this long history we have the developments which go to the making of what is sometimes called Modern Hinduism—the aspiring syncretic theism and repudiation of images by the Brahmo Samaj reformers in the nineteenth century, the equally vigorous but indigenous theism of the Arya Samaj, the mysticism of the saintly Ramakrishna, and the social concern and missionary zeal of his great disciple, Vivekananda; the practical piety of Mahatma Gandhi, proclaiming:

I am a reformer through and through and through. But my zeal never takes me to the rejection of any essential thing of Hinduism. . . . I have always regarded [the exclusion of outcastes] as an excrescence. . . . A religion that establishes the worship of the cow, cannot possibly countenance or warrant a cruel and inhuman boycott of human beings.[21]

It was characteristic of all these modern reformers that they sought to distinguish what was central and essential in Hinduism from what was just accretion. Mindful of Western criticism of their religion, they were themselves critical, but they believed that the conscience which moved them was essentially a *Hindu* conscience. Influenced or challenged by other believers in God now come to the shores of India, they affirmed that Hinduism had its own belief in God. Hinduism as they saw it and exhibited it was certainly not a frozen religion, but very much a living religion, responsive to new tides of life and thought.

In between these two extremes of Ancient Hinduism and Modern Hinduism there is the development of the "classical" Hinduism which the traders of the East India Company found when they arrived from Britain to establish their factories: the Hinduism of established caste regulations, sculptured temples, public festivals, and pilgrimages to the holy places; Brahman priests, learned pundits, devout hermits, wandering ascetics, temple dancing girls, and family worshipers at many household shrines dedicated to many gods; the cow held sacred,

as every form of life is held to be sacred; the Hinduism of the
sects in which the high gods, Brahma, Vishnu, and Shiva, take
precedence over the gods of the Aryan warriors; the Hinduism
of the great epic, the Mahabharata, which tells how the god
Krishna in human form befriended the warrior brothers of the
Kuru tribe in their great battle against their kinsmen, and of
the equally popular epic, the Ramayana, recounting the story
of another "Divine descent" as the exiled prince Rama, wandering the length of India rescues his wife Sita, the pattern
of Indian womanhood; the Hinduism of the various ways of
liberation (moksha) from the repeated experience of scarred
and troubled life in rebirth, as men seek their high destiny,
reunion with Brahman from whence they came, according
to their different capacities, some by way of high knowledge,
some by way of sustained meditation, some by way of godly
works, some by way of loving devotion (bhakti) to their
gracious God; the Hinduism of the various schools in which
the intellectuals ponder the high doctrine which has come
down to them from the age of the forest academies when earnest seekers for saving Truth left home and comfort to live
austerely in secluded groves, discussing among themselves the
mystery of the universe, discussions recorded in the Upanishad
scriptures with their central theme of underlying Unity: the
"secret self" of man (atman) in union with cosmic Brahman,
the Supreme Being beyond the high gods, Brahman hidden
yet manifest, Brahman the only, the One Reality, the formed
(*mūrta*) and the formless; doctrine interpreted in a pantheistic
or monistic direction by the Thomas Aquinas of Hinduism,
the great Sankara, towards the end of this period, and later
interpreted to mean theism by the Martin Luther of Hinduism,
Ramanuja.

All this is Hinduism, and more. Through the heart of it, as
we have remarked, a dividing line has often been drawn, dis-

tinguishing the "popular Hinduism" of the many gods from the "philosophic Hinduism" of the schoolmen which names Brahman-Atman the One Reality.

The question has been raised, however, whether this dividing line, though justified from one standpoint, is not misleading. It is a question put as the study of religions in general has brought into view the varieties of religious expression and the significance of what is said in story, song, and deed, and may perhaps be said in no other way. It is a question put again as growing Western knowledge of Hindu history has brought into great prominence a central Hindu theistic tradition in which much is told in this way of story and song: the tradition which has been named India's religion of grace, so distinctive that it has been called "another religion," not to be confused with either popular Hinduism or philosophic Hinduism, if by the latter is meant the monistic systems of Sankara and others.

This bhakti tradition of loving devotion to a personal, manifest God is reflected strongly in the Bhagavad Gita where the bewildered Arjuna, asking what is the way he should follow, is told that highest Brahman, the lord of all beings, abiding in the heart of man, manifest as personal deity, offers to man a way of "supreme devotion" to the Divine Being thus made known, a way of grace:

> If thy mind is on Me
> Thou shalt overcome all difficulties by my grace
>
> . . .
>
> Worshipping Me, revering Me,
> So shalt thou come to Me:
> I promise it, for thou art dear to Me.[22]

It is to this bhakti tradition that Ramanuja really belongs as he protests that we must climb up to Brahman through positive personal terms, the highest terms we know, and name Brahman personal God in the highest, protesting this with a vehemence and fervor which leads Rudolph Otto to describe him as "the fighter for God." [23]

But we come nearest to the heart and perhaps, too, to the mind of this tradition, also observing the extent of it, as increasing account is taken today of the significance of the hymns of a long succession of poets and singers from all classes and all parts of India. The great majority of these poets and singers are fundamentally theistic, affirming a God who is very near to man yet distinct from man. Thus the same Tukaram who writes

> There is no place, small as a sesamon
> But Thou, they say, art there

also writes:

> He who worships God must stand distinct from Him,
> So only shall he know the joyful love of God;
> For if he say that God and he are one,
> That joy, that love, shall vanish instantly away.[24]

The hymns of another great poet, Kabir, are sung today by Christians and Muslims as well as by Hindus. Kabir would have rejoiced at this, for, living at a time when Muslims were dominant in northern India, he could say

> O servant, where does thou seek me?
> Lo! I am beside thee
> I am neither in temple nor in mosque. . . .
> Kabir is the child of Allah and of Rām.[25]

Although this Hindu tradition developed during the centuries which brought Muslims and Christians to India, and reflects Muslim influence, the outlook of these hymn writers is definitely Hindu. It belongs to the soul of India no less than other Hindu traditions. Remarking its persistence and its influence today, we must say: This, too, is Hinduism, this central, theistic tradition which is between the popular Hinduism of the many gods and the philosopher's Hinduism of the Abso-

lute One, a tradition entering and affecting both of these realms,
yet to be distinguished from both, a theism which is not just
the theism of the schoolmen.

Whatever else this amended account betokens, it certainly
betokens a rich diversity. If the Hindu speaks of many ways—
or rivers—he certainly does so with full evidence of them in
his own tradition. Further diversity arises from the fact that
Hinduism is very much a *family* religion gathered around mil-
lions of household shrines, in which the deities honored vary
from household to household. And one might add that Hinduism, with its emphasis on personal experience, is not only a
family religion but also an individualistic religion. It is not
difficult to account, then, for the fact that the Hindu accepts
and values diversity. It is much harder to account for Hindu
unity and perhaps, too, an outside observer might add, to recognize it; he may feel that he can only take the Hindu word
for this sense of unity.

One thing is clear: whatever place definitions of doctrine
may have in determining the Hindu sense of unity, it is not
the place which might be assigned to it by some, if not most,
Christian theologians. Not only are conflicting interpretations
of scripture tolerated, but there is here no binding confession
of agreed-upon doctrine and no authoritative body appointed
to impose it. Some Hindu spokesmen today see disadvantages
as well as advantages in this situation. "If there has been no
heresy-hunting in Hinduism, there has been no restraining influence either," remarks D. S. Sarma. "The Brahmans have
been the custodians of religion, but they have never had, as a
class, any political or ecclesiastical power." [26] Some of the more
conservative bodies in India today are attempting to establish
such control in regard to the proposed reform of the caste system and other issues, but the concern here, it might be said,
is for orthopraxy rather than orthodoxy.

This being the situation, Hindu India seems to invite the study of what, in circles concerned with Christian reunion, have been called the "nontheological factors." Is the caste system to be included among these? If so, it might be claimed that it makes for the sense of unity as much as for diversity. For if it means different rooms for different people, at least they are all in the same house, and it has been remarked that the Hindu fears expulsion from his caste more than anything else in the world.[27]

There are also certain attitudes and practices common to most if not to all Hindus *qua* Hindus, some more definitely pertaining to their religious outlook than others. Among these, for reasons which will presently appear, we may remark in particular the attitude of profound respect for the "holy man," with which may be associated what has been termed "the guru principle." There is an illuminating example of this principle, as of much else in Hindu life, in Rabindranath Tagore's novel, *Gora*.[28] The novel begins by introducing the reader to the household of a retired Indian official who has come to what Hindu writers describe as the third stage in life, the *hermit stage* in which a man, having fulfilled his duties to the community, begins to withdraw from active life and "devote himself to religion." This elderly man keeps very much to his own room, which has an inscription above the entrance, The Hermitage, and spends long hours in the company of his spiritual teacher, his guru, who comes to see him.

The practice of turning to a particular guru as one's pastoral counselor is observed everywhere throughout India by all classes and at all times—not only in this "hermit stage" of life. But who is the guru? What are his qualifications? A visitor unacquainted with Hindu custom might well expect him to be some priest from the temple, a noted scholar, one of the many ascetics who have taken to the highways and byways, a specially appointed officer of the caste, or at least a Brahman.

But a guru may or may not be one of these. What then are his qualifications? The only answer the visitor may be given is "He is a holy man" and that, for the Hindu, is sufficient answer. Respect for the holy man is one of the most significant and distinctive features of Hindu life, and one we shall discuss later. Here it is sufficient to remark that it is one of the attitudes or practices which bring all Hindus, irrespective of caste, school, or sect, together.

Hindu unity perhaps comes more into view as we think of Hinduism in terms of its geography rather than in terms of its history. It is significant that while we have come to name various Hinduisms in terms of history, Ancient, Medieval, and Modern, we seldom do so in terms of geography. An Indus Valley Hinduism, maybe, and a bhakti tradition in southern India distinguished from that in the north, but scarcely such a differentiation as that suggested by the review of history. Hindus themselves may be indifferent to history—though not perhaps so indifferent today—but history has not been indifferent to Hindus. We might almost say that Hindu history has spelt diversity while Hindu geography spells unity, though we should need to qualify this by observing how physical barriers, mountain ranges, and deserts have tended to shut off one part of India from another, so that distinctively local cults have survived in isolated areas.

But taken by and large, geography has been a factor promoting the sense of unity. All the holy places of Hindu story are on Indian soil. There is here no looking to a distant Mecca or Jerusalem. These holy places are named again and again in popular scriptures, such as the epic which tells of the journeys of Rama and Sita. The Hindu in Madras no less than the Hindu in Patna looks to the river Ganges, holiest of the seven most sacred rivers, all of them in the one India. Again, for the Hindu in the south no less than for the Hindu in the north, the great Himalayan mountain peaks prompt the reflection that "hard to climb is the abode of Divinity." [29]

And anyone who has ever stood spellbound within sight of the cold snows of these high ranges which wall the hot, fevered plains can better understand the whole movement of thought and life in Hinduism which seems so nostalgic for infinitude and eternity, as well as that emphasis on mysterious, elusive distance expressed in the great neti neti (not this, not this) of Hindu thought.

It is very often suggested that this neti neti is inimical to any real belief in God. Something more is frequently implied in the criticism than a difference between Hindu and Western conceptions of God, though this too, may be asserted. What is suggested is that the *individual* Hindu thought cannot escape the infection of an ethos which is predominantly monistic in tendency. It is not just a question of beliefs modified consciously and deliberately in the course of intellectual exchange; it is a question of the Hindu believer's being more subtly influenced by the religious atmosphere in which he lives, by non-theistic attitudes as well as by nontheistic ideas, by deep undertones of which he himself may not be fully aware. Such criticism results from an analysis which brings into view something we are all too disposed to ignore, and that is the believer himself behind the beliefs. For the religious situation presents, not just with the meeting of abstract opinions, but with the meeting of the living men and women who hold these opinions.

But if all this is true in one direction, may it not also be true in the opposite direction? Is it not conceivable that Hindu monists may be similarly influenced by Hindu theists? Granted the theistic tradition presented by the Ramanujas and Tukarams of Hinduism, should it not be allowed that this tradition, too, may be infectious?

Nor have we exhausted all the possibilities of the situation by talking thus of one believer's infecting another. We have also to consider what may happen in the case of one and the same believer nurtured in the total context which constitutes

Hinduism. Where does he start? If Hinduism is essentially a family religion, anchored in household observance gathered around household shrines, it is surely here that the young believer is first introduced to the realm of faith, here, in an atmosphere centered in devotion to a particular deity. It is only later in life that he may have the sophistication to regard this deity as no more than a "symbol of one aspect of the Absolute." [30] Whether he becomes a philosophic Hindu or not, he begins, so to speak, as a popular Hindu. Whether he comes consciously and deliberately to qualify his theism by monism or to exchange his theism for monism, he begins with a symbol-directed faith which has not yet entered the realm of intellectual abstractions. We may then ask: Does any Hindu, does any religiously minded man or woman for that matter, ever entirely break away from what he believed in his nursery days?

In the case of the Hindu monist our question becomes more pointed as we also observe how he may continue to live his days, no matter how sophisticated he may have become, in that full atmosphere of Hindu observance and constantly remembered symbol and story which is indicated by Professor Raghavan in his account of Hindu life wedded to Hindu scripture, especially to the poetic, imaginative scriptures such as the puranas and the epics:

The literature of the Purānas has been alive and growing all through history and continues so even today. More than half of the public meetings announced in a busy, modern city like Madras are concerned with expositions of the epics and Purānas. Just as in the old days there were bards or minstrels who recounted the stories of the epics and Purānas, so today there are men who return to the same materials and explain them to the people who gather to hear them in the temples, the homes, and the meeting places of India. Hardly a day passes in any city, town, or village, without an epic or Purāna being read and expounded in the local language to large gatherings of people young and old, of either sex, and of all classes of society.[31]

May we not see in the public audiences to which Professor Raghavan refers, audiences composed of all classes of society, some sophisticated monists among others, and conclude that even the philosophic Hindu may be a popular Hindu at heart?

Again, having remarked the need to discern what is the intention of apparently theistic statements, we may turn the same argument around in the direction of apparently monistic statements. I recall a conversation with a Hindu scholar, an avowed follower of Sankara:

"Would you say Supreme Brahman is God?—a *personal* God?"

"Yes, indeed."

"Would you refer to Supreme Brahman as He or It?"

"Oh, never He. Always It. To speak of Supreme Brahman as He . . . that is too *anthropomorphic*." [32]

There is ground then, first, for the conclusion that we have to distinguish a central tradition of Hindu theism which comes in between the levels of popular religion and philosophic Hinduism, a more sophisticated theism maybe, but vital and infectious, and, second, for the conclusion that this theism may infect and in this way qualify the intention of monistic statements of belief. At the same time, it may be allowed that sophisticated theism is also similarly infected by the far-reaching influence or infection of what may be termed the Hindu urge towards mystical monism.

We have seen, then, in this Hindu context what may be called a principal body of doctrinal scripture, the Upanishads, presenting a conception of Supreme Being, Brahman-Atman, together with movements of life and thought which may lead to interpretation of this conception in a monistic or theistic direction. This interpretation is the doctrinal core of Hindu relativism.

We turn now to a closer examination of this Brahman-Atman

doctrine and some associated beliefs, including the belief in maya (the power of Brahman producing illusion) and the belief in the Divine Inner Controller (*antaryāmin*) dwelling within the spirit of man.

In turning to this subject we may have in mind several issues. There is the question of what Hindu relativism may mean to the Hindu himself, how it may motivate his present concern for unity in the national interest and his growing interest in world community. This has a bearing on what may be expected from the Hindu "forces of religion" in regard to world community. There is also the question of what Hindu relativism may mean to others, how it may be interpreted in ways which may contribute to our own better understanding of unity and diversity in religion. Does it, for example, lend support to the opinion that it is of small consequence what a man believes, as is sometimes maintained? Allied with the question of what Hindu relativism implies there is the possibility that a theistic version may prove more challenging to the Western mind than a monistic version.

There is also the question whether Hindu relativism results from an emphasis on how little man can expect to know in the realm of religion or an emphasis on how much he can aspire to know, the first a reference to human limitation, the second a reference to the nature of that reality to which religious faith refers. Is it that the Hindu thinks meanly of man or nobly of God? The two references are joined, but emphasis on the first may promote disregard for "religious forces" while emphasis on the second may promote belief and great expectations. The parable of the blind men giving different accounts of one and the same elephant as they come in contact with different parts of the elephant presents an oriental view of the situation. What does the Hindu conclude from it? That since all men are blind the least said and done about it the better? Or that since touch has made it known that there is this huge reality there is indeed much to be said and done about it—and that blindness is curable?

Whatever the interpretation of Hindu faith, monistic or theistic, nearly all Hindu thinkers would agree that interpretation gathers around what Professor Hiriyanna has called "the happy identification" [33] in the *Upanishads* of two major conceptions, that of transcendent, Supreme Brahman and that of immanent Atman, resulting in the classic formula Tat tvam asi (That art thou).[34] In this equation two lines of thought converge.

First, there is the line of thought leading to the conception of cosmic Brahman, that which was "at the beginning" and "became everything," [35] the "One without a second, the Non-Being from which Being was born," [36] the Ultimate Reality, the power or primary principle "which of itself burst into utterance" [37] and manifested itself as the universe.[38] This conception comes at the end of a long train of reflection as Hindu thinkers look outward and around them, asking how the world came to be, and how it is sustained. In the earliest Hindu scriptures, we have the first hints of this reflection with a picture of the gods making the world as men build a house, and the question: Whence came the timber for this building? In a later scripture there is the answer "Brahman was the wood, Brahman was the tree," followed by the burgeoning conception of Brahman as the underlying, enclosing reality—"Brahman is all this" [39]— the vast ultimate reality seen from a distance as the Himalayan mountain barrier is seen from the plains, towering, majestic, encompassing, merged with the sky:

> You are (the cloud) with lightning in its womb
> You are the seasons and the oceans
> Without beginning.[40]

Yes, "and to be found everywhere," discerned beneath and around, as well as above: the cosmic Mystery, that which

"holds the sun and the moon to their duty, earth and heaven
to their places; holds the moments, hours, days and nights, fort-
nights and months, seasons and years to their courses." [41] "It
is Brahman that is below and is above, that is to the West and to
the East, that is to the South and to the North. Brahman, indeed,
is this whole universe." [42]

The second train of reflection develops as the Hindu thinker
looks, not at the cosmos surrounding him, but within himself,
pondering the wonder of his own "power of being" and thus
developing the conception of Atman. Through his senses, it
is remarked, man tends to turn outwards "not inward into himself" but "some wise man, with his eyes closed and wishing
for immortality, saw the self behind." [43] From the conception
of an imperishable abiding self in each and every man, Hindu
thought passes to the conception that this "little self" is only
a trace, a "footprint" of a Great Self,[44] a Life-Power, one might
say, shared by all living beings. A classic parable in the Chandogya Upanishad presents the god Indra learning from Pra-
japati that the essential self in man which is "free from death"
is identical with the dreaming self freed from bodily limitations, with the self persisting through dreamless sleep freed
from mental limitations, but even this is not described for it is
"pure consciousness" (cit). The real self in man (atman) has
to be distinguished from the empirical self (jiva); it is existence
which is eternal and immutable (sat); moreover, it is that pure
bliss and love (ananda) which man may realize in mystical
ecstasy.

But in so doing man realizes what he can never fully describe.
Language fails him, because what is thus indicated is "that
which cannot be expressed by speech but that by which speech
is expressed." [45] For this "imperishable" within man, which is
"free from death," is the "unknown knower" [46] and "you cannot know the knower of the knowledge." [47]

Man is the more persuaded of this limitation of language as he realizes—and here we have the great equation, Brahman-Atman—that this, his innermost, his real self is the "innermost of everything." [48] That which is named self has now to be named Self; the atman in each is the Atman in all, the universal Self; and this Atman is Supreme Brahman; this power of being within man is the cosmic Power.

Uddālaka, Son of Aruna told his son Svetaketu . . . "My dear, when this man departs from here, his speech becomes one with the mind, the mind with the life-breath, the life-breath in fire, the fire in the Supreme Deity. This true Being, this subtle source of the world, that is the soul of everything that is Truth, that is the Self, THAT THOU ART, O Svetaketu." [49]

Now what we may very well observe is that the same sequence of reflection which leads to the "happy identification," Atman = Brahman, leads also to the further emphasis of the great negation of Vedantist thought, the neti neti affirming the distant, infinite, unimaginable, altogether lofty, astonishing Supreme Being, beyond limitation and beyond all terms implying the "qualities" which mean limitation: Nirguna Brahman.

"The indication of this Person (Brahman) is 'Not this, not this.' For beyond saying 'Not this, not this,' there is nothing else possible. Then as to the name (of the Brahman) it is the 'Truth beyond the truth.' " [50] The inquisitive Gārgī who is told that the knower cannot be known is rebuked: "Indeed, you are asking too many questions about a divinity about which we are not to ask too much. Do not, Gārgī, question too much." [51] "By what can this knower be known? This Self is the Lord of all beings, the King of all beings. Just as at the hub and the rim of the chariot wheel, all the spokes are filled, even so are all beings, all gods, all worlds, all lives, all selves laid in this Self." [52] If Hindu man is so impressed by the mystery of Supreme Brahman, he is no less impressed when he finds this mystery within himself. In seeking to know himself, his "secret self," he is more than ever persuaded that the final word for Supreme Being must be "Not this, not this." The Hindu, one might almost say, is an existentialist constrained to wonder.

To read these verses from the Upanishads which point to the equation Atman-Brahman is to recapture something of the sense of awe which accompanies the identification. There is no abandoning of the vision of the Infinite betokened in the conception of the cosmic Brahman. If the identification of Atman with Brahman means a higher valuation of man, it is not intended to mean a lesser valuation of Supreme Being or a reduction of God to the size of man.

This point needs to be taken into account when Hindu relativism is presented as equivalent to, or supporting, the kind of Western humanism which leaves no room for God. It is also relevant to the question raised as to the primary reference of Hindu relativism, for what I am here implying is that, as thus far seen, it is a relativism prompted more by thought of Supreme Brahman or God in the highest than by thought of human ignorance or confusion.

But here a question arises—or a number of associated questions. Is room left in this account for any significant naming of God at all? Such naming implies an ultimate distinction between man and God. Is the possibility of such distinction entirely removed by this association of the "secret self" in man with the being which is Brahman? Is it association and no more, or an identification which denies all distinction, that is, unqualified monism?

With this may be joined the question whether the neti neti is here an obliterating word or a qualifying word. If it is an obliterating word then we cannot also say of Supreme Brahman "At least this, at least that"; and there cannot be anything which can properly be called theism, for belief in an altogether unknowable God scarcely comes within this category.

Against this conclusion, it may be urged, however, first, that

when Supreme Brahman is identified with the imperishable
spirit of man, this much at least is affirmed: Brahman is spirit;
ultimate reality is spiritual; "spirit is the foundation of the universe, spirit is Brahman." [53]

Second, there are passages in the Upanishads which go further in this direction, more definitely supporting a theistic
interpretation. For example, there are passages which suggest
that the universe has come to be as the result of personal decision by a personal Supreme Brahman: "It thought 'May I be
many, may I grow forth.' " [54] In one passage it is suggested
that the world of beings has come to be because the Supreme
One desired company.[55]

And in one of the later Upanishads the terms suggest a personal God:

He encircles all things, radiant and bodyless, unharmed, and un-
touched by evil.
All-seeing, all-wise, all-present, self-existent, he has made all things
well for ever and ever.[56]

Third, the modern analysis of religious language suggests
that some fundamental passages may be interpreted in either
a monistic or a theistic sense. It all depends on what is intended.
To estimate this intention, it might be claimed, we have to take
into account the general, total context of thought presented
by these scriptures, which means we must make due reference
to passages in which the theistic intention seems clearly evident, even if they are comparatively few as against the more
numerous monistic passages.

We also need to consider how this teaching came to be, im-
agining ourselves among those earnest students of the forest
academies, gathered around a teacher. What, for instance, may
he do when he says "Brahman is all this" (*sarvam khalvidam
Brahma*)? Can we not see him, with sweeping gesture, pointing
to the surrounding scene, the forest, the trees, the streams, the
mountains in the background, the students themselves? He

may indeed mean what strictly monistic views imply, "Brahman is all that you see around you, and more, one and the same being in all this, without distinction," or he may mean, "Without Brahman, there would be, could be, none of this; Brahman is the Reality underlying all being." [57]

The theistic element in this scriptural heart of Vedantist doctrine is greater, then, than might be concluded from the comparatively few texts in which it is more explicitly affirmed. Among the freethinkers whose discussions are reflected in the Upanishads there were at least some who conceived a Supreme Brahman who was the personal God in the highest as well as those who felt constrained, in the final analysis, to go beyond such personal terms. And to see behind the written letter of this scripture the give and take of these personal discussions is to see more clearly perhaps how we have to allow for a qualifying theistic trend as well as for a qualifying monistic trend in Hindu thought. It is not just a question of one literature against another, the epic scripture naming the High Gods against the Upanishads gathered round the philosophers' conception of Brahman-Atman. It is a question of what may be gleaned from one and the same sacred literature, read and interpreted by a Ramanuja as well as by a Sankara, a theism of different origin and import from that expressed by the bhakti hymn writers.

Nor is it just a question of setting one system against another, a theistic Ramanuja against a monistic Sankara, as if the theme of highest God, personal God, in the Upanishads made no impression on any subsequent thinker except the advocates of avowedly theistic systems. Sankara's system is *qualified* monism; the qualification derives from the same theistic impulse, as room is made for a "lower knowledge," one of a personal God. Moreover, governing this as it governs other Hindu schools of thought is the final neti neti so that we find some thinkers of this school hesitating to say what ultimate union with Brahman will mean as they reflect that even the conception of Brahman as the "One" is a limiting conception in terms of the apparent here and now which has to be transcended. Thus one Hindu scholar can say that we should not conclude that man is to be "lost in Brahman" [58] and another can posit ultimate Brahman as Supreme Spirit transcending *all* "human forms." [59] The so-called prevailing monism of the Sankara school, then, may be seen to be shot through with theistic impulses and qualified accordingly.

Granted, then, this qualifying theistic impulse, how may it affect our view of the purport of Hindu relativism? For answer we may begin by considering the implications of two further associated conceptions presented in Hindu expositions of this doctrine of Brahman-Atman—the conception of maya (illusion) and the conception of *antaryāmin* (the Divine Inner Controller).

Thus far, it might well seem, Hindu relativism might be reduced to the opinion that one religious belief is as good (or as bad) as another since any finality which might be claimed for any of them is obliterated by the overwhelming neti neti. If so, there is little or nothing here to explain the new missionary purpose exhibited by some Hindu spokesmen today, for many of them announce that the Hindu view of life promotes a deep faith in God which, as they see it, is lacking in the West today.

At first glance the conception of maya may seem to take us even further away from such faith. As generally understood in the West, maya means illusion and signifies what a Christian means when he acknowledges that he "sees through a glass darkly." [60] It appears in Hindu thought as the explanation of man's present disposition to see only diversity and not the underlying unity. It appears to put such an emphasis on his confused state of mind that all his religious statements may be

taken to exhibit this confusion, which is sufficient reason for
a relativism which discounts all such statements but scarcely
for a relativism which is said to value them. The real referent
of Hindu relativism, it may then seem, is man himself, his sorry
condition, not any transcending vision of Brahman beyond
description.

It might then be concluded that what the Hindu is saying is
just what a good many others are saying: that you cannot expect from confused people anything better than confused statements of faith, so confused and so approximate that all statements must necessarily be mixed with error. Hence the Hindu
emphasizes experience rather than doctrine, warning others to
do the same. Now it cannot be denied that a good deal of what
is said about maya tends in this direction. In the discussion, the
spotlight is very much on the believer himself, as it is asked
why he should be so deceived by the apparent diversity, what
he must do about it, and what disciplines he must pursue in
order to overcome his confusion and recognize that his life is
indeed related to the underlying unity, Supreme Brahman.

We may next ask: How does man *know* about this overcoming of ignorance? He knows it, in the Hindu view, in the
light of statements made by those who *have* overcome, the
authors of Hindu scripture who *saw* the truth of the human
situation, the seers of old. This means that some religious affirmations are, to say the least, valued more highly than others.
Not all are regarded as equally confused. The reception and
interpretation of these scriptural announcements may indeed
be attended by further confusion, and even the "best minds"
by whom such interpretations (according to some schools of
thought) must be approved may be subject to confusion, unless there has been a similar "overcoming."

Overcoming of what? Their ignorance (avidya). But how
did this ignorance come to be? It is attributed to maya. Here
we come to the conception of maya as *power*—the power

(shakti) used by Brahman which produces the appearance of plurality. Since this appearance stands in the way of man's blessedness and has to be "seen through," the power producing it might be described as a power of evil, that which has to be overcome. Man is pitted against it. Maya in this sense functions in Hindu thought in much the same way as the conception of Original Sin in the Christian tradition. Although it is not something man has brought upon himself by any fall from grace, it is something he shares with all men, something he is born with, the "hump upon his shoulder," signifying his frustrating "congenital ignorance." [61]

But this is only part of the picture. From various channels of the Hindu tradition comes the conception of another aspect of this same maya, still conceived as power, the power of Brahman, but this time as *a power for good*. In the Bhagavad Gita, for example, the conception of maya is associated with divine incarnation intended to dispel confusion:

Though Lord of Beings
Resorting to my own material nature
I come into being by my own mysterious power (*Ātmanāyayā*).

. . .

For protection of the good . . .
To make firm footing for the right.[62]

And in the last canto of the great Song which concentrates on the assurance of divine grace upon which the warrior, Arjuna, can depend, this assurance is given in the same terms of beneficent maya:

The Lord abides, O Arjuna,
   in the hearts of all beings,
causing all beings to turn around by his power (*Yantrārūdhāni Māyayā*) [as if] they were mounted on a machine.[63]

Maya here is associated not with the evil of illusion but with the knowledge of the Lord abiding in the heart which means the beginning of escape from illusion. It is power prompting the movement of life towards release (moksha), gracious power.

Thus the power of maya is seen to work in more than one direction. In one of the Upanishads it is said to be "of three aspects, illumination, activity and delusion." [64]

Our quotation from the Bhagavad Gita, however, points to a further conclusion. This power works *within* man. In Hindu thought it is associated with that "secret self" of man which is the Great Self, which is Atman, which is Brahman. The "light which is within a person," which is "the same as that light which shines higher than this heaven," [65] it may thus be associated with maya. All this is in keeping with the polarity of Hindu thought and its monistic trend to trace everything to one original unity. Thus the urge to seek higher knowledge as well as the need for knowledge may be attributed to maya. This in part explains the Hindu respect for the quest of the intellect—one might say, reverence for the intellect. Here we may recall how it was remarked that Brahman conceived as Atman "the innermost" did not mean, for the devout Hindu, any diminution of Brahman, any flattening of the ultimate mystery which prescribes the qualifying neti neti. As he stands in wonder at his "secret self," this indwelling Atman, so too he may stand in wonder at that quest for truth which inspires him: it is, for him, something much more than might be implied by an equation with his natural intelligence; in theistic terms it is the very power of God working within him.

This is very well illustrated by a recent book by the Maharajah of Mysore. "The urge for expression that surged up within me," he writes, "was like an experience of irresistible Divine Grace [Isvarānugraha] but for which this work would never have seen the light of day. . . . The grace of the Lord . . . is the efflorescence of the divine in man . . . it expresses itself in the urge for philosophic vision." [66]

The Maharajah quotes scripture: "God, Isvara, is the master of power, *māyā*, and hence of all learning, *vidyā* or true knowledge." [67] The Maharajah's exposition, it may be observed, is in the Vedantist tradition generally described as "monistic" as it is also a commentary on a Gita which "tolerates no dualism." [68] But it also exhibits the qualifying theistic impulse of Hindu thought.

The conception of maya as gracious power associated with Atman shades off into another conception: that of the Inner Controller, and here especially, with a more evident impact of the theistic impulse, we move away from identification of this inward urge with human intelligence towards something more like a dialogue in the heart of man between God and man as this prompting power is more definitely personified. There is much the same tension of thought as that which may be observed in the Christian tradition between the conception of the Inner Light and the conception of the Holy Spirit bearing "witness with our spirits that we are children of God." [69] The conception of the Inner Controller means the same conviction of interior prompting. It is an important and integral part of the instructed Hindu's view of life. In the Upanishads the conception is associated with that of Brahman-Atman, Divine Transcendence, and Divine Immanence:

> He who, dwelling in all things
> yet is other than all things.
> . . . who controls all things from within
> He is your soul, the Inner Controller,
> the Immortal.[70]

In the epic scripture, the Bhagavata Purana, the same thought is expressed in the opening verse: "let us meditate on that Supreme Truth, which by its inherent light dispels illusion." In a later passage this illuminating Truth is personified as the Lord who "makes entry" as Dhurva, touched with the Lord's conch of knowledge, bursts into a hymn of praise:

> He who, entering me, revives
> with his power my dormant speech,

as indeed every other faculty of mine—
to you that Lord, the Being endowed with
all powers, I make this obeisance.[71]

But the same power is associated with an abiding Presence, "the
supreme Person residing in every heart" so that all hearts are
"constantly" moved towards God "as the waters of the Ganges
flow incessantly towards the ocean." [72]

All this has a very definite bearing on the intention of Hindu
relativism. It disposes of any conclusion that what a man believes is of no consequence and it indicates the ground of Hindu
tolerance.

When the doctrine is thus presented in theistic terms such
implications may be more apparent to Western minds familiar
with ways of thinking presented in the Christian tradition. To
begin with, there is the respect for human autonomy implied
in the view that man's mind reflects the divine, the light within
being the Light Divine. There is the view that the heart of man,
the dwelling place of the divine, is holy ground. Secondly there
is the inference to be drawn from the view that the purpose
of such divine indwelling is to prompt man towards the true
faith which comes with high vision. Whether we accept such
doctrine or not we can at least see how it may affect the Hindu
standpoint, how it may lead the believer to respect not only
his own power of vision but also the same power of vision exhibited in the lives of others. For it must mean a very great emphasis on the value of such vision wherever it appears.

To observe how and why the Hindu respects the authority
of his scriptures, regarding them as sacred, confirms us in this
conclusion. He does so because they come from men of vision,
the "seers" of old.[73]

Here we may very well return to what we remarked earlier
about the Hindu attitude of profound respect for the "holy
man" (sannyasi). It is important for our better understanding

of Hindu society, as Max Weber emphasized, when he pointed
out how the Brahmins reestablished their influence and power
in the twelfth and thirteenth centuries, the time of Muslim
domination, by fulfilling the role of guru, but how, too, this
influence and this power were challenged by the fact that
others besides Brahmins were accepted as gurus with the emergence of popular religious movements, especially in the Vishna-
vite sects. The guru was and is the instructor and spiritual
counselor of a comparatively small group. In some cases complete submission to his guidance was expected. Now it is understandable why a Brahmin should be accepted as such a guide.
He was able to pursue disciplines leading to the higher knowledge beyond the capacity and opportunity of the layman.
But how was it possible for others, lacking this learning, to
be accepted as gurus? The explanation is that the learning was
only a means to an end: holiness. Non-Brahmin gurus were accepted because they, too, were considered to have achieved
this holiness. There might be charlatans among them, but the
basis of esteem for the guru in general was this expectation of
holiness. In some cults they were even regarded as quasi-divine.
They were living saviors.

Now this profoundly significant respect for the guru or holy
man not only had important consequences for the development
of Hindu society, but it also provides a clue to the intention
of Hindu relativism. For we may well ask what is held to be
the criterion of this holiness? If a guru need not necessarily
be a Brahmin, or have similar learning or status, or belong to a
particular school or sect, what is expected and why is he accepted and valued? What does his holiness signify?

I recall an inter-faith conference in Ceylon, and a lively and
very honest discussion among the Buddhists, Hindus, Muslims,
and Christians who were there, with some sharp questions addressed to a Hindu speaker who gave an account of the life of

a holy man highly esteemed in South India. Why was he so esteemed? we asked, for we were told that he had a good many moral failings and he was not a scholar.

I have since asked this same question of other Hindu friends. In most cases they were not so ready to say as did this speaker at the Ceylon conference, most definitely, that the "morals" of a holy man might be dubious. They were just as persuaded, however, that the answer is not to be given in ethical terms. One of the most illuminating answers was given indirectly by a distinguished Sanskrit scholar. We were discussing contemporary Hindu philosophers, when he remarked "Yes, So and So is good, but it is not to him I'd go. No, I'd go to X." I asked why. "Because," was the reply, "he has given his whole life to it." He began to tell me of that life, and I then understood what he meant by "it." He meant vision.

Whether this is what all Hindus would *say* or not, it is a conclusion implied by their behavior, as it is also indicated by their history. Early in this history we find a special respect for men who are significantly called "seers" (rishi). They are believed to have seen further than most men into the heart of the mysterious Reality which constitutes and surrounds life. Their vision (darsan) is so valued that their recorded words become sacred, authoritative scripture. As time passes various disciplines are proposed whereby others may attain similar lifegiving vision. At the same time experience and generally accepted doctrine suggest that it is not a vision attained by all. But this vision itself is, if anything, all the more prized, especially as the conviction grows that there is indeed a higher life which signifies liberation (moksha) from the frustrations of this present, fitful life, and these men of vision know the way. These are holy men, holy because they perceive the holy. Along with this is the belief that it takes men of vision to interpret for ordinary men what other seers have recorded, that is, sacred scripture. These are the gurus, the teachers, qualified to be teachers because they are holy men. It is naturally assumed that such guidance should come from men (Brahmins) whose caste status is attributed to the fact that they are endowed with sattva (purity), higher intelligence (light). Some of them fail to give this guidance. At the same time, others not so born and so privileged, offer this guidance, or speak with such similar assurance and apparent insight that their counsel is sought. They too are considered holy for they too appear to have this treasured vision. It is the time when the bhakti hymn writers are abroad in the land like the minstrels of old, stirring the soul of India with the poetic insight of sacred song. And they are men and women of all classes. The holy teachers, respected gurus, are similarly found in different walks of life. They may or may not be Brahmins. They belong to different sects and stand outside the sects. They are not constituted "holy men" by any official appointment. Their one sufficient qualification is that they exhibit this power of vision. It matters not that some who claim the power are charlatans, living on the prestige established by others. The significant fact is that such prestige is established in this way.

From this Hindu attitude or practice, then, we may glimpse something of the deep Hindu conviction that life must be directed in terms of that eternity by which it is bordered. Hence the value attached to the word of men who are believed to have achieved vision.

A chosen instrument is not, in the Hindu view, a passive instrument. To understand this more clearly, however, we may need to read Hindu teaching in the light of Hindu practice, for there are aspects of Hindu teaching which, at least to Western minds, suggest passivity. There is, for example, the belief in karma. By the Hindu this is interpreted to mean that man is very much the architect of his own life, whereas to the Western reader it may appear that he is, in this present existence, very much limited in capacity and opportunity, by what he was and did in the far yesterday of previous births. Still more confusing to the Western mind is the image of the dancing Siva or the dancing Krishna and the conception of a divine sport (lila) which may seem to reduce life to a play, leaving little room for serious resolution. Hindu interpreters, however, take this imagery to mean that the Divine embrace includes the whole of life, and the gay Lord Krishna "playing most sweetly on his flute," sporting on the sands of the river with the cowherd lasses, is also the grave Lord Krishna concerned to "purge their minds of its evil." [74] In this Vishnu tradition, the high god is significantly named the "Great Master of Yoga."

It has been claimed that few things are more important for an understanding of the Hindu outlook than the conception of yoga. Yoga means union. As such it points not only to the goal of certain disciplines (union with Brahman) but to the demands of the disciplines themselves. The yogi is one who takes the lord's yoke upon him. Engaging in these disciplines from time immemorial, Hindus have seen in the mastery of certain yoga techniques a way in which man's body may become the instrument of his spirit, resulting in a spiritual freedom whereby he is the instrument of the divine. This is the significance of yoga postures and exercises. As time passed, various ways of yoga, suited to different human capacities, were distinguished. Thus the Bhagavad Gita discusses the three ways of intellectual search (jnana yoga), works (karma yoga), and loving devotion to a personal Lord (bhakti yoga). The fact that the way of loving devotion is presented as an easier yoke may lead to the false conclusion that it is free of demands and not a yoke or discipline at all. But this is not so. Whatever the way, there is the same call for firm resolution and serious engagement. The way of loving devotion cannot be told to one who is "not endowed with austerity." [75] In the Bhagavata Purana it is said: "By manifold paths and at the direction of manifold teachers, people worship you, the sole Lord, who is of the form of all gods, and even as all streams flow to the same ocean, so do all paths come to you in the end." [76] But it is far from the intention of such teaching to encourage the view that it does not matter what a man believes or what he does. On the contrary, the whole tenor of it is that the high vision by which life is ennobled is of supreme consequence.

Similarly illuminating is the interpretation sometimes given of another most general Hindu observance, the observance indicated by the term *ishta-devatā* (the chosen deity, the deity which is the immediate object of a man's devotion). This is frequently described as meaning that each Hindu decides for himself which of the gods he will worship, regarding all as forms of the divine. Some, however, interpret the practice differently. The choosing, they say, is not done by man. It signifies rather the way in which God has chosen to make himself known to this or that particular worshiper for "only by the man whom he chooses is he comprehended." [77] In line with this doctrine of divine election the holy man may function as a chosen instrument whereby dependence on that vision, without which the people perish, is held before men.

It follows, then, that as this vision is seen to be realized by, or given to, men who travel different ways—and sometimes unexpected ways—all, or most of these ways, should be left open and none, or few, forbidden. It is not a conclusion based on respect for *the way itself* (this or that tradition or doctrine) but for *that which may happen on the way* (the vision behind all true teaching, the vision encouraged by such teaching).

It neither despises nor exalts doctrines and systems of thought, and it can very well prefer one to another. It does not mean indiscriminate tolerance. Hindu history shows that, besides the proverbial "hospitality of mind" there has been, from time to time, stout resistance to alien teaching, especially to any teaching which proposes to clothe the Most High in a jacket of words. Nor is it a view quite so intent on religious experience for the sake of experience as is sometimes suggested. And it is certainly not intended to encourage irreligion, nor, again, the view, born of emphasis on man's confusion, that all religious statements are vain, for there is emphasis on men who have *overcome* confusion and emphasis on the grace of God which has enabled them to do so. No, the very reason why Hindus are hesitant about closing any road or marking it forbidden is the fear lest the vision whereby man lives might be lost. And looking out on the wider world today, and not least on our Western world, there are Hindus who believe there is indeed ground for this fear.

We have arrived at this conclusion by observing the manifold nature of the Hindu tradition, by emphasizing its rich diversity, a diversity seen to include a significant, central, theistic impulse penetrating and qualifying other tendencies; we have remarked how this theistic impulse qualifies the trend towards a monistic interpretation as the underlying unity is affirmed; we have considered a central body of doctrine in which this qualification is apparent; and, finally, we have moved from a discussion of ideas to a consideration of the implications of Hindu practice and attitudes.

Our conclusion is not the only possible conclusion. It would be strange if it were, in the case of a tradition presenting such diversity. But it is true, I believe, of the outlook of many Hindus today, and it goes some way to explain that resurgence of purpose and conviction which makes Hinduism one of the forces of religion to be reckoned with in the modern world. It presents a principle of believe and let believe which encourages the Hindu to cooperate with men of other faiths in the cause of world community, as it also challenges, very deeply, any disposition towards "dogmatism" in the Western world or anywhere else—a challenge forcefully presented by Dr. Radhakrishnan. His statement of the "Hindu view of life" may be very much his own view, as some of his critics maintain, a view affected by his interest in Western thought. But he certainly speaks for a great many thoughtful Hindu observers of the world situation when he declares roundly:

It is one of the major tragedies of the world that the great religions instead of uniting mankind in mutual understanding and goodwill divide mankind by their dogmatic claims and prejudices. They affirm that religious truth is attained in this or that special region, by this or that chosen race, condemning others either to borrow from it or else suffer spiritual destitution.[78]

In maintaining this view Dr. Radhakrishnan and others may very well conceive that they are making a contribution to the cause of world community.

And it is here, thus early in our survey, that we have our first hint of what we have called the confessional issue, that issue which arises when the conception of religious community presented by the "confessional church" pattern is called in question. If we are right in our description of the Hindu scene it is this confessional pattern of community which is the particular target of any Hindu criticism of the West. There may be differences of doctrine, Christian and Hindu. But from the Hindu standpoint such differences are secondary. He is prepared to tolerate them abroad as he tolerates them at home. It is not so much this or that Christian doctrine to which he objects as it is Christian *dogmatism* and the demand for subscription to doctrinal definitions as the condition of fellowship, so that the boundaries of community are set in exclusive terms of "You believe what I believe." Speaking from a community where such exclusive terms are rejected he would that others could share his liberty. He regards the contrary "dogmatic" attitude as mistaken, divisive, mischievous, and, in the final analysis, irreverent.

But this same final analysis may prompt a counter-criticism. Is the Hindu himself so far from adherence to basic doctrine as he may think? Is there not in the background of all his thinking the doctrine of neti neti, a doctrine which he maintains today not only with confessional fervor but with missionary fervor? The Hindu may perhaps reply that such a charge comes very near to playing with words. If the affirmation of neti neti is a dogma, then it is a dogma which, if accepted, puts an end to dogma*tism*. And that is what the Hindu is concerned to do. But does this neti neti also put an end to confessionalism? That is more doubtful, as we shall have reason to consider more closely in our next chapter, which deals with Buddhist relativism.

CHAPTER IV

Buddhism: Confessional Relativism

BUDDHISTS have so much in common with Hindus that we may not be aware at first of the significant differences between them. We are, it is true, immediately apprised of a difference in cultural situation and in the patterns of religious life when we pass from Hindu India to Buddhist Asia. But it is not so clearly evident that there is also a change in religious outlook. On the contrary, what may impress us more to begin with is the fact that we are still in a world where the religious outlook is tolerant in sharp contrast to the exclusive "dogmatic" attitudes frequently maintained in the West.

It may indeed be said of Buddhists as it is said of Hindus that they are tolerant of everything except intolerance. And this tolerance may be attributed to a relativism in regard to statements of religious belief, a relativism which appears to reflect Hindu relativism. Thus Hindus have been accepted as speaking not only for themselves but also for Buddhists when they challenge Western dogmatism. Or perhaps we should put it the other way around and say that Buddhists, since their missionary zeal has taken them farther afield, have been the chief spokesmen of this relativism so far as the wider world is concerned.[1] Be this as it may, Buddhists are certainly just as critical as Hindus of some Western religious attitudes. If anything, they are perhaps more critical today than before. Their challenge is the more articulate as they themselves are more exposed to challenge, more concerned to maintain their Buddhist culture in the changing modern world, more conscious of their identity as Buddhists and their missionary role. Some Buddhist leaders are convinced that the world of today is in desperate need of Buddhist doctrine and they are concerned to meet this need.[2]

All this is what might be expected. For the story of Buddhism begins on Indian soil. Yet Buddhist relativism has its own nuances. It goes a step further in attributing differences of religious opinion to differences in human condition and capacity. This again is what might be expected. For if Buddhism is the stepchild of Hinduism it is, as one Buddhist writer remarks, a rebellious stepchild.[3]

As to the Buddhist pattern of community, the broad line of division which can be drawn across the heart of the Buddhist world, marking off the northern Mahayana tradition from the southern Theravada (or Hinayana) tradition indicates a principal "wall of partition" of a kind not found in the more complex Hindu pattern. In this respect, what is presented by Buddhism bears closer resemblance to the Western pattern of a divided Christendom, in which Catholic is distinguished from Protestant. In other ways, too, there is resemblance between the Buddhist and the Christian tradition. If a broad line of division is thus discerned across the heart of both worlds there is also, at the heart of both, a story and, in each case, within this story a central symbol which encourages unity. As for Christians there is the Christ, so for Buddhists there is the Buddha. This means for Buddhists, as we shall presently emphasize, a significant and unifying reference to what may be termed the symbol of the Buddha character.

Again, as in the divided Christendom of today there are ecumenical movements designed to bring Christians more closely together, so in the Buddhist world of today there is the pan-Buddhist movement designed to bring the two halves of this world, Mahayana and Theravada, more closely together in new recognition of the one Path (eka-yana). One of the pioneers of this movement was the Chinese reformer T'ai-hsü (1890–1947) who joined with the revolutionaries to overthrow the Manchu dynasty and afterwards founded dozens of new societies, colleges, journals, leagues, and welfare agencies in his efforts to promote a revival of Buddhist life and thought. He also looked to the Buddhist world beyond China, promoting the exchange of Chinese monks and monks of Ceylon, and himself visiting Japan. And he looked beyond the Buddhist world itself, with missionary interest. He was convinced that "Buddhism alone could re-establish the moral standards needed by mankind" in this modern day when "an atmosphere of strife and murder seemed to have spread over our earth." [4] He was the more convinced of this world mission of Buddhism when he visited the West, lecturing in Europe and America.

T'ai-hsü died the year before the Communists established their regime, but his teaching is maintained today by his disciples in Formosa who continue to publish the magazine which he founded. The same international outlook is very evident among Japanese Buddhist scholars today, while the same joining together of missionary purpose and concern for Buddhist unity is reflected in the speeches of some of the leaders of the pan-Buddhist movement. In this association of the missionary motive with the movement for Buddhist unity we have another point of resemblance with the Christian world where the Ecumenical Movement which resulted in the World Council of Churches received much of its impetus from Christian missionaries. A significant event in this pan-Buddhist movement was the invitation extended to representatives of Mahayana Buddhism to be present as honored guests at the Sixth Great Buddhist Council convened by Theravada Buddhists, which was held in Rangoon. The Mahayana guests may well have been surprised by much that they saw in Burma during their visit. For the two traditions, Mahayana and Theravada, are indeed diverse in many ways. Some years ago I met a group of Buddhist monks from China on the high platform of the Shwe Dagon Pagoda in Rangoon, one of the great monuments of southern Buddhism. They seemed strangely out of place. Their black robes were in sharp contrast to the saffron robes of the Burmese monks who received them. They themselves may have felt out of place, for they must surely have missed the images of various Buddhas to which they were accustomed in their own northern shrines. The image of Gotama (Gautama) Buddha, yes; this indeed was here, many times repeated, with the selfsame features and generally in the same posture: but Gotama alone; none other. And if they discussed this and other points of difference with their Burmese hosts they probably found themselves quoting scriptures unknown to their hosts, while their hosts might have referred to a canon of scripture written in a classical language (Pali) of which, quite probably, the visitors had no knowledge.

To account for this diversity we have to turn, in the first place, to Buddhist history. There is, to begin with, the story which lies at the heart of Buddhism, a story we need constantly to have in mind if we are to see Buddhism as a religion and not, as some have presented it, a cold philosophy. Set against the background of that ferment of new inquiry which quickened the pulse of India in the sixth century before Christ, the Buddhist story is a story of a great renunciation and a great awakening. It is the story of the prince Siddhattha Gotama who renounced the comforts of his palace life to take to the forests and seek the saving truth. According to Buddhist tradition, he was moved to do so by seeing for the first time in his sheltered life a man wasted by sickness, a man bowed by old age, and, lastly, a dead man. The teaching he gave as the Buddha after his awakening or enlightenment, which he achieved as he sat cross-legged in resolute meditation at the foot of the bodhi tree in Gaya, was based on an analysis of human life in terms of this same three-fold spectacle of sickness, decay, and death. All, he taught, was change. All was suffering or frustration. The way to rise above this change and suffering and attain the liberation which was Nirvana was the Middle Way of the Noble Eightfold Path, a way between the extremes of asceticism and self-indulgence.

And this, according to Theravada Buddhists, was his conclusion of the matter. All that he taught during the rest of his long life was just an elaboration of this early theme; his followers were to continue resolutely in this same Path, each of them dependent on his own efforts. "The Buddha can point out the path; he can tell us of its difficulties and of the beauties which we will find as we tread the path; but he cannot tread it for us. . . . The Buddha says, 'By oneself is one defiled; by oneself is one purified.'" [5] The Buddha, indeed, is revered above all other teachers. His enlightenment sets him apart. His example is remembered and his teaching followed. In this sense southern Buddhists recite the formula, "I go for refuge to the Buddha." But it is refuge in a teaching, not in a savior, not in a God. What, then, of prayer? Southern Buddhists may indeed be observed with heads bowed in prayer like other believers the world over. But a Buddhist scholar explains it thus: "Prayer . . . will aid us in the concentration of our thought. . . . The concentration of our mind reacts on our will. . . ." [6]

Soon after Gotama Buddha's death there were conflicts of opinion among the members of the monastic order which he founded, conflicts resulting eventually in many different schools. One of these was known as Theravada, the doctrine (vada) of the Elders (thera). It is this name which southern Buddhists prefer today. For the name Hinayana (lesser vehicle) used by their Mahayana critics suggests disparagement, while the name Theravada brings to mind the Elders who resolved to abide by the Buddha's discipline. They are said to have recited the Buddha's teaching one to another at a Council convened immediately after his death. Thus committed to memory, the teaching, according to the southern tradition, was transmitted by word of mouth until, some five centuries later, it was written down in its present form of the threefold Pali Canon (Tipitaka) in order that the true doctrine might endure— written down in Ceylon, which was soon to become a principal citadel of Theravada Buddhism. At about the same time Buddhism was introduced to Burma, Thailand, and the countries farther east, while it gradually declined in India itself.[7] Although challenged by the later Mahayana schools, Theravada Buddhism eventually became predominant for many centuries in southeast Asia. Not only so, but it became the *national* religion in most of these countries. Princes included among their titles that of "defender of the faith." In Burma today, as for many centuries, there is the saying, "Burma custom is Buddha custom." Until the arrival of Christian missionaries in modern times there was no serious rivalry from any other form of organized religion. Traces of Hindu and Mahayana influence remained, and pre-Buddhist "animistic" practices continued.[8] But the prevailing culture was predominantly a Theravada Buddhist culture, as monasteries were established and the monks became the schoolmasters and counselors of the people and the chaplains and advisers of their rulers.

The pattern closely resembles the pattern maintained in European countries where one particular form of Christianity became the established national religion. This is a point of some consequence. It goes a long way to explain the fact that, in contrast to northern Buddhism, southern Buddhism is altogether a more compact, tidier tradition, with much less tendency to diversity. In Burma, for example, as in Thailand, there was a central ecclesiastical authority concerned to maintain the Theravada discipline. The influence of the monastic order was preserved by the period of residence in a monastery spent by each young layman following the initiation ceremony which marked his coming of age. As there were very few sectarian divisions in the Theravada tradition, it was a unifying influence, the more so as the source of all instruction, whether for monk or layman, was the one body of canonical scripture, the Pali Tipitaka. "The Tipitaka," remarks the Maha Thera U Thittila, "contains everything necessary to show forth the path." [9]

Thus Southeast Asia presents a Bible belt of Buddhism gathered around a monastic order remarkably free from sectarian division, conservatively resolute to maintain this "way of the Elders," a way determining the cultural outlook of this region for centuries without serious invasion or interruption from the great world outside. Western intruders in modern times have disturbed this pattern, but it is being renewed today. In view of this past history, it is no argument against true zeal for religion to observe that religious revival is here associated with national restoration. Many Buddhists in Ceylon, remarks the Venerable Ananda Maitreya Nayaka Thero, sought independence "for the sole purpose of gaining back their national religion." [10]

Throughout this whole region, then, there is a predominantly Buddhist culture. The strength of this culture is the monastic order and its outward and very visible sign is the saffron robe of the respected monk, who, as schoolmaster and counselor of the laity, has been far more closely related to the life of the people than might be supposed from accounts which present the monk as an isolated recluse solely intent on his own perfection. Everything here, then, points to a realized Buddhist unity rather than diversity. The Sixth Great Council held a few years ago was a significant reaffirmation of this unity.

The very opposite holds true in the case of Mahayana Buddhism. Nearly everything here makes for diversity. This

has been so from the beginning, for Mahayana teaching antici-
pates, promotes, and authorizes diversity, a diversity further
encouraged by the circumstances of its development and the
direction of its expansion.

Mahayana teachers claim that this development is what the
Buddha himself expected, and indeed initiated. They present
a revised version of the Buddha story. According to this version, the Buddha's teaching of the Noble Eightfold Path was
not the conclusion of the matter. He had more to say, a
greater (maha) way (yana) to proclaim. But he waited until
the end of his long ministry to proclaim it. Such was his wisdom, such his compassion, such his "skillful means" that he
waited until his disciples were ready to receive this teaching,
waited until he had led them, step by step, along the Path.
Then, before he passed to Nirvana, speaking to his disciples
from the heights of the Vulture's Peak, surrounded by the
heavenly hosts, bathed in radiant light, he manifested himself
as the Eternal Buddha, "the Father of all the Worlds," not
only calling men to follow the Path, but in the plentitude of
his power, far greater than any poor strength of their own,
upholding, inspiring, strengthening them in the Path. By the
same token, all earlier instructions were only partial and the
"lesser way" (Hinayana) was only an introductory way. By
the same token, again, our understanding of the Buddha's
teaching (dharma) is relative to our progress in the way.

This revised version, however, comes from scriptures written later in Buddhist history, and written, not in the Pali of
the Theravada canon, but in Sanskrit. And there are many
such scriptures. For the Mahayana tradition in the course of
time has branched out into many schools and sects, each with
its selected scripture from a much larger corpus than the
Theravada Pitaka. In these respects Mahayana Buddhism reflects the Hindu pattern as it may also be said to be born of
further encounter with Hindu thought. While the Mahayana

Buddhist, like the Theravada Buddhist, points back to earlier beginnings, the historian refers in particular to the new ferment of inquiry which developed in northern India some five hundred years after the Buddha's death, continuing for nearly a thousand years, with school succeeding school. In the first centuries of this development we have the writing of the scriptures of the new "transcendental" wisdom (the Prajñā Pāramitā Sutras), and the speculations of the "central" Madhyamika philosophy. The great dialectician Nagarjuna conducts from Nalanda a lively debate with his Brahmin opponents across the Ganges River. It is a time of adventurous journeys undertaken by the first Mahayana missionaries along the central Asian trade routes north of the Himalayas to introduce Buddhism to China.

The period overlaps the first centuries and similar missionary expansion of the Christian tradition. Did the two traditions, Buddhist and Christian, meet? The question is often raised, for there are affirmations and emphases in both traditions, which suggest such a meeting.[11] In particular there is the bodhisattva version of the Suffering Servant and its associated ethical ideal of adventuring, ministering, long-suffering benevolence which is distinctive of the Mahayana tradition as compared with the Theravada (though not so entirely absent from the latter as is sometimes supposed).

What is more relevant in our present discussion, however, is the impact of the Hindu faith on the Mahayana development especially. For here we have a return, it might seem, to the qualifying neti neti (not this, not this) of Hindu thought, and with it, a return to the neti neti and relativism making room for diversity, which is also fundamental in Buddhism.[12] Nagarjuna may cross swords with Hindu opponents, but is he not nevertheless essentially with the Hindu tradition when he speaks of that ultimate reality, Sunyata (the Void), which is beyond all the something as it also is beyond all the nothing conceived by the mind of man? For this reality, which is Nirvana, which is the Buddha, which is dharma, "escapes precision." Hence the view that "all is relative," since we simply do not know "what is finite and what is infinite." As in Hindu thought, this emphasis of the sheer transcendence of a unity which is beyond cries halt to dogmatism and promotes a branching out into a rich diversity.

As this Mahayana teaching makes its way northward and eastward to China, Korea, and Japan, it enters a pattern of further diversity and adds to this diversity. For in these countries the Buddhism which splinters into sects (or schools, if you will) is itself a sect, or at least just one expression of "organized religion" among others. Buddhism is never here for any length of time a national religion unifying the life of a whole people. In China it takes its place beside Taoism and Confucianism and is modified by both.[13] In Japan there is Shinto.[14] "A magnificent High Church," says Stcherbatsky.[15] But Stcherbatsky's eloquence has led him astray here. Churches maybe, but not *a* Church; sects established by a succession of great reformers from the Chinese Chih-I to the Japanese Honen, sects generally amiably tolerant of each other, so that the Buddhist monks are still initiated into a single order.[16]

But Stcherbatsky is right when, in the same paragraph, he speaks of "radical revolution" and "the break between new and old within the pale of what nevertheless continued to claim common descent from the same religious founder." The difference between Theravada and Mahayana Buddhism is all the more evident because there is so much diversity *within* the latter.

As to the central core of teaching in each tradition we may summarize the difference in broad terms by remarking that whereas in the Theravada tradition the term Buddha means the historic founder, in the Mahayana tradition it signifies the Eternal Buddha manifested in many forms so that various

Buddhas are named besides Gautama. There is a trinitarian conception of the Buddha conceived as the exalted absolute (dharmakaya), as the Buddha walking this earth (Gautama and others: nirmanakaya) and as the Buddha (samboghakaya) generating joy and love for dharma (truth; law; light) in much the same way as the Holy Spirit is conceived to inspire believers in the Christian tradition or as the indwelling God is conceived to move them in the Hindu tradition.[17] At the popular level there is something like a return to the high gods of Hinduism as many Buddha-beings are named and pictured, including Amita, who presides over the Pure Land in the western quarter of the universe and has vowed to save all sentient beings; Maitreya, the future Buddha who now dwells in the Tushita heaven; Bhaisajyagura Buddha, the "Master of Healing," residing in the Pure Land in the eastern quarter; Avalokiteshvara (Kuan-yin) who takes many forms, including a feminine form, in seeking to relieve human distress; and even Ksitigarbha (Ti-tsang) who is the patron of criminals.

The last two named are bodhisattvas, Buddha-beings so filled with compassionate concern that they remain in this world of woe, delaying their own full realization of Nirvana for the sake of others, a conception elaborated and emphasized in a way which inspires in the believer the conviction that, far from being entirely dependent on his own efforts, he is living in a universe thronged by invisible Buddha-beings engaged in an untiring ministry for his benefit. There is indeed, in this Mahayana tradition, a religion of "other power," as well as religious observances more nearly resembling the observances found in other traditions than in the case of Theravada Buddhism.[18] If it is questionable whether there is any room for prayer and worship in the Theravada tradition, where the historic Buddha is revered rather than supplicated, there is no question about such room in the Mahayana tradition (although it is not always occupied). A popular pamphlet published in Shanghai some years ago, for example, details specific cases of answers to prayer in times of distress.[19]

What is frequently claimed is that Mahayana Buddhism thus presents a larger view of man as a being already possessed of the Buddha-nature, which only needs to be realized and developed, as well as a larger opportunity for man and a nobler ideal. The larger opportunity appears as the Buddha is seen to assist all sentient beings by "skillful means" adapted to their several conditions and capacities. The nobler ideal is presented in terms of the virtues of the self-sacrificing bodhisattva who delays his own full Nirvana bliss for the sake of others. This is set in contrast to the Theravada ideal of the disciplined monk intent on his own salvation. There is also the suggestion that, at least in Japan, the bodhisattva ideal has meant a more active benevolence as clergy and laity alike are encouraged to engage in social service, whereas in Theravada countries the monks remain secluded in their monasteries while the laymen are left to practice the meager morality indicated by the few precepts prescribed for them as against the 227 regulations prescribed for the monks. There is here, however, a good deal of exaggeration. The ideal of service for others cannot be foreign to the minds of Theravada Buddhists who so frequently recall not only the teaching but the example of the historic Buddha, as well as the virtues emphasized in the Jataka stories of his previous existences. Nor is there quite such a gulf between Theravada laity and clergy as is sometimes supposed. The monks have exercised a more active teaching ministry than is sometimes recognized. As to the contrast drawn between the Theravada monk concentrated on his meditation exercises and the householder immersed in worldly affairs, we must remember that the householder has also been encouraged to withdraw from the world for days of retreat, a practice significantly revived today. At the same time, it may be allowed that more is said about the householder's religion in the Mahayana tradition. There is also the difference between the two traditions which is indicated by the fact that some Mahayana sects have married clergy who are very much family men, engaged in what might be termed in the West a parish ministry, while all the Theravada clergy are celibate monks. There are many other points of contrast, especially if we include in the Mahayana tradition the tantric Buddhism of Tibet with its mantras, tutelary deities, symbolic rites, and mystic formulas, very different indeed from the sober Theravada way.[20]

In brief, northern Buddhism, with its many Buddhas, many scriptures, many schools, and its history of new departures and frequent reformers establishing new sects, exhibits much greater diversity than southern Buddhism. The Theravada tradition with its one body of scripture and comparatively few sects is altogether a more compact system of belief and practice.

Accompanying differences in practice and doctrine there is a fundamental difference in attitude. The Mahayana attitude is essentially progressive, whereas the Theravada, wedded to the way of the Elders, is conservative.

The coming together of the two traditions today may be largely due to that shaking of the foundations of the modern world which, in each case, has meant a challenge to the dominant attitude. Faced by the challenge of new conditions, the Theravada teacher is being asked, for example, what he has to say to those who must build the "welfare states" of today. What is his social gospel? [21] The same pressures mean that the Mahayanist must ask what he has to say to the world as a Buddhist. What is there in his tradition which must be preserved and announced and distinguished from what others, including Christians, Marxists, and the evangelists of the "new religions" in Japan, may be saying?

Thus disposed to come together, and brought together by the changing conditions of the modern world, Buddhists today

are asking anew what they have in common. It is not enough
to name the one Path. That has been named all along, not least
by Mahayana Buddhists. But this naming of the one Path has
not sufficed to check increasing diversity, sometimes to the
point of division. Nor is it enough to say that all acknowledge
the one goal of this Path: Nirvana. Nor, again, does it suffice
to add that all name the enlightened teacher who pointed out
this Path, since his pointing has been so variously interpreted.
We are still left asking what the Buddhist who places his whole
trust in Amita Buddha's saving vow has in common with the
Buddhist who looks only to the teaching of Gotama Buddha
to whom no such vow is attributed.

With the confessional issue in mind, we may begin with
some attempts which have been made to draw up a common
Buddhist confession or creed. It is significant that these attempts have been largely promoted by Western converts, just
as Western scholars have attempted to distinguish what the
Buddha himself taught from what his followers have taught
in his name.[22] Whether Buddhists themselves attach a similar
value to the definition of doctrine is, however, questionable.
One of the first attempts to draft a confession or creed to which
all Buddhists might assent was made by the American found-
ing president of the Theosophical Society, Colonel H. S.
Olcott, in 1891. Colonel Olcott listed fourteen "fundamental
Buddhistic beliefs." Printed as an appendix to his *Buddhist
Catechism*, they were approved by "accredited representatives"
from Japan, Burma, Ceylon, and Chittagong at a congress held
in India.[23] But the important Shin School is missing from the
list of Japanese sects who signified approval. Half a century
later, when Mr. Christmas Humphreys, of the London Buddhist Society, attempted a similar statement, listing twelve
principles, he made special efforts to word his statement in
a way acceptable to Shin Buddhists. The difficulty was to
reconcile the proposition that every man must "work out

his own salvation" with the Shin teaching of trust in Amita Buddha's saving vow.[24] Mr. Humphreys claims that he was successful, and his publishers claim that his twelve principles, translated into fourteen languages, "are in process of being accepted as the basis of world Buddhism." The *basis?* I wonder. It is arguable that what we have here is a very Western valuation of doctrinal agreement. To Western minds such a confessional platform might well seem a necessary if not a first step towards the realization of Buddhist unity. But it is very much open to question whether Asian Buddhists approach the issue in this way or set the same value on announcements of interpretative doctrine as the gateway to unity.

It is true that the more speculative Mahayana Buddhists seem at times to come near to doing this. Thus T'ai-hsü, the Chinese reformer, coupled a modest claim for Buddhists with an exalted claim for Buddhist doctrine when he said, first, that it was *probably* Buddhism alone which could provide a basic, unifying morality for the modern world and, second, that it could do this by providing the cosmic view inherent in its doctrine of interdependent causation (pratiyasamutpada).[25] But another Mahayana scholar, Professor Nakamura, explicitly allows that Buddhists themselves interpret such doctrine differently.[26] Early in his statement on Buddhist unity and diversity he makes it clear why this is so: "Only a Buddha can apprehend the whole truth. . . . Thus in Buddhism there is no dogma which opposes other dogmas." [27] As to Theravada Buddhism, U Chan Htoon of Burma, the present leader of the pan-Buddhist movement, expresses the same attitude when he remarks that ex cathedra pronouncements by religious leaders are unknown in Buddhism. Far from suggesting a unifying confession of faith, he says flatly that Buddhists have no "blind faith in any particular creed." "Dogmas," he says, "will always remain an insuperable obstacle to religious unity." [28]

Mr. Humphreys himself describes Buddhism as "a form of

relative truth" and he could cite many quotations from his own work to prove what he would doubtless claim, that his twelve principles are not intended as an ex cathedra, dogmatic confession, after the Western manner. Nevertheless, there is the savor of Western confessionalism, with its respect for clean-cut conceptions, in the suggestion that twelve agreed-upon principles will provide *"the* basis of World Buddhism." [29] We have here, I think, an interesting example of what is happening today as Western and Eastern attitudes in regard to such definition encounter each other.

What is presented by the Buddhist world itself is not only the difficulty of achieving doctrinal unanimity but a large question concerning its possibility, desirability, or necessity. If there are moves in this direction, they are qualified by Buddhist relativism. I emphasize this as one of the things which lead us to look further for the sense of Buddhist unity.

The trail takes us, in the first place, away from creeds to scripture, especially in the Theravada half of the Buddhist world. There are no ex cathedra announcements, says U Chan Htoon; the *"sole authority"* is the text of the Tipitaka.[30] This lay opinion is supported by both ecclesiastical opinion and practice. As at other great councils, the principal business of the monks assembled for the Sixth Council held recently in Rangoon was to examine the scriptures and promote their study. The reference to scripture, however, is scarcely a reference that can be said to further the sense of unity for, as we have observed, "there is no one scripture which is accepted as having the same authority for everyone who calls himself a Buddhist." [31] There is also the fact that the emphasis on direct insight and silence in Zen Buddhism reduces, in this tradition, the reliance upon scripture.

The reference to scripture, however, points us on our way to what may very well be our final conclusion: *that the most central and unifying reference is the reference to what may be termed the symbol of the Buddha character.* This statement requires explanation of both the word "symbol" and the term "the Buddha character."

The word "symbol" is variously employed today. I use it here with reference to the distinction which may be drawn between the expression of a primary apprehension of that which arouses religious response and the expression of reflective thought concerning this response. The symbol, so to speak, stands behind the doctrinal proposition. It is there before all credal elaborations and systematic presentations, a language of first awareness or impression, often a picture language, intimating more than is actually pictured. In this sense of the term *symbol*, what is immediately expressed by the name *Buddha* may be said to constitute the prior and central symbol of Buddhism, as what is immediately expressed by the name *Jesus Christ* may be said to constitute the prior and central symbol of Christianity. As a Christian may be described as one who seeks to "have the mind of Christ" [32] so a Buddhist may be described as one who seeks to have the mind of Buddha.

In either case much that is presented in this way is presented in the form of story. In Theravada countries Buddhism means not only a constant remembrance of the Buddha's teaching but a constant remembrance of his life and example. The *shinbyu* (initiation) ceremony in Burma, for example, when the young Buddhist comes of age and leaves home to live for a time in the monastery, is gathered around the story of the Buddha's great renunciation. It may begin with a procession as the young novice rides through the village, attired in princely costume. He may be mounted on a white pony, for does not the Great Story tell how the Prince Siddhartha thus left the palace on the day of his renunciation "on the back of his favorite horse . . . a magnificent animal . . . the hair of a beautiful white, resembling a newly cleaned shell"? There is a dramatic moment, following the return to the young man's home where the monks and other guests have assembled for the ceremony. This is the moment when the princely clothes are thrown aside, the boy's head is shaven, and he appears before the guests in the saffron robe of the Buddhist novice. For is it not also told how the Prince Siddhartha, seeing that his rich and shining robe did not answer his purpose, accepted from a friend "one dress required . . . for his future calling," having first with one hand unsheathed his sword, and with the other seized his comely hairs, cutting them with a single stroke to become a tonsured recluse? [33]

For the young Buddhist, thus gaily attired and proudly mounted, riding through the village, this dramatic reenactment of the great renunciation surely means to "have the mind of the Buddha." It is all, so to speak, "in character." For the parents and guests, too, it is surely a recalling of the story, a moment of high poetry and of all that pertains to the poetry of this religion.

There are many other occasions when the story is recalled and many other ways in which all that the Buddha stood for is brought to mind. The instruction received in the monastery, as in earlier boyhood at the monastery school, is in part precept and in part story. There is the *Song of the Eight Victories*, in which the Buddha's battle with Mara, the tempter, is recalled:

> By liberality did he
> The Sage attain to victory
> (Such was his chosen armoury!)
> Māra, by all his host attended,
> (With thousand flashing swords defended,
> On his war elephant so proudly seated)
> In panoply of steel the Sage defeated.

Each stanza of the song ends with a refrain bringing home to the young disciple the teaching that he, too, should be clothed in a panoply of steel and have the same resolute mind:

> Be yours his glorious victory
> And yours its ample blessing be.[34]

There are other stories, stories of how the Buddha in his long ministry led his disciples in the Path by example as well as by precept, of how "like a battle elephant" he calmly pursued his purpose, quietly resolute, undisturbed in the face of false accusation, winning men to his side that they might "preach the Noble Doctrine for the good and welfare of the many," all of them in character, the character of the compassionate sage. Nor are these stories forgotten when the monastery schooling is ended. There are many occasions, formal and informal, when men and women gather together, listening to monks who tell again "the story of that great life, bringing it home to you with reflection and comment till you forget that he of whom they speak lived so long ago." [35] Nor is it only the monks who do this. "He who has lived in Burmah," wrote Bishop Bigandet a century ago, "must have often heard . . . laymen repeating, during sometimes a whole hour, formulas in Pali, or religious stories in Burmese, which they had learned in the school." [36]

Besides the storyteller there is the artist. What is told in word is also told in drama, picture, and sculpture. Here we may very well take into account the influence and significance of the sculptured Buddha image. Every day is lived in the presence of this image. There is not only the image in the monastery precincts but also the one in the wayside shrine and the image in every household. In Theravada countries the features are always the same, the features of the calm, serene Gotama. How well I remember that image, even today (some thirty years after the time I lived in Burma), and I am a Christian! What must it mean to the Buddhist who lives in that presence, and lives in it for a lifetime?

My Theravada friends are quick to say that it does not mean idolatry, nor yet worship as worship is conceived in other traditions. "True Buddhists . . . do not worship an image nor pray to it. . . . Just as people love to see the portrait of one dear to them when separated by death or distance, so do Buddhists love to have before them the representation of their Master, because this representation enables them to think of his virtues, his love and compassion for all beings, and the doctrine he taught." [37]

"To think of his virtues." This explanation, it may be observed, goes beyond that frequently offered in the case of the veneration of images by Hindus. The instructed Hindu, it is sometimes claimed, knows very well that the image of his chosen deity points to no other reality than that which is in the mind of the devotee. It meets a psychological need as "the heart of man hungers for a (personal) god of love, grace, and mercy." [38] In the context of Theravada Buddhism, however, the image of the Buddha has an *ethical* function. It points beyond itself and also beyond what may be in the mind of the devotee to what he ought to have in mind, what he ought to recall to mind, what has been set before him in a life which has been lived: the *virtues* set before him. This is one reason why I speak of the symbol of the Buddha *character*.

Besides the story of the historic Gotama, Theravada Buddhists chant and repeat other Buddha stories, *Jātaka* stories referring to previous existences of the Buddha, before that existence in which he attained enlightenment. These are also stories "in character," presenting aspects of that character which provides the model of conduct; they tell of the character which the Buddha-to-be was forming on the way to enlightenment: the character which his followers must form in their own progress towards this enlightenment. Many of them, in particular, exhibit the quality of compassion. And here we have a bridge between the Theravada and the Mahayana traditions, first, in the suggestion that there may be reference to more than one life, more than one model or presentation of what is essentially the same character, and, second, in the Theravada anticipation of the bodhisattva compassion emphasized in Mahayana teaching (though this anticipation is not confined to the stories of previous existences; it is inherent, too, in the story of the historic Gotama).[39]

These considerations meet the possible objection that in turning to the Mahayana account we turn to an altogether different presentation of the Buddha. It may be objected, in the first place, that in the elaborated Mahayana Buddhology the Buddha is so glorified, whether as the eternal father of all the worlds, the Buddha of the "triple body," or the Amida Buddha of the Western Paradise, that he becomes the distant, exalted Buddha rather than the historic Buddha, setting before men the "human" example and the teaching. It is because of this that I refer to the Buddha *character* rather than the Buddha example. Having done so, I then observe that, even as the Exalted One, the Buddha is presented as exhibiting essentially the same character, a character of mercy joined with wisdom. This is the constant theme of all the Mahayana expositions.[40] Even as the Exalted One he fulfils the same ethical function as in the Theravada tradition. The virtues of the Buddha provide the norm of conduct.

Nor is the historic teacher, the Sakyamuni, Gotama, hereby ignored. In Shan-tao's popular parable of the hesitant pilgrim, treading the perilous way between fire and flood, chased by beasts and robbers, he is the voice crying "Go" together with the encouraging voice of the awaiting Buddha in the Western Paradise crying "Come." Moreover, the nirmanakaya doctrine means that there is reference to the Buddha manifest in sentient form, thus not only announcing the teaching but exhibiting the Buddha virtue. In the Mahayana scripture, the Buddha Carita, ascribed to Asvaghosa, it is said of the historic Buddha that, even before the moment of his enlightenment no one in his company, as he came from his palace on the day of his renunciation "indulged in an improper thought as at the presence of Religion herself embodied." [41] The king of the Magadhas "beheld him . . . distinguished by his beauty of form and tranquility as the very creation of Religion itself." [42] If it is objected that Gotama Buddha is not the only image and manifestation in the Mahayana tradition my reply here is that, whatever the form or name, there is still the presentation of the Buddha character: the Buddha compassion, the Buddha wisdom—"his wonderful wisdom." The purpose of Amida's saving vow, for example, is to enable sentient beings to realize this character.

But what of the objection that Mahayana Buddhism, with its conception of the benevolent bodhisattva delaying his own full salvation for the sake of others, presents an altogether different ethical ideal and conception of the Buddha character from that presented by the Theravada conception of the arhat narrowly concerned to "work out his own salvation"? Much has been written about this difference. I grant that it exists. I grant, too, that it has been emphasized by Buddhists themselves. On the one side, the Mahayana development has been hailed as a rediscovery of the missionary purpose, human concern and active benevolence taught and exemplified by the Buddha as against a "faith monopolised by monks" intent on their own emancipation with scant regard for the laity. On the other side, the Theravada tradition has been interpreted as true to the original ideals of resolute world-renunciation, individual responsibility, and equanimity as against the "secularism" of a tradition which allows a married clergy and, in the name of compassion, condones compromise.

This difference, however, may be exaggerated. Furthermore, what I have named is not some rigid *definition* of the Buddha character but the *symbol* of the Buddha character, with all the room it provides for difference of emphasis and interpretation. We have here not the wedding of two abstractions, compassion and wisdom, to form a character, but, in the first place, a character presenting two aspects so named, the *Buddha* character. To be a Buddhist is to be Buddha-minded. Other bonds of unity may be named but it is this central reference, more than any other, which brings the Buddhist world together, as it also means a unity which allows for diversity.

It is a central reference which may be seen to function in much the same way, in this respect at least, as the belief in divine revelation and the reference to the Christ in the Christian tradition. To say this is not to identify the conception of the Buddha with the Christian conception of God. Such an identification is repudiated by Theravada Buddhists. Even in the Mahayana tradition where the Buddha is "glorified" and named "the Father of all the worlds" and regarded as omniscient, omnipotent, and omnipresent, the conception comes short of such an identification. No Buddhist says, "I believe in Almighty Buddha, maker of heaven and earth." On the contrary, it is flatly said: "Buddhism has never believed in a creator-Buddha or a creator-god." [43]

Nor can the conception of the manifest Buddha be identified with the conception of the manifest Christ. What is rather signified by the fact that both are named "the Light" is a similarity of function. In both cases there is a central reference which motivates and informs conduct as it promotes unity.

At the same time, it may be observed that the central reference to the Buddha character functions in this way only *as a symbol*, with all the flexibility of interpretation and hence the unity and diversity which a symbol allows. In a recent discus-

sion of the role of symbol in religious society, Dr. Peter Munz
has suggested that when the "symbol-picture" of the central
reference is maintained, as against the reduction involved in
dogmatic definition, the possibility of unity in diversity is
preserved.[44] We shall return to this point in a later chapter.
Meantime, the conclusion may be drawn that what the Buddhist world contributes in particular to our discussion of unity
and diversity is an illuminating example of the situation and
possibility which Dr. Munz has in view. *As a symbol*, the reference to the Buddha character draws the Buddhist world together, while allowing for diversity.

It remains to consider in what way this allowance for diversity differs from that observed in the Hindu tradition.
Buddhist relativism, it has been suggested, while it reflects
Hindu attitudes, does so very much on its own grounds, presenting its own challenge. What are these grounds?

For an answer we may very well turn in particular to the
Mahayana tradition where there is the greater diversity. In a
particular scripture, The Lotus of the Wonderful Law, this
diversity is explicitly justified. Probably written in the second
century A.D., acknowledged as one of the most influential and
one of the noblest of all the Mahayana texts, the Lotus (Saddharma Pundarīka) [45] presents the view that the Buddha did
not say all that he had to say until the very end of his ministry.
It also explains why he thus delayed. He did so because his
disciples could not at first have received this full teaching even
if he had given it. He did so, because as the all-wise Buddha
who understood them, as the compassionate one, he was patient
with them, and as the "Father of all the Worlds" he could
afford to wait; he was possessed of the skillful means required
to bring them to full understanding. But now that they had
this understanding and could know this Great Way (Mahayana) this was the way they must follow, not the Lesser Way

(Hinayana) which was all that they could understand before. This Lesser Way is not denied; it is true as far as it goes, but it does not go far enough. Of this they can be assured, for the Buddha who gives this word is the Sakyamuni, the historic Buddha received into glory, the eternal Buddha, none other.

All this is told in one of the most exciting books in religious literature. To feel the pulse of this excitement is, I think, to conclude that it was written fairly early in Mahayana history. It reflects the adventure of thought, the missionary zeal, and the evangelical fervor of the new movement. It is "truth embodied in a tale," and it is meant to "enter in at lowly doors" as it moves from the poetry of apocalyptic imagery to parable. The central theme is the presentation of the earthly Sakyamuni Buddha as the glorified eternal Buddha, omniscient, omnipotent, omnipresent, announcing to all sentient beings "Ye shall all become Buddhas." This theme is unfolded in a great spiritual drama with the whole universe as its stage. It is a crowded stage, with all the saints, all the Buddhas, all the bodhisattvas, all the gods, all the beings of the earth, all mankind, and even the demons from the deepest hills gathering to hear the great announcement. Astronomical figures, as these hosts are introduced and named, help to build up the tension of expectation until words and numbers fail and the writer can only compare the assembling hosts with the sands of the river Ganges.

Expectation is aroused from the first. Something astonishing and tremendous is going to happen! Of this we are assured as the curtain rises and Sakyamuni Buddha, the great teacher, is seen, in this last moment of his ministry, seated on the high Vulture Peak, holding, as it were, a celestial durbar "surrounded, attended, honored, revered, venerated, worshipped" by 12,000 and more disciples, by 80,000 bodhisattvas, 60,000 gods, by Brahman and his 12,000 followers, by dragon kings and demon kings and all their attendents. All gaze on the Buddha in "astonishment, amazement and ecstasy," as from the center of his forehead comes a great ray of light, penetrating to the highest heavens and to all the worlds. What does this mean? it is asked. The reply is given that it means that something indeed is going to happen: the Buddha is about to make his final revelation, "to blow the conch of the Great Law, to beat the drum of the Great Law, to expound the meaning of the Great Law"—no less.

Another question is raised. If there is need for this further revelation why was it not given sooner? Why were the Buddha's followers given only a lesser way (Hinayana)? A good part of the earlier chapters is given to the answer to this question. *The ways of Buddha to man are justified.* In other words, what we have here is an exposition of the Buddha character. It gathers round a doctrine which is very central to Buddhist relativism: the doctrine of *upāya kausalya* (the Buddha's skillful or tactful means). The Buddha, it is taught, is indeed concerned that all men should come to full understanding of saving truth. Such is his compassion. But such is his wisdom that he is aware, too, of different conditions and capacities. He sees men at various stages of spiritual progress in the Path. And, as he is alert to the condition of each and all he adapts his "means of grace" to each particular case.

Here the thread of high drama is broken to introduce three parables. One of these is the parable of the Prodigal Son. But, as in the case of the similar Christian parable, it might also be named the parable of the Solicitous Father. More so, perhaps, in this Buddhist context, for in this story, which is much longer than the New Testament story, the central figure is very much the father. The central theme is the father's character of concern and sagacity. The son is presented as returning after a long absence to find his father so advanced in affluence and position that he does not recognize the princely landowner as his father. The father, however, immediately recognizes the son. But he also recognizes that the son is reduced to so menial a condition that he is in no fit state to be received and treated as the heir. The son indeed is so abject and apprehensive that at first he tries to run away again. There follows an account of how the wise persistent father, by various devices, gradually and without revealing his identity, restores the son's condition and character until at last the day comes when he can be given full responsibility and proclaimed the heir. Even so, it is concluded, the Buddha, "knowing that our minds delighted in inferior things, by his tactfulness taught according to our capacity. But still we did not perceive that we were really Buddha-sons." [46]

A similar moral is drawn in a second parable, and in a third, which tells of the life-giving rain cloud in a universe where plants and trees are seen to be different though "produced in the same soil and moistened by the same rain." Even so there is the one Law, but as the Great Teacher (Tathagata) "sees clearly . . . the varying stages in which all beings are . . . so . . . he carefully leads them on,

> honored and humble, high and low
> Law-keepers and law-breakers
>
> · · ·
>
> Orthodox and heterodox,
> Quick-witted and dull-witted.[47]

But it is not enough to have further knowledge of the teaching. There now must also be further knowledge of the teacher: the Buddha must be known as the Eternal Buddha. The climax of the drama comes when there suddenly arises from the earth a stupendous shrine reaching to the highest heavens. Innumerable Buddhas appear, a mighty voice is heard, a portentous action is taken, an invitation is given, a challenge is issued. The mighty voice, the voice of the Ancient Buddha, declares:

> Excellent! Excellent! World-honored Sakyamuni!
> All is true that thou sayest.[48]

The action is the action of the Sakyamuni ascending into the heavens, opening the door of the shrine "when there went forth a great sound like the drawing of the bolt on opening a great city gate." The Ancient Buddha is seen seated upon his throne. The challenge is a challenge to all true Buddhists to publish and maintain this Mahayana doctrine against the opposition which may be expected from "men of false views, who proclaim heretical doctrines," those who arrogantly assert that they have already attained what has to be attained, those who

> wear the patched robe in seclusion
> scorning dwellers among men,

that is, the Hinayana conservatives.[49]

Hinayana teachers are significantly criticized as those who think they have already attained. When it is recorded that five thousand (Hinayana) disciples withdrew from the assembly at the first hint of the new teaching, it is remarked: "The root of sin was deep in them, and their haughty spirit was so enlarged that they imagined they had already attained." [50] The Buddha comments that he is glad to be rid of this chaff. "It is good that such extremely haughty ones as these are gone away." "Never by a smaller Vehicle [Hinayana] could a Buddha save any creature. The Buddha himself is the Great-Vehicle [Mahayana].[51] In contrast, those who remain and hear the parables telling how the Buddha by skillful means prompts men to cultivate "supreme aspiration" are said to realize now that this aspiration is what they lacked:

> Gaining but a trifle of Nirvana
> Contented we sought no more.[52]

Only now that they have this further teaching, have they "attained to clear vision."

> Now at last we are
> Really hearers of the Sound

Who take the news of Buddhahood
And make all creatures hear.[53]

It should be observed, however, that the presumptuous claim
to attainment of "clear vision," when there has been no such
realization, is regarded by *all* Buddhists, Hinayana as well as
Mahayana, as a cardinal sin. It is one of the grounds on which
a monk may be expelled from the monastery. Where there
is a difference is in the application of this principle. Mahayana
teachers (as here illustrated) apply it to those who are wedded
to the "Hinayana" conception of the Path. Hinayana teachers,
on the other hand, emphasizing the intuitive knowledge which
is to be expected only at the end of the Path, see in the Mahayana speculations a presumptuous discounting of present
limitations and a vain dalliance with metaphysical questions
which belong to "the puppet show" or the "entangling jungle." [54]

Here, it might be concluded, in the doctrine of nonattain-
ment, we have a principal ground of Buddhist relativism—a
ground not so very different from that presented by Hinduism,
allowing for the change of idiom. Like the Hindu doctrine of
maya (illusion), which is also reflected in Buddhism, it emphasizes human confusion.

All that is said about the Buddha's use of skillful means adds
to this emphasis. Human beings are seen as the Buddha is said
to see them—limited by their condition, at various stages of the
Path, not yet possessed of that clear vision which comes only
at the end of the Path or with full realization of their Buddha
nature. As such, they are still beset by illusion. Even the saintly
Shinran is constrained to write: "Although I say the Nembutsu,
a welling joy is hard to come. . . . Strong indeed is the fire
of illusion that burns us." [55]

By Shinran this condition is seen to point the need for greater
faith in Amita Buddha's saving power; by others it is construed to mean a greater personal striving. But by all it is seen

to exclude presumptuous "dogmatism." In man's present condition there can be no more than a partial, relative grasp of truth. Each can only speak from his own limited viewpoint.

By the same token there should be liberal toleration of others. This does not necessarily involve heeding what they may have to say. There may be respect for the insights of great teachers as they are seen to recall men to the need for vision. But on the whole the toleration of other schools and believers is joined, in Buddhism, with indifference to their views. We can scarcely gather here what may be gathered from some aspects of Hindu thought and practice: the conclusion that the many roads should be kept open for the sake of the vision which may come by any one of them, a vision of benefit to all. The basis of Buddhist toleration is respect for the believer himself rather than for what he says.

It may be one of the paradoxes of Buddhism that this should be so, for it is hard to reconcile with some interpretations of the doctrine of anatta (non-ego) which may seem to reduce the individual believer to the vanishing point, though in the full context of Buddhist thought and practice, it hardly seems to be the intention of such teaching to do so.[56] Be this as it may, there is a strong element of individualism in Buddhism joined with an emphasis on personal experience similar to that found in Hinduism—personal experience related to the grasp of truth as each believer makes his own progress in the Way. The Buddha only points the way, insists the Theravada teacher. Perhaps the Mahayana teacher sees the Buddha doing more than this. But in neither case is anything said which divorces the grasp of truth from what is personally experienced by progress in the Way.

Thus, as each believer is seen to have his own, very own experience, and so much is seen to depend on it, each must be allowed and encouraged to develop this experience and expected to have his own say—as far as it goes. Buddhist history, with its branching out into different schools, shows that there has indeed been this diversity of "say."

Thus far the Buddhist view may seem to be much the same as the Hindu view, allowing for a change of idiom. It reflects in particular that aspect of Hindu teaching which emphasizes the human condition, as it also reflects the Hindu aversion to any "dogmatism" which ignores the limitations of this condition. Thus Buddhism certainly underwrites the challenge of Hindu relativism.

But something is added, something more than a change of idiom. There is the determinative reference to the symbol of the Buddha character. As this reference makes for unity in the Buddhist world, so also it provides a distinctive support or sanction for the Buddhist respect for diversity. It is a normative reference. It confirms the relativist approach to religious beliefs, makes tolerance an imperative, and sharpens the edge of the challenge to "dogmatic" attitudes. How this is so is evident in the *Lotus* scripture. The implication is plain: the Buddha character manifested is the pattern of perfection for sentient beings who are here assured that they are "Buddha-sons," that is, that they have the Buddha nature. The prodigal son in the parable is encouraged by skillful means until the day comes when the father can say to him "*I and you are of the same mind.*" [57] The employment of skillful means has exhibited the character of this mind. To be a Buddhist is to "aspire" to have this mind. At the same time it is to be aware that one has not yet attained it.[58] This forbids dogmatism. It means a relative attitude to one's own present grasp of truth.

Again, to observe the Buddha's patience is to emulate that patience. This means tolerance. Thus, when the Lotus scripture closes with a call for evangelists, it is a call for evangelists who will be as tolerant as they are zealous. They will "disparage none." They will

"ever be gentle, patient
And compassionate to all,

wearing the armour of long suffering." [59] For this same scripture which presents the Exalted One, the Eternal Buddha surrounded and worshiped by all the heavenly hosts, also proclaims:

The Dwelling of the Tathagata
is the great compassionate heart
within all living. The Robe of the
Tathagata is the gentle and forbearing heart.[60]

What is thus set forth in Mahayana scripture was announced more tersely in the illuminated inscription placed over a vast, floodlit statue of the Buddha in Theravada Ceylon:

THE TRUE LIGHT OF THE WORLD [61]

All Buddhists everywhere would subscribe to that. Not *a* light. *The* light.

Such a claim may seem perhaps an instance of the very intolerance and dogmatism which Buddhists challenge. But we must note the nature of the reference. It is significant that the inscription was placed above a *statue* of the Buddha. It bespeaks that constant recalling of the life and example of the Buddha which, as we have observed, is promoted by the many statues of the Buddha always repeating the same familiar features in the Theravada countries. The reference is to a *symbol:* the symbol of the Buddha character.

And it is frequently made. For example, at the time of the Sixth Great Council held in Rangoon a Burmese Buddhist, U Tin, looked out on the modern world and deplored its spate of dogmatisms and ideologies. "Fanatical creeds are now much more in fashion," he said. "Of all isms in human history fanaticism is the most dangerous." Quoting the Pali scriptures, he affirmed that the whole temper of Buddhist life and thought was against such "dogmatism." "As the followers of the Buddha we must not be dogmatic. . . . As the followers of the Buddha we must show our tolerance and good will to all those who hold views or beliefs different from our own." [62] *As the followers of the Buddha!*

The speech was a criticism of the West. But it was addressed to Buddhists. It might therefore be taken as equally critical of any tendencies towards dogmatism which Buddhists themselves might exhibit. For Buddhists can, like others, sin against the light, their own light. The same Lotus scripture which calls for missionaries who will disparage none disparages Hinayana conservatives. With Buddhists, as with others, zeal for what is regarded as a true version of the faith may mean disparagement of other versions. Thus a widely esteemed Shinshu Buddhist exposition is named *The Book Deploring the Heterodoxies*.[63] And the Chinese reformer, T'ai-hsü, in one of his writings came near to pinning the Buddhist evangel to a particular doctrine, the doctrine of interdependent causation. As for Theravda Buddhists, some of them are just as wedded to the letter of the Pali scripture as some Christians are wedded to the letter of the Bible.

Today, Buddhists are exposed to new pressures. Confronted by the dogmatic attitudes of others, they are tempted to respond in kind. Drawn into the modern world in which it might appear that their Buddhist culture can be maintained and defended only by firmer definition of what Buddhists "stand for," Buddhists may be further influenced in this direction by the zeal of Western converts, by the revival of missionary purpose, and by the challenge of other religious communities presenting confessional statements which invite a response in kind.

Nevertheless, the "true light of the world" named by Buddhists is not a scripture or a dogma but a symbol: the Buddha. It is allegiance to this symbol, flexibly interpreted, which is drawing the Buddhist world together today. Buddhism remains a religion with a story at its heart: the story of the Buddha.

With this story in mind, Buddhists "as followers of the Buddha must not be dogmatic . . . must be tolerant. . . ."

To take account, then, of religious attitudes in Buddhist Asia is to meet the same relativism encountered in Hindu India, which challenges some of our Western attitudes. But it is also to be presented with further questions, for we have here a different pattern of religious community. Buddhist community may be properly described as confessional. It is centered in a confession of faith—faith in the Enlightened One. As such it may seem to invite comparison with Christian rather than with Hindu community. Yet it avoids the dogmatism which is usually associated with the pattern of the Christian confessional church. We are thus led to consider more than one form of confessional community. We may speak perhaps of Buddhist and Christian confessional forms, but before doing so we shall need to consider whether there is not in Christianity itself an outlook and conception of community more comparable with the Buddhist outlook and conception than that associated with the "confessional" church.

Meanwhile we may at least conclude that Christians and Buddhists have rather more in common, and Hindus and Buddhists rather less in common, than at first appears. To observe this much is to begin to question the idea that in dealing with religion we are dealing with two worlds only, and with two worlds sharply separated.

CHAPTER V

Islam: Confessional Practice

FROM THE TWO great religions of the orient, Hinduism and Buddhism, we turn now to what are significantly grouped together and described today as the "three great *Western* religions." [1] Judaism, Christianity, and Islam, with special reference in this chapter to Islam.

It would be more accurate to say, perhaps, that we *return* to the West. For in our introductory chapters it was a Western pattern of religious life and thought which we had more immediately in view as we observed how it is invaded and challenged today by Hindu relativism. In the last two chapters we have seen how this challenge of relativism emerges from a context and history very different from that of the West, a pattern exhibiting both a greater diversity and a more deliberate *approval* of this diversity. It is this resonant note of approval which, as much as anything, is distinctive of the Hindu outlook. Western patterns, too, present diversity. But, generally speaking, the Western conscience is uneasy about it. At least this is so, or has been so, outside modern America where we have come to expect, tolerate, and even praise religious diversity. Elsewhere and in earlier days there has been in the West a strong suspicion of religious diversity as likely to promote division. This has amounted at times to the conviction that, when it comes to religion, diversity should not be there. The emphasis has been on unity. There has also been a tendency to identify unity with uniformity.

But Hindus have not only tolerated diversity; they have seen it as essential to religious vitality and vision. Nor has this estimate of diversity been confined to any one school or interpretation of Hindu thought. It is characteristic of the Hindu attitude in general.

In the Buddhist world we found, as might be expected, a reflection of the Hindu attitude. But there was also difference. We found patterns of life and thought more nearly approaching those with which we are familiar in the West. In southern Buddhism especially, there was some evidence of that same "confessionalism" identified with the West which is so challenged by the East. All told, indeed, we found more differentiation in this Eastern pattern than may have been anticipated. The question therefore arises: Is there quite such a contrast between East and West in regard to the religious situation today as is often assumed? Differences there may be, but are they of such a kind and so located, that a dividing line separating the religious world into two halves can be sharply drawn? The question is certainly important for any appraisal of the forces of religion in relation to prospects of world community, and we may very well hesitate before we answer Yes or No. Even if it is decided that there is some reason to draw such a line, conclusions may be modified in the light of further qualifications in regard to the Western scene, which we shall now consider, qualifications similar to those made in regard to the Eastern scene.

A first issue pointing in this direction may be a question concerning Islam. Is it properly described as a "Western" religion and grouped together with Judaism and Christianity? There is certainly a disposition to do so today.[2] And it is significant that there is this disposition. It is indicative of new attitudes, between Christians and Muslims and also between Christians and Jews.

The new attitude of Christians to the Muslim world is reflected in the tributes now paid by Christian writers to the historic founder of this faith, the Prophet Muhammad, his personality and character. It is a far cry from the day when Dante consigned Muhammad to the twenty-eighth sphere of his Inferno, as the archprotagonist of damnable schism,[3] a far cry too, from the day when Christians could see him only as a depraved sensualist with a scandalizing harem; a menacing, militant fanatic; a hypocritical politician manufacturing scripture to suit his ends; or a deranged visionary. Instead there is today Christian tribute to the largeness of Muhammad's humanity,[4] the "sincerity of his piety," [5] his single-minded devotion and "nobility," his "stature and uniqueness," [6] combined with sober and scholarly appraisal.

Along with respect for the Prophet has come new respect for the tradition of faith which he is said to have founded, and a better understanding of this faith. One evidence of this better understanding is the fact that we now hesitate to describe Muhammad as "the Founder." For that is not how the orthodox Muslim would describe him. Nor would the Muslim speak of "Muhammadanism." [7] His faith is Islam, the faith of utter surrender to the Divine Will, which is what Islam signifies, as the term Muslim signifies one who voluntarily submits to the Divine Will. "God is most great. I bear witness that there is no god except God." This comes first in any true account of the Muslim faith, and some Christian scholars today seem not less concerned than devout Muslims themselves that it should be held so and remain so.[8] Muhammad may have given it the name, Islam, but the faith itself and the command to live by it came from heaven—for Muhammad himself, for the men of Mecca, for the people of Arabia, for all mankind.[9] The second clause of the Muslim confession, the affirmation that "Muhammad is the Apostle of God" is meant to implement the first: it signifies commitment to the revelation conveyed through Muhammad, God's instrument, God's slave.[10] Christians have greater respect for such firm witness to the one God when they feel it to be very much needed in the modern world. By some Christians it may still be held that the Muslim confession is no more than the distorted testimony of heretics, but there is a hint of approval, perhaps, when Islam is described as "theocentric but in a super-heated state." [11]

The present Christian interest in Islam does not halt with the written word. There is new and friendly engagement. The Institute of Islamic Studies in McGill University in Canada, bringing together Christian and Muslim scholars in cooperative research, is a case in point. From Africa, too, where Christians and Muslims are rivals in missionary enterprise, there is word of sustained discussions welcomed by Christians as being in the interests of better understanding.[12] At other levels, too, conditions in the modern world have tended to promote new attitudes, with Christian administrators, traders, and soldiers returning to their homeland to praise Muslim virtues.

There is still, no doubt, a long memory of the day when the advance of Islam threatened all Christendom. The prejudices thus begotten die hard, and it has been remarked that the Christian approach not only to Islam, but to other religions in general, still bears the impress of attitudes formed during the Crusades.[13] Nevertheless, all told, there are many signs of very different appraisal today.

As to the Muslim view of Christians and Christianity, here, too, the memory of the Crusades is still distorting. The Western imperialist, says one Arab writer, is the old Crusader in modern disguise; the struggle between East and West, Islam and Christianity, is "perpetual." [14] A Syrian friend told me recently of his Christian community existing alongside a Muslim community with little if any exchange between them, each darkly suspicious of the other, each with long memories of the Crusades. Nor has any Muslim scholar, so far as I know, produced an appreciation of the Christian position similar to some of the books written in appreciation of Islam by Christians, although at least one Muslim scholar has spoken urgently of the need for such.[15]

At the same time, the cooperation of Muslims in the McGill enterprise, the African conversations, and other joint enterprises are significant, and there are additional signs of a new approach. In India I was frequently reminded by Muslim friends of how much we had in common. Some Muslims, indeed, claim that there is no need for any new approach on their part, since Muslims have always respected Christians as "people of the Book." This may be said, indeed, to show that Muslims are superior in tolerance, but it is also said in affirmation of good will. "The Bible, the New Testament and the Qur'ān are three concordant books," writes Muhammed 'Abduh emphatically. "Religious men study all three and respect them equally. Thus the divine teaching is completed, and the true religion shines across the centuries." [16]

As to Jews and Christians, it might be claimed that there never was a time when there was better understanding between them or more conscious purpose to come together. Nontheological factors have contributed very largely to this. The Nazi persecution not only shocked the Christian conscience, but promoted something more than sympathy elsewhere; it stimulated a new regard for the Jewish contribution to modern civilization. I need not enlarge on this subject as the relevant facts will be known to most of my readers. But particular reference might be made to the influence of such thinkers as Martin Buber on Christian thought, and the cooperation of Jewish and Christian scholars in Biblical studies. There is also the difference of outlook in new countries where Jews, instead of being a conspicuous minority facing a dominant majority, form one of many such minorities constituting the nation.[17]

Nor need I enlarge on the tensions created by the establishment of the new state of Israel, affecting present relationships

not only between Muslims and Jews but also between Muslims
and Christians. What may be more significant in the long run
is the fact that despite these tensions there are writers today
who suggest that all who "take the idea of God seriously," [18]
as do Jews, Christians, and Muslims, are thereby drawn together and must needs stand together against the militant Marxist atheism of our day and other forces which oppose their
faith. Whether the defensive attitude here implied is altogether
healthy we must presently consider, and we may very well
do so by first remarking one possible consequence of such a
defensive outlook as it is presented in the context of modern
Islam.

The emphasis on the ideological affinity at least indicates one
reason for grouping Islam with the Western Judaic-Christian
tradition in spite of the fact that Islam, with sixty percent of
its people living east of Karachi, appears on the map as very
definitely "a religion of the East." There is also the fact that
Muslims grew up alongside Jews and Christians to begin with
and the further fact, related to our present subject, that if all
three exhibit diversity they are not nearly so happy about it
as Hindus and Buddhists. This is clearly so in the case of Islam
with what Professor Gibb has described as its "characteristic
quest for unity." [19]

It might be said that there is not only a difference of *attitude*
to diversity, but also a difference in the *extent* of the diversity
which may be observed, East and West. The three great Western religions, severally and together, do not present nearly so
many highways and byways of faith nor such complexity of
pattern as are found in Hindu India. Each has a more definite
norm of practice and belief. Each tends to view diversity as
a mischievous deviation from this norm, a deviation to be ac-
tively resisted and overcome. Each, in this broad sense, may
be described as a confessional religion, centered in a controlling
confession of faith, whether implied by associated practice or

more explicitly declared in credal form. Such, at least, may be our first impression, an impression of a Western world which may admit diversity but, on the whole, reluctantly and within limits.

But we have now to see how first impressions of the Western pattern may need to be modified. Is there here quite that absence of diversity, as within its three major traditions and as between them, that may be suggested when the West is presented in terms of sharp contrast with the East? Or quite that rigidity of faith which is said to be challenged by oriental relativism? Or quite the firm presentation of the counter-challenge we may have been led to expect? Or is there reason here, also, for further differentiation?

We begin with Islam. Of all the major religions, it might be thought, Islam, with its impressive characteristic unity—its *aggressive* unity, one might say—stands in the greatest contrast to the complex oriental pattern and most firmly presents the counter-challenge inherent in the Western outlook.

Islam may be briefly described as the religion centered in the divine revelation believed to have been communicated to the Prophet Muhammad [20] and communicated by him to the people of the two Arabian cities, Mecca and Medina, in the seventh century A.D. in successive chapters or suras of varying length. These chapters, memorized or written down by his followers were collected after Muhammad's death to form the sacred scripture, the Qur'ān (the Recital), also known, in English, as the Koran. The substance of the teaching thus given was a call to surrender or commitment to the Will of the one and only God (Allah).

God—there is no god but He, the Living, the Everlasting. . . . He knows what lies before men and what is after them, and they comprehend not anything of His knowledge save such as He wills. His Throne comprises the heavens and earth. . . . He is the All-high, the All-glorious.[21]

He is "the first and the Last, the Manifest and the Hidden" [22] yet "closer to man than his own neck vein." [23] There is emphasis on the Divine Unity: "whosoever giveth a partner to God hath conceived a monstrous sin." [24] There is persistent warning of divine judgment, with reference to the Last Day when the graves will be opened and men will be called to account. Man is to live constantly in the fear and service of God, giving him sole allegiance. But there is also emphasis on divine mercy: God is the Bountiful, the Provider, and the Qur'ān itself is the greatest bounty, the sufficient sign of divine mercy,[25] the sign to which Muhammad himself pointed when one was demanded.

Emphasis on the divine sovereignty is fundamental to the whole Muslim outlook. The name Muslim signifies a believer and the quality of this belief is indicated by the name, Islam, which was chosen by Muhammad: it means wholehearted surrender to God, utter allegiance. Other apostles have declared this besides Muhammad, including Abraham, Moses, and Jesus, but Muhammad's message is final; he is the last, the Seal of the Prophets. What distinguishes the Muslim from other believers in God is the conviction that the Qur'ān communicates the *final* revelation of the divine will, superseding all others. Thus at the heart of Muslim faith and practice there is the confession: (a) "There is no god but God," and (b) "Muhammad is His Apostle."

As revelation announces divine dominion, so it means law. With the Qur'ān which contains many precise regulations, comes divine direction. "For Muslims the Qur'ān is not only the . . . instrument of prophecy . . . it is at the same time the fundamental law . . . the criterion of truth . . . the best model for behavior." [26] In course of time, the Qur'ānic instruction was further developed by reference to the practice (sunna) of first generation Muslims, especially Muhammad himself, rulings handed down through the years and thus named the

Traditions (Hadith). Even so, new questions arose. These were answered by appeal to reason in accordance with established principles (*fiqh*) with special regard by the majority of Muslims to expert opinion presenting the "consensus of the community" (ijma). The directives thus derived constituted the "straight path" (Sharia) or general pattern of Muslim law. Muslims, it has been said, have been more concerned with the discussion of law than they have with the discussion of theology. There are no clergy in Islam but the scholars versed in the law (ulama) have wide influence and they have exercised an important function in the life of Islam.

They have done so because law is essential to community and community is essential to Islam. From the beginning Islam has meant community—regimented community, one might say as one observes the Friday assembly for prayer in the mosque, all the worshipers engaged not only in the same recital but in the same motions, sometimes standing in rows behind a prayer leader, following him in successive postures, arms raised together like a regiment at drill: a great demonstration of unity as the whole life ouside the mosque, life in the community, is meant to be a similar demonstration of unity in the service of the One God. All life is gathered together in the embrace of Islamic teaching, every aspect of it joined and directed. All is worship. Paying one's taxes is worship. Farming is worship. Duty in battle is worship. All is gathered together in the one community, the Islamic community, not a church within a state, but itself the state, Islam constituting a state. The Muslim name for citizen, *mukallaf*, implies as much; it means one on whom is laid full responsibility for the performance of his religious duties and observance of the Sharia which is "the pattern of communal order." [27]

At the same time this duty is an intensely individual responsibility. Each believer must stand by himself before God. "The fate of every man have we bound about his neck. . . .

Neither shall any laden soul be charged with the burden of another." [28] Each is required to observe the five "essential duties," also (significantly) named the Five Pillars of Faith:

1. The confession of faith: There is no god but God (Allah); Muhammad is the Apostle of God.
2. The prayers offered five times a day (facing toward Mecca).
3. Almsgiving.
4. Fasting, especially during the month of Ramadan.
5. Pilgrimage to Mecca (unless prevented by physical or other sufficient cause).

There are today between three and four hundred million such believers, all looking to Mecca, all hoping to make the pilgrimage to Mecca and a great many of them achieving it, so that to be in Mecca is to feel oneself at the heart of a world within a world, a world of faith, impressively united and widely distributed. This distribution, it has been suggested, might well be indicated by a splash of ink on the map of Arabia,[29] extending northward through Syria and Asia Minor into Southern Russia; westward along the coast of Africa to Spain and across the Bosphorus through the Balkans to Albania; again in a northeasterly direction through Iraq and Iran to China; then, again, eastward through Afghanistan to India, turning southeast to Malaya, Indonesia, and the Philippine Islands. At Mecca today, therefore, many different races are represented, many different languages are spoken. But when the sacred scripture, the Qur'ān, which "came down from heaven," is recited it is recited (except in Turkey) in the original Arabic, the language, it is believed, ordained by God as Muhammad was ordained by God and as the Islamic community has been ordained by God to fulfil his purpose in history.

In brief, the first thing that may well strike us about this widespread religion is its impressive unity, centered thus in the unifying conviction of the divine unity and the divine sovereignty, in the reference to the one great teacher, the one scripture, in respect for the one great pattern of conduct maintained by the practice of the same five essential duties including the daily prayers with all faces turned towards Mecca.

It is somewhat surprising therefore to read of Islam's characteristic *quest* for unity as if Muslims, like other believers, had also a sense of a unity lost or broken to be renewed or a further unity yet to be achieved. But when one turns to the thirteen centuries of Islamic history one finds that this history might very well be written in terms of increasing diversity, coming near to the point of division and, in some instances, passing that point.

Diversity, indeed division, came early in this history, though in Muhammad's own time unity, it might be said, was manifestly sought and largely achieved. There are two periods in this first chapter, the Mecca period and the Medina period, and some have suggested that there are two Muhammads, the essentially religious Muhammad, the Prophet who "warns" the men of Mecca, and the astute, political Muhammad, the leader who established at Medina the Islamic state and became its ruler and the commander in chief of its army. But to see it thus is not only to misrepresent Muhammad; it is also to misunderstand Islam. By Muslims the message announced at Mecca is seen to imply from the beginning the Islamic community and its politico-religious expression, the Islamic state. This is seen by the men of Mecca, too. Hence in large part their original opposition.

Muhammad is already in middle life when he announces his message. In vigil on Mount Hira, he has been commanded to

> Recite: In the Name of thy Lord who created,
> Created man of a blood-clot. . . .[30]

While it is a recital which causes dissension in Mecca, it also means, from the beginning, unity—the unity of the resolute minority who gathered round the Prophet in strong loyalty.

Nothing more clearly attests the character of Muhammad himself than the stalwart character of some of those who now came to his side, including his two successors, Abū-Bakr and 'Umar.

The Muslim calendar begins with the year of Muhammad's "emigration" from Mecca to Medina, A.D. 622. The terms of the invitation which he received are significant, as is the undertaking he required before he accepted it. He was invited as one who might end the tribal feuds which disturbed Medina, and he required the pledge:

> We will not worship any but the one God. . . .
> Nor will we disobey the Prophet in anything that is right.[31]

From now on there is to be new law, new sunna at Medina. In a ritual symbolic of purpose and community, Muhammad joins together in ties of brotherhood a number of pairs of men, one a citizen of Medina, the other an immigrant from Mecca. Tribal feuds are renounced. Islam is visibly existent, the religion which is Islam, the state which is Islam, one and the same, and Muhammad the Prophet is Muhammad the ruler, defending Medina against attack, marching across the desert in victorious return to Mecca, his dominion incredibly enlarged within ten crowded years until, by the time of his death, it includes a great part of Arabia. It is a remarkable history.

Islam now appears as a sudden military power emerging from the dust of the Arabian deserts moving swiftly westward to strike at the heart of Christian Europe. Within ten years of Muhammad's death there is a Muslim empire which includes Syria, Iraq, and Egypt. Within a hundred years Muslims have swept through northern Africa, crossed the Mediterranean to Spain, and threatened France. Two and a half centuries pass and this Muslim empire includes Asia Minor, parts of central Asia, India, and west Africa. Two centuries later Muslims have advanced into the Balkans, into Russia and Siberia, and southeastward as far as Indonesia. It is a sustained progress which suggests consolidated strength, and although there have been setbacks and withdrawals, this advance continues today as Muslim missionaries go forward into the heart of the new Africa.

To the neighboring world thus invaded the secret of Islam's advance might well seem to be its marshaled, unified strength, especially in the days of Muhammad and his immediate successors (caliphs), his two resolute lieutenants, Abū-Bakr and 'Umar. Yet even in this early day there was faction. The internal history of Islam, indeed, might be written in terms of increasing diversity tending to splinter the new community and coming very near to breaking it.

The weak rule of the third caliph and the disputed election of the Prophet's cousin and son-in-law, Ali, as his successor, resulted in civil war. Where all is political and at the same time religious, as in this state of Islam, no sharp line can be drawn between political and religious motives and consequences. Ali's rule may have been challenged for reasons that had little to do with so-called pure religion, but he was assassinated by the puritanical Kharijiti sectarians for reasons that had everything to do with religion. One consequence was certainly sectarian dissension within Islam at an early date. Ali's followers, the Shī'a Muslims, constituted not only a political party but a sect, later branching into several sects, developing, in course of time, doctrines repudiated by their opponents, the Sunni Muslims, who today constitute by far the largest sect in Islam (ninety percent of the Muslim world, according to some estimates).

The conflict between the partisans of Ali and the Umayyads, however, resulted in more than sectarian diversity. It presaged the dispersion of rule in Islam's far-flung dominion. From then on there was no question of central authority or leadership, religious and political, combined in the person of one man, as in the case of Muhammad and his immediate successors. Future caliphs were not in this category. Political power was divorced from spiritual power, and some caliphs had very little of either. Much of their political power passed to princes who were virtually independent. As to religion, it was now the day of the jurists and the theologians, the jurists developing and interpreting the comprehensive body of law (the Sharia) which became "the main unifying force in Islamic culture," [32] the theologians, especially at Medina, gaining in prestige as they stood for the ideal of the church-state, now deserted in practice, and produced statements of "orthodoxy."

Both the development of law and the development of theology, however, meant further diversity. The Sunni Muslims produced four principal "rites" or schools of law, and as many schools of theological opinion, while the Shi'ite sects developed doctrines which seemed to their critics a far remove from anything taught in the Qur'ān.

Doctrinal diversity, it might be said, was only to be expected. The same thing had happened in the Christian world some centuries earlier and for much the same reason; advancing Islam was encountering Greek thought; the "simple Gospel" brought from Arabia was now entering a more sophisticated world infected by Hellenistic and Asian speculations.

Then there were (and are) the Sufis. It has been suggested that the Sufi ascetics and mystics virtually constituted another religion, some of them having more in common with Hindu monists than with orthodox Muslims.[33] On the other hand, it has been held that the Sufis were the very heart of Islam, the religion of popular piety and warm devotion, in contrast to the elaborations of the upper-class Muslims and the small circle of the theologians. On this I cannot pretend a sufficient knowledge of Sufi mysticism to warrant an opinion, but it is at least clear that the Sufi beliefs, practices, and orders meant a diversity which sometimes stretched orthodox toleration to the breaking point.

Sufi teaching ranged from a veneration of saints to doctrines of union with God which challenged orthodox views of the distance between man and God, while Sufi practice meant the institution of "brotherhoods" or "orders" introducing new and various avenues of allegiance. Even al-Ghazali, who in the eleventh century cast a mantle of comprehensive orthodoxy over much of Sufi opinion and practice, saw dangers in the Sufi emphasis on mystical intuition. From al-Ghazali's time onward, Sufi influence, now generally accepted, was widespread throughout Islam, and Sufi patterns and teachings varied from what was substantially orthodox to what was wildly extravagant and often superstitious, verging on the magical. In the middle of the eighteenth century the Wahhabi movement, gathering force in the deserts of Arabia and converging on Mecca itself in 1806, challenged both Sufi "heresy" and orthodox "compromise," promoting a fundamentalist return to the Qur'ān and a "purification" of Islamic life and thought.

Islam today is Islam faced by the challenge of Western secular thought and all the pressures of the modern world, with new tensions in Islam itself as conservative vies with liberal to meet the challenge. Thus, throughout its history, Islam has known far more of diversity than is sometimes recognized.

There has been enough diversity to call for toleration if the community was not to be broken and for some limit to toleration if the community was not to lose its identity. It is the claim of Muslim apologists (and also of an increasing number of Christian writers on Islam today) that Muslims have indeed been tolerant. In support of this claim, reference is made to the considerate treatment of Christian and Jewish minorities in

Islamic states. As for the treatment of Muslim dissidents, it is claimed, few religions have been more accommodating. Excommunications have been rare. Compliance with rule and regulation was expected, but a Muslim could very easily change from one "rite" to another. At al-Azhar, the great center of instruction in Cairo, not one but four rites have been taught. Thus, tolerant of each other, Muslims have kept together, brothers in the faith, attracting new converts to the faith by their evident solidarity.

But what, it may be asked, of Islam's "holy war"? Surely this needs some explaining. Whatever else may be said, tolerance and conversion at the point of the sword are scarcely compatible. So it is frequently argued.

The doctrine of jihad or holy war, it has been said, has been abandoned by the Muslims today. "It no longer has any hold upon Muslim thinking. It has been all but swept away by a more liberal view." [34] This conclusion, however, depends on what is meant by the holy war. To give a "liberal" interpretation of the concept, as some Muslim apologists are doing today, is perhaps to give it deeper significance rather than to sweep it away. And this deeper significance may be very relevant to our present inquiry: it may pertain to our better understanding of Islam in the first place and our assessment of Islam's relation to prospects of world community. We shall consider first the "classical" Islamic view of the holy war, and next how it may be presented today.

Obligation to engage in the holy war was regarded by some Muslims as a sixth "essential duty," one of the Pillars of Faith, set alongside confession, daily prayers, almsgiving, fasting, and the pilgrimage to Mecca. It is significant that the duty of holy war is formulated in broad terms in one of the chapters of the Qur'ān, between the regulations for the Fast and the injunction to perform the pilgrimage to Mecca: "Fight in the way of God with those who fight with you, but aggress not: God loves not the aggressors. . . . Fight them, till there is no persecution and the religion is God's." [35] Muslim writers claim that their history has been this all through, a "striving" or "fighting in the way of God." Present duty, too, they may add, must be read in these same terms: a holy war, not with aggressive intent, but with intent for the benefit of all mankind, a holy war which, rightly interpreted, is seen to be the way of peace.

The view that the holy war has been pursued with intent to the benefit of mankind may conceivably be related to an honest conviction that to come within the new commonwealth of Islam was the best thing that could happen to any man. It was the best thing for the feuding tribes of Arabia and the best thing for the peoples beyond Arabia. As the Muslim saw it, there were two realms, *Dār al-Islām* and *Dār al-Harb* (*harb* meaning, literally, war). He himself was fortunate to be in the first. It meant being within the pale of law, and to be within the pale of Islamic law was to be indeed a recipient of divine bounty, for law, so to speak, brought religion down to earth. "Islam is both belief and legislation which organizes all the relationships of man. . . . Belief without a code of laws to put it into effect would be merely theoretical and ineffective." [36]

There is an interesting presentation of this view in Sayyid Amir 'Ali's *The Spirit of Islam*, the more interesting because Amir 'Ali was himself, from a liberal, progressive standpoint, critical of excessive legalism. But he held nevertheless that a religion had to be "eminently positive" to have a salutory influence. In this respect he considered Muslims to be in better case than Christians. "The glory of Islam consists in having embodied the beautiful sentiment of Jesus into definite laws." Jesus himself died too young to do this. His work was unfinished. "It was reserved for another teacher (Muhammad) to systematise the laws of morality." [37]

Now in this view it was very much to the gain, not only of the tribes of Arabia but also of Christians and others, to be brought within the Muslim empire and within the beneficent writ of its law. Even if they did not become converts, they experienced the benefit of the order thus established, while those who did become converts would have the benefit of life in the congregation of God (umma). Benefit of law meant benefit of community.

As to this benefit of community, even Christian writers have been vocal:

The success of Muhammadanism, where it still appears as a rival to Christianity, as among African tribes, is largely due to something highly meritorious . . . that is, that it incorporates weak races into a great world-wide fellowship, of which they at once feel the sustaining force. The principle of brotherhood they see among the Muhammadans really exemplified. They feel its support.[38]

Should we then revise our view of Muslim history, and see it as a history of conquest pursued *for the benefit of the conquered?* If so, Muslims would not be the first or the last imperialists to claim and justify dominion on such grounds. They might conceivably construe the call from the minaret—"Come ye unto good"—in similar terms: "Come ye, the tribesmen of Arabia, the peoples of Africa, the peoples of Spain, come ye, pagans, Jews, Christians, unbelievers and half-believers, come ye unto the good, this good we Muslims know and enjoy, come ye unto our community, come ye within the pale of this benefit of Law."

Yes, it is conceivable.

But it is not so conceivable within the *full* context of Muslim thought and life. "Come ye unto good." We have here only one phrase of the call from the minaret, as we have also only part of what is in the Muslim mind. "Come ye unto the good," yes. But the call from the minaret begins:

> God is most great.
> God is most great.
> I bear witness that there is no god except God.
> I bear witness that Muhammad is the Apostle of God.
> Come ye unto prayer—

and only then, *following* this, following "Come ye unto
prayer," only then "Come ye unto good." The call of the
minaret is a call to *worship*. If there is any thought of good
or benefit in the Muslim mind, benefit for himself or for others,
benefit from law, it is thought which must be interpreted in
this context of worship—worship and allegiance. That law is
good, that Muslim dominion meant the rite of law, that to
be within the realm of such law was good for those brought
into it, even by conquest, that Muslim dominion was on the
whole beneficial dominion, all this may be plausibly argued:
but it is *not* what the Muslim meant by *holy* war.

Regard for human benefit, it is true, is not entirely absent.
The warrior slain in this cause is promised a rewarding paradise, and the community thus extended may indeed be considered the best for mankind. But neither individual reward
nor social weal is presented as the *primary* concern. *The primary concern is that the confession of faith should be maintained and extended without let or hindrance.* And it is enough
that God has willed it so. This is implied by the Qur'ān contexts where the overruling consideration is the "advancement"
of the faith. As believers are exhorted to "employ their substance and their persons" in this cause, so they are exhorted
to "go forth to battle," to fight for the religion of God. As
the cardinal sin is to ascribe "partners to God," as the confession "There is no god but God" means witness to the truth
denied by this sin, so it is enjoined:

Kill those who ascribe partners to God wherever you find them,
and take them, and confine them, and lie in wait for them at every

place of ambush. . . . Fight those who believe not in God and the Last Day and do not forbid what God and his Messenger have forbidden—such men as practise not the religion of truth, being of those who have been given the Book.[39]

The fundamental and sufficient premise for the holy war, then, is the holiness of God. The holy war was pursued in the interests of a recruiting campaign for God. It was not in itself this campaign. On the contrary, Muslims today are swift to repudiate any idea of conversion at the point of the sword.[40] What is rather held is that the sword may have to be used to prevent interference with the campaign, to ensure the liberty of prophesying. "Will you not fight people who . . . purposed to expel the Messenger?" [41] In this sense, if in no other, the wars of Islam may be presented as essentially *defensive* wars, true to the injunction to avoid aggression. They are frequently so presented by Muslim apologists, sensitive to the modern criticism that the Muslim is bellicose.

But there are Muslims today who go a good deal further. Their concern is not so much with past history as with present duty. Nor are they merely apologetic. They are not merely replying to critics. They are asking what significance this conception of holy war may have for Muslims today. Granted that Muslims *have* engaged in holy war, what fundamental principle for human conduct may here be discerned? What kind of holy warfare may be contemplated today? And for what objectives? These are some of the questions asked.

One reply, given by Dr. Ahmad Galwash in a book with the al-Azhar imprint, emphasizes the principle of resolute resistance to evil.[42] What, he asks, is the alternative? "Abject toleration" of evil? Such abject toleration would mean the encouragement of "all sorts of nefarious designs and mischievous courses." He is very critical of what he conceives to be the Christian doctrine of nonresistance indicated by the injunction "Love your enemies and do good to them that hate you." If Muslims had acted on this principle of non-resistance, he argues, standing by while the worshipers of the one true God were destroyed, they would have thereby allowed "the only living faith to be swept out of existence." Instead of this, Muslims acted on a definite principle of resistance, for "if evil is not to be resisted, it would be allowed to grow unchecked and eat away the very vitals of humanity." Christians themselves, he adds, have not, as a matter of history, acted on this principle of nonresistance. They have recognized that Jesus gave contrary advice when he said, "Think not that I came to send peace on earth . . . not peace but division." Otherwise Western civilization would have been destroyed. No, there cannot be the "abject toleration" which results from the view that resistance to evil is sinful.

Where evil arises, Dr. Galwash concludes, the right means, "harsh or mild, suited to particular cases," must be taken to resist it.

This reference to the right means, however, may lead to the observation that the term jihad does not in itself imply the use of the sword. It means simply "striving." There may be other and better means of striving against evil than resort to war. A remarkable example of an interpretation along these lines is provided by Khan Abdal Ghaffar's "red shirt" movement in support of India's independence. Here we have Muslim support of Mahatma Gandhi's principle of nonviolence, turbulent Pathans of northern India engaged in a striving, a jihad, for the cause of India's independence, yet accepting a remarkable discipline which means anything but physical force. Nonviolence with the principle of jihad, resolute resistance to evil, invoked! [43]

Or the same principle may be construed to mean, in Iqbal's phrase, "a passion for righteousness," and be thus interpreted by a Muslim journalist in India: "Fight the devil in your own bosom first . . . fight the devils of disease and poverty . . .

fight ignorance and illiteracy, fight the fat capitalist who defrauds and exploits the poor . . . fight those who deprive you of your birthright of free manhood." [44] Or, again, jihad may be interpreted, as by some Sufi teachers, as an "interior" warfare, as each believer's own spiritual warfare, a conception comparable with the Christian John Bunyan's account of the war on the battlefield of "Mansoul." Here, it might be thought, we have a more definitely "religious" or "spiritual" conception of jihad, as compared with a "moral" interpretation. But to say this is to misrepresent the whole Muslim outlook. Any divorce between morality and religion is entirely foreign to the Muslim mind.

On any showing, then, the Muslim interpretation of jihad is fundamentally theocentric. The holy war is God's war. It is in allegiance to the divine will that the holy war must be pursued. They are to "Fight in the way of God."

The fact that we have been led to observe this confessional emphasis by a discussion of Muslim practice introduces a further question. Relevant to both our better understanding of Islam and our discussion of religion and community in general is the question of *how* the confession of faith is maintained and expressed in Islam. Is it maintained by required subscription to a creedal statement? Have we in Islam an example, not only of confessional religion, but of dogmatic religion? Are we here confronted by that dogmatic attitude which arouses the criticism of Hindus and others, an example of the Western insistence on "You believe what I believe"? Nay, more, an insistence on "You say what I say"? Does Islam present an example of community rigidly determined on the basis of adherence to dogma? Is it true to say, as does Dr. Kraemer, that Islam is "creedal and doctrinal to the core"? [45]

These questions arise when it is observed that theology in Islam takes second place to law. Muslim life is shaped by codes rather than by creeds. This does not mean that Islam has no theology. But theology was a comparatively late arrival on the Muslim scene. Interest was concentrated on right practice rather than on right doctrine. As Islam marched out beyond Arabia, theological discussion was quickened by the meeting with Hellenism, Christian thought, and Gnostic and other speculations, but even at a fairly late date it would have been difficult to say which opinion was accepted as unquestionably orthodox and which was not. Nor, apparently, did it matter much. What was more important was the definition of law.

There was a Muslim creed, but it was minimal. Even today the extent to which creedal assent determines community is debatable. Testimony varies and a good deal seems to depend on where it comes from. Muslims from some parts of the world will say that, so far as creedal assent goes, it is enough for a man to confess his faith in the one God and affirm that Muhammad is the Apostle of God to be accepted as a Muslim. Others will say that assent to at least six articles of belief is required: "belief in God, Angels, revealed scriptures, prophets, the Day of Judgment and the destiny of man for good or evil." [46]

Instead of saying, therefore, that Islam is "creedal to the core" it would be nearer the truth to say that Islam is "codical to the core." [47] But it might nevertheless be allowed that Islam is "doctrinal to the core." For the codes of Islam certainly reflect basic Muslim beliefs and teachings. Muslim practice would not be what it is without its reference to fundamental belief. To take, for example, our discussion of the holy war, the killing of "idolators" (those who "ascribe partners to God") follows from a doctrine of divine unity.

The fact that what holds the Muslim community together is its body of law rather than any body of doctrine is suggested by Muslim terminology:

There would seem to be no word in Arabic, or indeed in any Islamic language, meaning "orthodox." The word usually translated "orthodox," *sunni*, actually means rather "orthoprax," if we may use the term. A good Muslim is not one who conforms to a given pattern, whose commitment may be expressed in intellectual terms that are congruent with an accepted statement (as is the case generally in Protestant Christianity), but one whose commitment may be expressed in practical terms that conform to an accepted code.[48]

Professor Smith adds, in a footnote, that while, in course of time, there were indeed theological discussions and creedal debates in Islam, these debates were not "fundamental"; "they did not affect the community so basically as in Christian history, or as other issues affected Islam."

Have we here, then, in this Muslim tradition, something which may be better compared with the Buddhist pattern of confessional community than with the Christian? A good many may think at first that any such comparison with Buddhism is wildly impossible since Buddhism is associated with a tolerance and a relativism which are held to be foreign to Islam. Muslim and Buddhist attitudes, it might be thought, are flatly opposite. Nevertheless there is something to be said for such a comparison, especially if we confine it to Theravada Buddhism. In both traditions there is a fundamental confessional allegiance, in both a minimal creed, in both an emphasis on right practice and in both it is this emphasis on right practice which makes for the sense of community. In both it may be claimed that handsome is as handsome does. And what is considered handsome— the faith confessed—is expressed very largely in the discussion of what has to be done: the Sharia discussion in Islam, the discussion of the steps of the Path and the vinaya disciplines in Buddhism.

I recall once putting a question on the subject to a Muslim friend. I set in contrast a Christian who might affirm belief in the one God while failing, in his conduct, to exhibit the virtues a Muslim might expect from such profession and a Buddhist who made no such profession, yet exhibited these virtues. I asked my friend whether, in such a case, he would feel greater affinity with the Christian than with the Buddhist. He hesitated for a while. Then he replied that he would have more in common with the Buddhist. He would doubt whether such a Christian had any "real faith" in God. He proceeded to emphasize the Muslim concern for "right practice."

Perhaps we should not press the comparison too far. Nor should we press too far what is said about the Muslim's adherence to code rather than to creed, since Islamic scholars are not altogether agreed on this issue. But the very fact that the issue arises and is subject to debate points to the possibility, as does our description of Buddhism, that there may be more than one form of confessional community, including a form not so wedded to theological statement as that found in the pattern of the Christian confessional church.

Study of the Islamic community points to a further possibility which is relevant to our discussion: the possibility of confessional community where there is a relativist rather than a dogmatic attitude to statements of belief. This appears when we ask what is the nature of the Muslim's commitment. Granted that it is the intent of his practice and his law to express such commitment, what does the Muslim stand for? What does he "confess"?

This question is raised by Wilfred Cantwell Smith in a penetrating discussion of modern Muslim apologetics. He notes that some Muslim writers today are very much on the defensive. They are sensitive to Western criticism, sensitive to questions and doubts expressed by young Muslim intellectuals, sensitive to all that challenges the Muslim faith in this present age, and generally concerned to *defend* the faith.

"The fundamental *malaise* of modern Islam," writes Professor Smith, "is that something has gone wrong with Islamic history." [49] Islam is no longer advancing, conquering and to conquer, is no longer a growing empire. This is cause not merely for chagrin, but for dismay, for searching of heart, perhaps even for doubt. For history, to the Muslim, is profoundly significant. The Muslim sees his community as fulfilling a divine purpose in history according to a divine plan. When all went well with Islam he was the more assured that this was so. Here Professor Smith's analysis recalls Max Weber's analysis of Calvinism. There is the same need for assurance of the divine election and it has been found in much the same way: by identifying success with divine approval. The achievements and astonishing victories of the early period of Islamic history might therefore be read as proof that the divine plan was rightly interpreted and faithfully effected.

The first great shock to this assurance came with the Mongol invasions and the fall of Baghdad in 1258; "it could be felt that the great endeavour to realize God's purpose was petering out." [50] The second great shock has come with the modern period, with the waning of Muslim political power in the eighteenth century, the invasion of the Muslim world by the Western powers in the nineteenth century, and the challenge of Western thought and life and all the disturbing events of this present century. To the first great challenge Muslims responded creatively. It remains to be seen whether they will do so in response to the present challenge.

At present a good many seem to feel that the Muslim world, subject largely to forces outside Islam, has lost its grip. Islam is no longer in control of history, but confounded by it.

One result of this condition is the stream of apologetic literature which has been appearing for the last fifty years, especially in the Arab world, much of it on the defensive against Western criticism. The penetrating question which Professor Smith raises is whether this concern to defend Islam has meant a departure from the very thing for which Islam stands: commitment to the living God. Sensitive to the gulf between history as it ought to be and Islamic history as it has come to be, have some apologists neglected that very reference which might narrow this gulf? Or, concerned to hold young Muslim intellectuals to the faith of their fathers, have these writers, in point of fact, presented and defended something which is less than that faith?

Professor Smith cites two Cairo editors. For the first, Islam is "a celestial vision, of which the earthly history is but an imperfect expression." [51] What he is concerned to defend and present is not past history, not Islam as an institution, "not an historical entity handed down by tradition, but a transcendent Idea," "an idea in the mind of God," [52] not what has been, but what ought to be. His primary, overruling interest is commitment to the living God.

For the second editor, however, Islam is usually an institution or "a set of ideas in men's minds, a heritage, a society. It is not a moral imperative but something tangible, an historical reality," [53] and what he is concerned to promote and himself exemplify is "the service of Islam"—this Islam on earth. "Virtually his entire endeavor is to convince or reassure his public that Islam is all right." [54] The emphasis is on Islam's record and what *Muslims* have done. There is very little reference to God and no evidence of the sense of commitment manifested by the first editor. Readers are invited to admire and approve. Faith in Islam as an institution or as a "set of ideas" is virtually substituted for faith in God.

Professor Smith's critique is confirmed in substance by a letter written by a Muslim in India rebuking a Christian editor for using the term "Muhammadanism." Islam is not just Muhammad's teaching or Muhammad's ideas. It is above all sorts of so-called -ities or -isms. Islam is "entire self-resignation to the Supreme Will." It is "Eternal Religion." [55]

The dogmatism which exalts what man has to say about God is here, then, repudiated. We should not perhaps go as far as to say that Islam substitutes for such dogmatism a relativist attitude to such statements. But there is a significant economy in the use of such statements. We are at least on the threshold of relativism. We have in Islam an attitude which, on the whole, is averse to theological speculation. Indeed, in spite of much that is opposite in the two religions, there is some ground here for a comparison of Islam with Buddhism. As for the Buddhist (at least for the Theravada Buddhist), it is enough to know the Law and obey it. In both traditions the major concern is with practice. The Muslim Sharia has its counterpart in the Buddhist Vinaya disciplines. In brief, both religions present a confessional form of community in which the creedal element is minimal and the confession of faith is mainly expressed in, and sustained by, practice. If in the one the relativist attitude to statements of belief is more pronounced, there is in the other at least a near approach to this attitude.

Returning to Professor Smith's critique of Islam, we may note how it points not only to *what* may be lost when commitment to a "set of ideas" is substituted for commitment to the Eternal; it also points to *how* this fundamental commitment may be lost. His analysis indicates that it may happen when a religious community becomes overly defensive. It also indicates that it may happen when religious teaching is too narrowly addressed to contemporary challenge and particular criticism: sensitivity to history may mean becoming lost in history. He further suggests that the form of religious community is seldom pure. Even if the Islamic pattern presents an emphasis on code rather than creed, Islam on the defensive shows that the contrary emphasis on a "set of ideas" remains latent.

We shall have reason to refer again to these several points as we move further in our survey. We shall observe, for example, a Jewish rabbi describing the "commitment" of his own tradition in much the same terms as those in which Professor Smith describes Islamic "commitment." Turning next to the Christian world we shall thus be on the alert for similar issues there.

Meanwhile, in regard to Islam itself, we may conclude, first, that Islam appears on the page of world history as very definitely and self-consciously shaping that history, doing so explicitly in the name of religion and in the power of religion. No tradition exhibits more clearly the force of religion in human society. What are sometimes called nontheological factors are not absent. But those who try to explain the course of Islamic history in any terms except terms which allow for the strength and effect of the Muslim's religious conviction can do so only by ignoring or distorting evidence to suit theory.

Second, this power is clearly associated with emphasis on a *particular* reference. There is emphasis on a particular divine revelation, a reference consciously maintained by allegiance to a particular pattern of life (the Sharia) expressing and implementing a particular confession of faith: Islam is a *confessional* religion. Those who argue that religious motive is most effective and dynamic when there is an emphasis on what is particular or special may cite Islam as a case in point.

Third, however, there is the suggestion that Islam's confessional strength depends on Islam's commitment to something more than a set of ideas. It is a commitment which allows for more of diversity together with tolerance of diversity within the pale of Muslim community than at first appears. Thus, a degree of tolerance, qualified by Islam's characteristic quest for unity, may partly account for Islam's impressive solidarity.

As to what contribution may be expected from Muslims in regard to world community, there is the fact that they are certainly disposed to think in such terms. But the world they envisage is a world coming within the pale of their own community. The world community which they conceive is community on their own terms or, rather, the terms of their faith, their commitment. Today, however, the Muslim world embraces considerable non-Muslim minorities. Whether from this experience Muslims may come to accept the idea of world community which can be realized only by cooperation with men of other faiths remains to be seen. Meantime they bear witness to the need for a resolute "striving" (jihad), which some may see as the first condition of any prospect of world community.

CHAPTER VI

Jewish and Christian Confessions

WITH THIS CHAPTER we come to the two religions which have had most to do with the shaping of life and thought in the Western world: Judaism and Christianity. Since a good deal has been written on this subject, the reader's familiarity with salient facts may be assumed. Therefore I shall not attempt any general survey in regard to unity and diversity in either of these two traditions. As to Judaism it is enough for my present purpose to observe that Jews today retain, most of them, a remarkable sense of their identity as the "chosen people," despite their checkered history, their widespread dispersion, and the fact that wherever there are two Jews together one can expect three opinions, as they themselves testify. As to Christians, it suffices to observe that while one today looks to Rome, another to Geneva, another to Athens, and another to Canterbury, all still look to Jerusalem, or that while Christians may be members of Baptist, Congregational, Catholic, Greek Orthodox, Anglican, Methodist, Presbyterian, and many other churches most of them would still say that in the final analysis there is only one Church, the Church of Christ.

First, then, with regard to Judaism, second, with regard to Christianity, we shall here be dealing more specifically with questions raised in previous chapters. There is the question of Western attitudes to religious beliefs, challenged by Hindu relativism. Are Western attitudes as dogmatic and divisive as might at first appear? There is the confessional issue, raised by what was observed first in the case of Buddhism, second in the case of Islam. Granted religious community gathered around a unifying confession of faith, how may such a confession be expressed and maintained and with what consequences? Does Christianity present more than one form and conception of confessional community? That is the particular question raised by the criticism of Muslim discussions. Granted that what may be confessed is something more than a "set of ideas," does a departure from this something more, when men are overly concerned to "defend" their faith, mean a consequent loss of the very dynamic of faith which it seeks to maintain? These are among the issues to be considered as we turn now, first to Judaism, second to Christianity, and third to a new interest in the West today which engages both Jews and Christians: an interest in what may be termed "depth religion."

In discussions of religion today there is a tendency to group Jews and Christians together with broad reference to the "Judaic-Christian tradition," a description which emphasizes the fact that Jews and Christians have indeed much in common. Both, for instance, refer to the same sacred scripture, the Old Testament. But such usage tends to obscure the fact that from Old Testament times onward there are two separate traditions of *further* history, with further history for the Jew as well as for the Christian. In each case there are developing patterns and conceptions of community relevant to our discussion. We shall therefore consider each tradition separately.

In regard to Judaism, there is the important point that further history here means the Talmud. "It is quite impossible to understand Judaism," writes Rabbi Finkelstein firmly, "without an appreciation of the place which it assigns to the study and practice of the Talmudic Law." [1] He goes on to remark that the devout Jew regards this study as a very means of communion with God. This conviction, central to Jewish life

and thought through the ages, is symbolized in every syna-
gogue by the eternal light which burns before the Ark wherein
is kept the scroll of the sacred law (the Five Books of Moses),
a scroll most carefully prepared, written on sheets of parch-
ment in black, indelible ink by a tutored scribe who must say
to himself as he copies the text and as he writes the divine
name, "I am about to write this book as a sacred scroll of the
Law; I am writing this word as the sacred Name." [2]

It was this same conviction, this same reverence for the revealed law which inspired the discussions pursued in the rabbinic academies of Palestine and Babylonia, discussions which
resulted in the two great collections of commentary and precept which together constitute the Talmud, completed some
five centuries *after* the beginning of the Christian era. The
rabbis engaged in this work were regarded as the successors
of the Sanhedrin or Supreme Court, which was the authority
in regard to Jewish Law and custom before the destruction of
Jerusalem, A.D. 70. Their opinions recorded in the Talmud have
had authority second only to the Bible itself for the great majority of the Jewish people. The Bible is interpreted in the
light of the Talmud.

The Talmud, however, is anything but a systematic presentation of the Jewish faith. It is a collection of books, published
in twelve folio volumes, reflecting the discussions of about a
thousand rabbis over a period of eight hundred years on nearly
every subject under the sun from agriculture to matrimony,
religious observances, civil and criminal laws, doctrine, and
scriptural exegesis, with here a homily, there a maxim, here
personal reminiscence, there a story, and much else. What gives
this collection its unity is its evident purpose: to bring every
aspect of human life under the writ of divine law. Its dominating concern is with conduct. But this concern is governed by
a reference to history—particular history, the history of the
peculiar, the chosen people—history which is seen to be gov-

erned by divine will. These scholar-guides of Jewry confer together in their academies as men who are persuaded above all else that they are bound by Divine Covenant "to walk in all the way which the Lord your God hath commanded." [3] They recall the direction:

When thy son asketh thee in time to come, saying, What mean the testimonies, and the statutes and the judgments, which the Lord our God hath commanded you? Then thou shalt say unto thy son, we were Pharaoh's bondsmen in Egypt; and the Lord brought us out of Egypt with a mighty hand. . . . And the Lord commanded us to do all these statutes, to fear the Lord our God, for our good always. [4]

Theological system may be foreign to the Talmud, but the mood of all this discussion of norms and rules of behavior is through and through theocentric and confessional.

As in the Talmud, so it is with the community to which the Talmud gives direction. There is here no Nicene Creed or Westminster Confession. It is a community held together by agreed norms of practice and ritual observances, rather than by any structured or codified theology. The so-called creed of Maimonides (formulated as late as the twelfth century) may be generally accepted as the norm of orthodoxy, but it has not the same authority as a Rabbinic pronouncement on ceremonial law based on Talmudic texts. On the contrary, there has been liberal room for diversity of theological opinion: room for an Alexandrian Philo profoundly influenced by Hellenistic thought, room for the medieval thinkers stimulated by the rediscovery of Aristotle, room for Maimonides and his rationalism, but also room for the poetry of Yehudah Halevi, anticipating Pascal,

> And my heart seeth thee and hath faith in thee
> As though it had stood by at Sinai. [5]

All told, Judaism is indeed a rich tradition. It reflects elements of Sufi mysticism. It embraces the Kabbalists' exotic theosophy, and Hasidic pietism (the background of Martin Buber's thought). In America today there are seminaries and congregations which espouse Reform, Conservative, and Orthodox teachings.

In contemporary Judaism there is a wide variety not only of opinion but also of practice, as some Jews adhere more rigidly than others to traditional observances. Yet Jews today, still dispersed thoughout the world (though they now also have their own state), speaking many different languages, responsive to and contributing to many different cultures, are bound together by other than racial ties. Notwithstanding all diversity, there is here a unity of faith. As Leo Baeck so forcefully puts it, the Jews "all live in one religious home." [6] At the heart of their faith there is the central, biblical confession: "Hear, O Israel: the Lord is our God, the Lord is One." [7] It is a confession which is repeated every morning and evening, as well as on his deathbed, by every practising Jew.

But if we want to know what this confession fully signifies, we must look to the *practice* of the Jewish religion rather than to any creedal formulation. We must also look to the discussion of this practice, in brief, to *the law*. In this respect Judaism has much in common with Islam. In both cases the confession of faith is maintained by an elaboration of law rather than by an elaboration of theology. In both cases the spiritual leaders of the community, the rabbis of Judaism and the ulama of Islam, have been described as "essentially lawyers."

There is, however, one striking difference between the two traditions. Whereas for a great part of their history Muslims have been an expanding, advancing, conquering community, the Jews have more generally been on the defensive. The wonder is that the Jews, dispersed and persecuted, have survived at all. Today there are only about twelve million of them, as against nearly four hundred million Muslims and eight hundred million Christians. For many centuries, Jews have made few converts from other religions and have not attempted to do so. The missionary motive has been absent. Many Jews, indeed, disavow it as incompatible with the tolerance they profess. There are, however, some signs of a change of attitude in this respect. A leading rabbi in North America once told me that when he observed the Christian missionary enterprise he felt challenged. "We Jews should be doing the same," he said. He did not mean by this that Jews should be seeking to convert individuals, but rather that Jews should be thinking more in terms of their mission to the world and their contribution to civilization. He believed that in North America, which is still very much a "new world," still very much in the making, Jews had a special opportunity to share in the shaping of the democratic way of life.

For long centuries, it has been suggested, Jews, parceled among the nations of the world, have been paralyzed by the thought of their dependence on what others might do. Their fate has been "linked to the fate of mankind." [8] Some today may see in the new state of Israel an emancipation from this involvement. Others interpret this very involvement as a call to greater service. Some find greater significance in the fact that nearly half of the Jewish people are citizens of the new America than they do in the fact that the other half has now returned to the Palestinean homeland. Interpretations vary. What is chiefly significant is a change of attitude, a conviction that Judaism has retained "a body of insights all its own" [9] which the world needs today. There is new consciousness both of the opportunity and the responsibility to contribute these insights.

This change of attitude has been developing for some time. It has been accompanied by a good deal of self-criticism. Fifteen years ago, for example, Rabbi Stern of Montreal exclaimed at a Jewish Congress that there had been too much talk of survival. Jews could not be content with "sheer physical survival." Nor could they be content with any merely "negative approach" to life. In contemporary Jewish communal life there was a great deal of "feverish activity." But was it not largely misdirected activity? he asked. Quoting Santayana, the rabbi suggested that the Jewish community might be redoubling its efforts because it had lost its aim: "It is indeed deplorable that in present day Jewish communal life so much of our energy is given over to techniques in fighting anti-Semitism. . . . Let us not reduce almost the whole of Jewish life to an anti-defamation league." [10]

But he also remarked "the radiance of spirit" coming from the new Palestine where Jews were resolved "to build a pattern society." He spoke of the unique contribution to the common life made by the Jewish citizens on the American continent. With these examples in mind, he urged a return to "the joy and poetry of Judaism." He asked for "a new dedication to Jewish values," not merely in the interest of the Jewish community but for the sake of the whole world. For on Judaism, true Judaism, "hinged the salvation of humanity." [11]

Along with this Congress address we may very well consider a sermon preached by Rabbi Stern to his own congregation. The subject of this sermon was The Idolatry of Ideologies. Picturing the children of Israel in the wilderness as "madly dancing around a golden calf," forgetful of the God to whom but yesterday they had pledged allegiance, he also pictured the contemporary Western world "dancing madly around our ideologies." He saw here another consequence of the defensive attitude. Concern to protect the Western democratic way of life against "the ideology of Communism" was promoting a reply in kind: the fashioning of a similarly inflexible orthodoxy in defense of Western democracy. Communistic or democratic, he insisted, ideology meant idolatry, allegiance to "a body of ideas," a golden calf of man-made ideas idolatrously regarded as infallible.

When people ascribe infallibility to an ideology and make that ideology the only promise of salvation, then, indeed, that system of thought, whatever name it may bear, becomes a menace. . . . For the orthodoxy of any ideology results in the closed mind and leads its adherents to become persecutors and inquisitors of those who dare to differ.[12]

They become forgetful, he added, of the sovereign God, the Father of all. True religion and human progress alike depended "on mobility of thought and not fixity of thought." [13]

Rabbi Stern's appraisal amounts to this: that Judaism today, and perhaps thoughout its history, exhibits two opposite tendencies or aspects. On the one hand there is resilient Judaism, accepting contemporary history as it also interprets past history in the light of its central confession of faith, its transcending reference to the living God, a Judaism alerted today to new adventure by contemporary challenge and opportunity. On the other hand, there is a Judaism, tempted to meet this same contemporary situation by defensive strategies and a defensive ideology alien to its own vital poetry of faith.

As we consider Rabbi Stern's appraisal, we may very well recall the view of similar tendencies in modern Islam with which we concluded our last chapter. In the case of Islam also, it was suggested, a defensive ideology signified a loss of authentic aim. Concern to justify Muslim achievements and ideas was substituted for concern to respond to the divine will. Both of these criticisms refer to great confessions of faith, dynamic and invigorating when what is confessed is commitment to the living God. Both suggest a loss of vitality when such commitment is exchanged for subscription to formulations of human thought. Both portray the consequent rigidity as inimical to the very genius of the faith which is defended in this way.

Now it is precisely such Western ideological rigidity which is challenged by oriental relativism. Here, however, we see this rigidity challenged on its own terrain by *Western* critics. What is more, the criticism is expressed in terms which imply that relativism is not only compatible with confessional religion but essential to its health and vitality. If what is confessed is the overruling, sovereign will of God, none other, then any human grasp of this divine intent, any human formulation of its content can only be regarded, and must be regarded, as no more than approximately adequate or relatively true. It is subject to frequent correction. The reference may be to a particular announcement of divine revelation, but between this announcement and finite, human interpretation of its purport there is a distance. No halt can be called to this interpretation. Such is the argument implicit not only in the criticisms we have considered but in the persistent searching for the Divine Will indicated by the Talmudic and Sharia discussions.

"He who adds, subtracts," said Rabbi Hezekiah. We may take this cryptic Talmudic saying to mean that none of the Talmudic maxims, discussions, or conclusions are meant to subtract from that transcending reference to the will of the Most High which prompts these discussions. In both cases Dr. Goldin's apt phrase applies: "All of this is governed by a kind of eager reaching out towards the divine imperative." [14]

Such a "reaching out" is indicated by the very elasticity of the Talmudic discussions, with one opinion set against another, one subject ranged alongside another, and liberal allowance for digression.

The scholars . . . sit in groups; some forbid and others permit; some declare a thing unclean and others declare it clean; some pronounce a thing unfit and others pronounce it fit. Lest anyone say to them [In that event] I shall sit back and not study, Scripture declares, They are given from one shepherd: one God created them, one leader gave them, the Master of all things uttered them! Thou, too, therefore, make thine ear like a hopper and take in the words of them that pronounce unfit and the words of them that pronounce fit.[15]

This mood of the Talmud (allowing diversity in the light of the transcending reference which forbids premature closure) penetrates the community. Here too there is a tolerated diversity, yet also cohesion.

We have, then, in Judaism a qualified relativism and elasticity which promotes the unity of the confessional community as well as its vitality. It is sometimes maintained that when a faith is more precisely and elaborately formulated the adherents of that faith are thereby more firmly held together; they know what they stand for; they know just where the line is drawn and they can be made to toe the line; deviation is avoided and community maintained. But almost the opposite seems here to be the case. Jews have held together despite the absence of such an elaborated orthodoxy, or maybe *because* of its absence. Recognizing the distance between the heights signified by divine revelation and what men may make of divine revelation, they have been the more disposed to tolerate what other Jews may make of it, allowing them continued room within the same household of faith. Much the same may be said of Muslims. As in Islam, so in Judaism, the relativism expressed is a qualified, restrained relativism. It is gathered around a particular reference. But so, too, is Buddhist relativism, as we have seen, a relativism restrained by its central reference to the Buddha character. We cannot, then, draw such a hard and fast line between Eastern and Western attitudes as is sometimes suggested. Such a line can be maintained only when grounds for qualification are ignored or minimized.

Our recognition of this qualified relativism does not mean, of course, that there is no trace at all in Judaism or Islam of that "dogmatic" rigidity which is criticized and challenged by the East. On the contrary, the criticisms we have cited point to such a tendency in both Judaism and Islam.[16]

A good many would say, however, that it is in the Christian tradition, which we must now consider, that the dogmatic tendency is most evident. Indeed, they might add, the Christian tradition presents a counter-challenge: oriental relativism is described, criticized, and dismissed by some Christians as oriental obscurantism. It is Christians who appear to be most persuaded that without precise definition of belief there can be no real community in religion. It is in the Christian tradition that we have the greatest rash (or wealth) of creeds and confessional statements, the greatest incidence of heresy hunts, the greatest intolerance of diversity, the greatest tendency to exclusive dogmatism, and the greatest repugnance to all that savors of indecision in thought or life. It is the Christian who most insists that the believer must "make up his mind," "know what he stands for," and, in the words of the Epistle, "follow the pattern of sound words," guarding the truth that has been entrusted to him.[17]

Perhaps we should beware, however, of overstatement here. As already remarked, firm definition of belief has not been confined to Christians. Nor are Christians the only target for criticism in this respect. Toynbee, for example, ranges Muslims alongside Christians as he comments on attempts to translate prophetic vision into the terms of "metaphysical blue-prints." [18] Nor again, if we take into account the whole length and breadth of the Christian tradition, can we ignore the degree of flexibility which remained despite all attempts at such blue prints. A distinction, too, may be drawn between the church in the West and the church in the East. It is maybe the church in the West which is the more disposed to marshal adherence to clear-cut doctrinal formulas.

Nevertheless, it is a Western world influenced by the tradition of Christian thought which is mainly in view when there is criticism of "dogmatic" attitudes. Such attitudes, it is charged, result in "narrow," "intolerant" definitions of religious community which exclude from such a community those who do not subscribe to preferred and elaborated statements of belief. That there is ground for such criticism cannot be denied, ground which appears when a confession of faith maintained in flexible, poetic terms, open to further and various interpretation, is distinguished from a confession tied to statements expressed in more precise, less flexible terms which are accepted as binding.

Christian history, it is maintained, presents a passage from poetry to prose, a passage from confessionalism broadly expressed to what may be called "subscriptionism": a confessional allegiance joined with a demand for subscription to clear-cut statements of belief. How this came to be in the Christian West and with what consequences we have now to consider. To do so in brief compass will mean a somewhat cavalier treatment of issues on which Christian scholars are divided, including the whole, larger question of the tension between Hebraic and Greek elements in the Christian outlook as the Christian community, cradled in Judaism, is seen to make its way in the larger gentile world of Greco-Roman culture.

It may be well to consider, to begin with, just what is involved in this passage from "confessionalism" to "subscriptionism." It is a passage which is generally attributed to the impact of Greek philosophy in the first four centuries of the Christian era. When Toynbee, for example, speaks of the "pinning down of the Gospel," he refers to the effect of the introduction of Greek metaphysical terms into the Christian vocabulary. He implies, as others have done, that the very process of translation affected the Christian outlook. He refers to an "attitude of mind, widespread and pervasive" [19] which accompanied the adoption of Greek terms.

The philosophically educated elite of the Graeco-Roman public wished to believe that it possessed, in its metaphysics, a complete and final blue-print of scientific truth. . . . It was this impracticable demand . . . that constrained Christians and Muslims to translate their gospels out of the prophet's poetic medium of expression into the philosopher's scientific medium.[20]

According to this view, shared by a good many other writers, it was not just a question of Christians using such terms as *ousia* in their creedal formulas nor such bridge-terms as *logos* in their efforts to communicate the Gospel to the pagan world. It was a question of Christians becoming infected by a whole "attitude of mind," a mind given to the production of metaphysical "blue-prints" or "scientific charts of the Universe" which could be regarded as "complete and final." Thus there was the "precipitation" of systems of theology similarly aiming at a total view of man and his environment, mundane and supramundane. There was further enclosure and definition of the Christian faith. There was not only a tendency to wed such definition to some metaphysical system, but also a searching of the scriptures for first principles or main premises of the faith and a statement of these premises in precise terms. Christian thinkers, in philosophic engagement, sharpened what they regarded as God-given wits in order to state more clearly and definitely just what they believed and did not believe.

It is this zeal for precise definition [21] which marks the passage from the greater flexibility of confessionalism to the rigidity of subscriptionism. Subscriptionism involves three things: (a) a summary statement of the faith professed by the religious community; (b) a valuation of this statement as sufficiently precise and true; (c) a demand for subscription to the statement thus valued as the condition of membership in the community. The provision of a summary statement of the faith is only a first step. What is of chief consequence is the valuation of the statement as sufficiently precise and true to be used as a test of membership or a ground for inclusion in, or exclusion from, the household of faith.

As for the first step, the step towards definition and summary of the Christian faith, this can scarcely be attributed entirely to the impact of Greek culture. Inherent in the very character of the Christian confession itself, as in the situation of the early Church, there was a need for some degree of clarification. From the beginning Christian community was gathered around a particular announcement. It meant a confession of faith, which was restrained by the "religious facts" [22] to which it referred. If there was more flexibility in the apostolic teaching than is sometimes recognized, with more than one "pattern of sound words," there was also the restraint (as well as the stimulation) involved in the central announcement of the confession that "Jesus is Lord." Confess this, writes St. Paul, and "you will be saved," [23] and it was the missionary hope of the new community that "every tongue" would indeed confess this "to the glory of God the Father." [24] Pliny the Younger bears witness to this "particularity" when he reports to the Emperor Trajan that the one thing no genuine Christian can be brought to do is to "curse Christ." Christians sing hymns to Christ "as to a God." [25] The writer of an early homily (*2 Clement*) similarly testifies: "Brethren, we must think of Christ as of God."

But such "thinking" did not, in itself, imply sharp definition. The reference to "Christ as of God" might also be seen as stimulating richness of thought and flexibility of interpretation.

In these earlier centuries any disposition to a firmer definition of what Christians stood for was part and parcel of a whole movement towards consolidation. An early regard for Christian unity meant an early movement to check deviation, a movement which included steps towards a more definite organization of the community and the definition of canonical scripture besides the formulation of the creeds. It is in this light, if in no other, that we may read the injunction: "Avoid divisions. . . . All of you follow the bishop . . . that everything which you do may be sound and valid." [26]

At the same time, the Christian faith was still a faith based upon, and continuing, the Hebrew recital of the "acts of God" as told in essentially "poetic" scripture. It does not affect the point we are here making to observe that Hebrew scripture had already been translated into Greek by the time of the Christian era. Nor does the fact that the parent Hebrew tradition was itself already infected by Greek thought. It is not just a question of comparing or contrasting Hebrew and Greek *ideas*. What matters is that the Biblical writers were not philosophers. It is the way, the essentially poetic way, in which truth is presented in the Bible which here concerns us. For this way betokens an attitude of mind fundamentally different from that of the Greek philosophers, with their quest for more precise and more sufficient statement. It is therefore in regard to the second step we have named, the valuation of summary statements of the Christian Faith as precise and true, that the impact of Greek thought is more especially emphasized.

But what was it that actually happened in the first four centuries of the Christian era? There was never any total disappearance of the Hebraic element in the Christian outlook. What happened was the beginning of a dialogue within the Christian pale, a dialogue between Greek and Hebrew. This dialogue continued throughout the whole course of Christian history. Every new engagement with Greek thought, as in the case of medieval scholasticism and again in the case of post-Reformation Protestant scholasticism, meant renewal of the impetus towards precise and systematic statement. But insofar as such statement was still based on the Bible, there remained within the Christian tradition the resistance movement of Hebrew poetry. Dogmatism was qualified by a Christian relativism of the kind suggested by the Pauline references to "the deep things of God," the "searching by the spirit," and the distinction between the "wisdom of this world" and the "mind of Christ." [27]

Thus within the Christian tradition there has been a persistent tension between two attitudes of mind in regard to statements of the faith. The Gospel has never once and for all and beyond question been "pinned down." It has again and again broken free from any attempt at such confinement. Toynbee's extrapolation of the Parable of the Sower—"and some seeds fell upon a conveyor belt and were carried into a factory where they were processed, refrigerated, and sterilized"—presents only part of the story.[28]

Nor should a presentation in terms of Greek-Hebrew dialogue be taken to mean that there was no poetry in the Greek mind, no Platonic imagery besides Platonic definition. Nor again, can it be held that there was nothing in the Hebrew outlook which might encourage an exclusive attitude. We cannot disregard, for example, all that has followed from the Old Testament belief in "the jealous God."

Furthermore—and the reader versed in ancient history may well have been waiting for this acknowledgment—the Christain encounter with the pagan world meant much more than the encounter with Greek philosophy. Even if there had been no Plato or "wretched Aristotle" to arouse the Tertullians, no Athens to set in contrast to Jerusalem, there was much else in the total complex of pagan life and thought, including the Gnostic speculations and the challenge of the mystery religions, to prompt the movement towards a firmer definition of the Christian faith.

Much the same can be said about the Christian environment during the subsequent course of Christian history. Although there have been times when the Western world itself has been designated "Christendom," there has always been a world influencing and challenging this life and thought in ways which have revived and sustained the tendency towards subscriptionism. All that is here claimed is that the impact of Greek thought is one of the things which enables us to see more clearly, and in part account for, the tension within Christianity itself, the tension between a zeal for definition and a hesitation to press definition too far.

At the one extreme we have dogmatic, exclusive attitudes not only towards adherents of other faiths but sometimes towards other Christians, together with a limitation of diversity, a frowning upon deviation, and a suspicion of all religious statements not clearly rooted in Christian premises. At the other extreme we have a relativist attitude to Christian statements themselves, a tolerance of other statements, a professed readiness to "embrace Truth wherever it is found," and a hospitality of mind in some cases so akin to the Hindu hospitality of mind that it may allow not only for Christian Platonists but for the possibility of "Christian Buddhists, or Christian Confucians, and even perhaps Christian Vedantists or Christian Moslems." [29] In between these two extremes we find a good many Christians shifting uneasily from one foot to the other.

All told, however, the tendency towards dogmatism has been sufficiently marked to warrant the criticism of Dr. Radhakrishnan and others when they include Christians among those who have "identified religion with dogmas and beliefs" and have "fought wars over abstract theological differences." [30] Christians have certainly taken their beliefs seriously.[31] They have been ready to die for them and to put others to death for them.

The Christian conception of religious community is in accordance with this emphasis on "right belief." "You believe what I believe; therefore we belong to the same household of faith." The conception is through and through confessional. The Christian Church, wrote Cardinal Bellarmine, is "a body of men united together by the profession of the same Christian Faith." [32] Theologians of all denominations, Protestant as well as Catholic, would say much the same. They would associate Christian unity specifically, as does the Cardinal, with the profession or confession of faith.

Even such a loosely federated body as the World Council of Churches, it has been said, would be unthinkable without some minimal confessional agreement:

The World Council is open to churches which accept Jesus Christ as God and Saviour. . . . Without this categorical affirmation . . . the ecumenical movement would lose all its meaning. The ecumenical movement is both based on and seeks unity in Jesus Christ, not just any kind of unity.[33]

No question arises, then, as to the confessional character of the Christian religion and Christian conceptions of community. Questions *do* arise, however, as to the way in which the Christian confession may be expressed and the consequent forms of community. Does such confession necessarily involve the dogmatism with which it is frequently associated? Does it necessarily mean adherence to elaborated and precise definitions? These questions are suggested by what we have observed in dealing with Buddhism, Islam, and Judaism. We have now to see how they are also posed by what may be observed *within* the Christian tradition itself. Consider, for example, Dr. Nicholls, the Anglican theologian whose comment on the World Council of Churches we have quoted above. He applauds the Council's "categorical affirmation." This may be taken to mean that he applauds its "confessionalism." But a few chapters later on we find him very critical of a confessionalism which he describes as heretical and bad. "Our confession of the faith," he says, "is continually menaced by the heretical tendency to claim that we alone know how to confess it." [34] Here, we have reference to two kinds of confessional religion, both of them within the Christian tradition, with rejection of one kind as too narrowly and rigidly dogmatic.

The term "confessional" is in fact used in two senses, one broad, the other narrow. It may be used, as we have used it in these chapters, either with broad reference to communities held together by a particular "categorical affirmation," as in the case of Buddhism, Islam, and Judaism, however this affirmation may be expressed. Or we may speak of confessionalism with reference to attitudes and practices associated in particular with the so-called confessional churches. These churches, following the Reformation, indicated their doctrinal positions in systematic statements of belief which went beyond shorter statements of the creeds approved by church councils held in the fourth and fifth centuries. Thus the Lutheran Confession of Augsburg (1530) not only reaffirms the accepted creedal statement about "remission of sins" but also goes into detail on the subject of "original sin." It also expounds a dogma of "justification by faith" and other dogmas. Similarly, the Westminster Confession (1643) maintained by the Church of Scotland elaborates the Calvinist doctrine of predestination. Every minister of the church has been required to subscribe to this confession and instruct the laity accordingly. In England there was similar subscription to the Thirty-Nine Articles of the Anglican Church. Since the Reformation, Roman Catholics have similarly adhered to the statement of doctrine formulated at the Council of Trent (1545–63).[35] The term confessional church, then, may be used with narrow reference to churches where there is adherence not only to the Christian faith but to some particular interpretation of the faith. Such churches may be seen to encourage a confident dogmatism. They bring to a head, as it were, the tendency towards dogmatic insistence which was developing in the Christian world long before the Reformation.

It is confessionalism in this narrow sense which Dr. Nicholls rejects, while accepting confessionalism in the broader sense which is exhibited by the World Council's "categorical affirmation." He is not averse to dogma as such. In fact he regards "theological relativism" as "even worse" than narrow confessionalism. The fact that such a position can be held *within* the Christian tradition is significant. It exhibits the tension between extreme dogmatism and liberalism to which we have referred. It also points to the possibility of more than one Christian conception of confessional community. The fact that Dr. Nicholls is an Anglican is also significant. It might be said that it is precisely from such a quarter that such a statement might be expected. For it is questionable whether the Anglican Church can properly be named a narrowly "confessional church." Anglicans have virtually ignored their "confession" (the Thirty-Nine Articles). Many would say that what rather holds them together is their Book of Common Prayer, in other words, not doctrinal agreement but agreement in worship or religious practice. Observing this, we may be led to look in other quarters besides the Anglican for variations in the Christian confessional pattern. There is the difference between the Western churches (Catholic and Protestant) and the Eastern churches (Orthodox). The Orthodox churches are certainly creedal. But they do not go beyond the definitions of the historic creeds. "The Orthodox Church recognizes and accepts as an Ecumenical Symbol *only* the Creed of Nicea-Constantinople." [36] This creed, as we have said, is a minimal statement compared with the more elaborated "confessions." Some observers point to a corresponding reluctance on the part of Orthodox teachers to press dogmatic definition too far. "It is the conviction of Eastern Orthodoxy that the deepest things in the faith are not precisely definable, but mysteries to be reverently felt out by mystical insight." [37]

Next, we may turn to some of the "free churches" formed since the Reformation. We find some of them agreeing with the Orthodox Church that the Nicene Creed is "the sufficient statement of corporate faith" while adding that, even so, this can only be accepted if there is "reasonable liberty of interpretation." [38]

Finally, with such bodies as the Quakers we have a pattern which some might say is not confessional in any sense.

Besides such deviations from the confessional church pattern, account should also be taken of new movements of opinion within the confessional churches themselves. The formulations of doctrine remain but the demand for full subscription to them has in some cases been modified so that all that is now required is a general assent to the standpoints maintained by these statements.

All told there is sufficient deviation from the strict confessional church pattern to point to the conclusion that within the Christian tradition itself, as well as outside it, there is more than one way in which confessional allegiance is expressed. As to the consequent forms and conceptions of religious community, there are at least some patterns within Christianity which invite comparison with what was observed in Buddhism, Islam, and Judaism.

Glancing again, then, at the map of the great religions, now that we have added these brief surveys of Judaism and Christianity, we may broadly distinguish, in "confessional" terms, at least three patterns of community. There is first the non-confessional pattern of Hindu India (and the Quakers?). Second, there is the broad confessional pattern. Third, there is the pattern exemplified by the confessional churches presenting an emphasis on conformity to agreed dogma. We shall return to this classification later. Our main point for the present is that the possibility of such a classification calls in question any simple identification of confessionalism with the dogmatism which is the target of oriental criticism.

As to the Christian tradition, the fact that it presents forms, conceptions, and attitudes which may be included within the second category of broad confessionalism suggests that here is greater affinity with some oriental attitudes than might at first appear. Sober critics of Christian dogmatism are prepared, of course, to allow for exceptions which prove the rule or for Christians who are "better than their creed." But our descripion points to something more than such exceptions. It indicates a greater complexity in the Christian pattern than is sometimes recognized. It refers to a tension within Christianity which means that the say of the dogmatist has never been the only say. It allows for the fact that there are Christians like Professor Hocking and Fredrick Heiler who feel no less strongly than Dr. Radhakrishnan that Christianity as well as other religions includes an aversion to "dogmatic fetters" and exclusive attitudes. At the same time our description points to enough dogmatism in the Christian tradition to provide grist in plenty for the mills of the critics. As one Christian writer freely acknowledges, "toleration and 'reasonableness' have been very late comers on the European scene," a scene largely set by Christianity.[39]

If one were asked whether Christians today were becoming more or less "dogmatic" it would, indeed, be difficult to reply. In some quarters there is certainly a flexing of dogmatic muscles within the Christian tradition. This has come about in several ways.

The ecumenical movement, for example, the very movement which might be expected to discourage dogmatic, exclusive attitudes since it is designed to promote unity, has had one immediate result which has surprised some observers.

A curious thing is happening in contemporary Protestantism. Alongside an ecumenical concern for the reunion of Christendom is a growing denominational self-consciousness that threatens to perpetuate the ancient divisions. Whether this is creative or destructive has been a topic of considerable debate. . . . Many Protestants feel that the new emphasis on denominationalism . . . jeopardises ecumenical concern. . . . Another group of Protestants feels that . . . the ecumenical cause will best be served as each denomination holds up for public inspection, discussion, and possible amendment its own particular gifts to "the coming great church." [40]

A good deal may be seen to depend here on what each denomination considers that it has to offer. Anglicans, who were among the first to suggest such an offering, may very well have thought that their own "comprehensiveness" is just what is needed and what is implied by their history. But other denominations may feel constrained to contribute something very different as they consider their "particular gifts." Looking back on their own denominational histories they might say that what they find here is a zeal to maintain sound dogma at any cost, even at the cost of schism. Asked to count this cost, they might very well reconsider the soundness, importance, or statement of some of their particular dogmas. That is one thing. It is another thing, however, to expect that such a looking back should lead them to change their whole attitude to dogma. On the contrary, what has happened has been a new insistence on doctrinal fidelity and the need for clearly defined standpoints, with a good deal of talk about the dangers of obscurantism and the temptation to "sacrifice principles to expediency." True, there has been some reaffirmation of the biblical relativism which affirms that definition in this realm cannot, and should not, be pressed too far. But by and large what has resulted from ecumenical conversations has, if anything, been a renewed emphasis of the possibility and importance of doctrinal statement.[41] This is seen in the very general demand in all churches today for a "teaching ministry."

Again, in any theological discussion the men who are prepared to say clearly, definitely and forcibly just exactly what they stand for have a certain advantage. And most of them take it. Their example, too, is infectious. Spokesmen of denominations not hitherto notable for doctrinal clarity and firmness have replied in kind. Asked to say what they stand for, they have taken it for granted that the answer must be some more or less elaborated and precise confession. Where such a confession is lacking in their own tradition, they have sometimes been the more ready to accept it from others. The general trend is indicated by Dr. Nicholl's significant comment that "theological relativism" is "even worse" than confessionalism.[42]

"Theological relativism" is said to mean the idea that "there is only a possibility of a multiplenty of relative truths, one of which is as good as another." This brings us to a second factor which has promoted a return to "dogmatism." We observed in our introductory chapter that the challenge of Hindu relativism has been obscured by its identification with a relativism which is homemade in the West itself. The Hindu challenge is obscured by this identification because (if we are right in the conclusions drawn in our third chapter) Hindu relativism does not involve any disparagement of religious beliefs. But our Western relativism does very often imply such disparagement. It seems to take the ground away from any possibility of certainty (or even certitude) in realms where man desperately seeks for certainty. Modern man is fighting to retain this ground or to find new ground for certainty.

It is altogether natural for him to do so, for the quest for certainty corresponds to the human need for security, and the felt need of security is one of the characteristics of this shattering twentieth century. "But where," asks Professor Levi in his recent survey of the present philosophical scene, "where in the modern world is this intellectual security to be found?" [43]

One proposed answer is: the doctrine of Marx and Engels. It is an answer which appears to provide exactly what Professor Levi says is demanded: "a body of established truth which not only charts the structure of the natural world but also fixes without question man's place within it." [44] Now whatever else this Marxist answer may be it is certainly definitive, apparently confident, clear, creedal, and dogmatic. It defines community in vigorous terms of "You believe what I believe." Whether Marxism is properly described as another religion or a Christian heresy is debatable. There are Messianic tones in it which lead some to observe that Karl Marx himself was, after all, a Jew with a Christian upbringing. Others see and emphasize in Marxism the sense of togetherness and direction along with the fervor which is associated with religion. It is worth observing, however, that what is more evident to a great many oriental critics is that Marxism is another "Western ism." It is in this respect that they compare it with some aspects of Christianity. They see it appealing to modern man in much the same way as Christian dogmatism.

That resurgent Christian dogmatism does have this appeal is evident. One significant testimony to this effect comes from the principal of a theological seminary in England who gives his impression of changes in the students' outlook. As compared with students twenty years ago, he observes, students today "are much less secure and this fact makes them inclined to look for a more authoritarian approach both in theology and in ordinary life." [45] In other words they are the more ready to accept, cherish, and maintain the dogmatism which they can still find in the Church just because they cannot find it in the surrounding culture of the age. Nor need it be concluded that they are doing so blindly. Besides a psychological need there may be an intelligent rejection of relativism as it is generally presented and understood in the West. Or what may be thus signified may be a growing "resistance movement" within the Church similar to the resistance movements of earlier ages when the pressures of the cultural environment promoted the very dogmatism which today is challenged by contemporary relativism.

A revival of Christian dogmatism, however, is by no means the whole story. It is nearer the truth of the Christian situation to present it in terms of continuation of the tension which we observed earlier. If one response to the cultural relativism of our day is the No of a resurgent dogmatism, another and very different response is a relativism which, while it may be stimulated by what is happening elsewhere, is largely of the Church's own making. This relativist movement finds expression in a growing critcism of the shallows of intellectualism combined with a growing interest in what may be called depth religion.

The subject of depth religion, however, raises so many issues
that its consideration means a new chapter. Until we have
given the subject this consideration our description of the
Christian world, and of other worlds, too, is incomplete. And
others besides Christians are affected by some of the issues
raised by this subject.

CHAPTER VII

"Depth Religion" and Western Dogmatism

THE TERM "DEPTH RELIGION," admittedly an ambiguous
term and one which calls for closer examination, as will presently be emphasized, is suggested by the frequent recurrence
of the word "depth" in discussions of religion today.

From time to time in the history of human thought and
inquiry, some new way of looking at things seems to emerge
quietly, unobtrusively, one might almost say stealthily, without
any special announcement or fanfare of trumpets. No one person seems to have proposed it. Instead, it seems to be introduced from various quarters by various writers, some of them,
it would appear, not fully aware of what they are doing. Yet
somehow they converge in a whispering campaign which is
so effective that what they say becomes widely accepted and
repeated, and all this with little inquiry as to the validity or the
truth of it. This is what seems to have happened in the case of
depth religion.

How this is so may be indicated by a number of examples
selected more or less at random from various contexts. Before
giving these examples, however, I want to make four things
clear.

First, it is not suggested that every use of the word "depth"
means a reference to depth religion. With other kindred terms
it is often used in a broad superlative sense merely to indicate
something worthy of special respect as when the depth of the
Buddha's teaching is said to be one of the Five Wonders.

Second, it is not suggested that the reference is, in each case, precisely the same. That, indeed, is one of the issues to be clarified.

Third, I am aware that there is nothing new in the suggestion that religious teaching is profound, in the sense of either (a) referring to a situation or an experience which means a better understanding of life, or (b) implying more than appears on the surface.

Fourth, my purpose is limited. In naming some of the issues presented by the interest in depth religion, I am not here concerned to propose any resolution of these issues, though I may refer to ways in which other writers propose to do so. The purpose of this chapter is rather to show how the present interest in depth religion reflects and encourages the movement towards relativism while, at the same time, the issues presented by this interest may promote a countercriticism of relativism, and maybe a revival of dogmatic attitudes.

I begin with what first aroused my own interest,[1] and that is the remarkable agreement on this matter between two writers who in other ways are very opposite: Arnold Toynbee, advocate of what is called the *liberal* view of the great non-Christian religions, and Dr. Hendrik Kraemer, considered by his disciples to have put all the liberals to rout by his broadside of dialectical theology, *The Christian Message in a Non-Christian World*, an assault which he has since vigorously maintained.[2]

Toynbee and Kraemer both see in the religions of the world a mixture of good and bad. Both see the strengthening of this good and the overcoming of this bad by a depth of apprehension which they set in contrast to anything achieved by theological or other rational inquiry and speculation. Kraemer, it is true, draws a sharp line between an apprehension of divine revelation and the kind of intuitive apprehension which Toynbee has in mind. But in their reference to a corrective word which comes from depths beyond levels known to pedestrian reason they are strangely together.

Toynbee's study of universal history has led him to emphasize an experience of what he calls "withdrawal and return." As he sees it, the health of civilization largely depends on a creative minority, consisting of men who from time to time withdraw from the shallows of everyday living to a realm of deeper awareness and understanding. From this experience they return to the world of affairs with a new vision and purpose which may infect others. Quoting Bergson, Toynbee describes these creative souls as those who have "felt the truth flow into them from its source." [3] With this we may compare what he says elsewhere of religions which "become more vital when they send their roots down below the intellectual surface to the subconscious depths of Human Nature." [4]

Along with this emphasis on what may be *gained* by going below the intellectual surface, there is a reference to what may be lost or obscured on the merely intellectual level. Toynbee refers to "the pinning down of the Christian gospel in creeds" and to "cramping and warping intellectual trammels." [5] This judgment is based on a distinction drawn between "the truth of the sub-conscious" and the "truth of the intellect"; between two organs in the human psyche, one conscious and volitional, the other "a sub-conscious emotional abyss," "each with its own way of looking at, and peering through, the dark glass that screens Reality from Man's inward eye"; between the intellect's step by step science and poetic, prophetic utterance expressing "flashes of intuitive insight shooting up out of the subconscious." [6]

What is here implied is that religious vitality and insight depend on an intuitive apprehension which is related to subconscious depths. Dogmatic formulations are disparaged and some readers may very well conclude from Toynbee's account that the intellect is more of a nuisance than a help so far as religion is concerned.

With this we may compare Dr. Kraemer's analysis. In certain respects it is remarkably similar despite the fact that, in emphasizing divine revelation as his starting point, he speaks of it as "basically different from religious intuition or divination." [7] For Kraemer assigns a corrective role to a more immediate apprehension of divine revelation which he distinguishes from intellectual presentations. He also associates this corrective apprehension with "what happens in the depth." Like Toynbee, he draws a line between what may be realized on the intellectual level and what transcends it. A distinction is made between the biblical message and our man-made systems, theological as well as philosophical, not only in regard to scope but in regard to the *way* the biblical message is presented, and also in regard to the way it is apprehended. "The central point in Biblical epistomology is not reason but 'the heart.' " [8] Whence comes what Kraemer calls the "primordial decision" and response of faith.[9] "The biblical theological approach is exclusively concerned with . . . what happens in the depth between God . . . and man." [10]

Some of the terms Kraemer uses when he proceeds to draw a distinction between religions and the religious consciousness are also significant. He speaks of "the silent, unconscious or conscious drama of the encounter of God and Man" which takes place in the religious consciousness.[11] He refers to all religions as "responses to God, conscious or unconscious." [12] He refers to "deep Ahnungen [intuitions] of Divine Love" and to "the spontaneous God-intuition which in crucial moments surges up in man." [13] He writes of "apprehensions akin to biblical apprehensions," which, he says, may be found in the different religious traditions. At the same time the major *differences* between one religion and another are related to some fundamental apprehension present in each.[14]

Some of these references to "the depths" again and again recall similar references and emphases in Toynbee's pages. Yet Kraemer is far from being a Toynbee. He is accepted in quarters where Toynbee is suspect. Rightly or wrongly, he is generally considered a "conservative" drawing a sharp line between the Christian faith and all other announcements which the liberal Toynbee, with the tolerant Symmachus as his patron (if pagan) saint,[15] and with his account of the "Christian-Mahayanian way of life" [16] would certainly question.

Nevertheless, if we regard not so much the conclusions arrived at as *what is taken into account in the process of arriving at these conclusions,* there is remarkable agreement between these two writers. Both have recurring references to "the depths"; both agree that the health of religions (Christianity included) depends upon a return to the "depths"; both are consequently critical of the shallows and pretensions of intellectualism as both emphasize an apprehension of reality attained in the depths. And in both cases these depths are associated with what occurs beneath the level of consciousness.

In brief, what is thus presented is (a) depth religion and (b) the limitations of intellectual definition in the realm of religion. The reference to depth religion, joined as it is with the recognition of the unconscious, is evidence of the way in which contemporary studies in this field of religions are affected, as we observed in an earlier chapter, by studies in related disciplines (in this case by modern psychology). The caveat against intellectualism is also significant. It recalls an earlier observation: that in the West itself we have today a trend of thought towards relativism, a trend of Western origin, apart from what may be ascribed to the influence of oriental thought, a trend away from the dogmatic rigidity associated with subscriptionism. In the case of Kraemer this trend may not at first be apparent. But it comes into view as we remark the distinction he draws between the biblical message itself and the systems of the theologians who are just as much tempted to sin against the light, in his view, as the philosophers. At the same time he is no less critical of *oriental* relativism. We are thus prepared to find him speaking elsewhere of two kinds of relativism, life-weakening and life-liberating.[17] Two kinds or not, the conclusion in one respect is the same: we have here, developing in the West itself, a relativist attitude averse to any rigid dogmatism and critical of any "idolatry of ideology." And this relativism is associated with, and largely prompted by, the recognition of depth religion.

But both presentations, Kraemer's and Toynbee's, raise a good many questions. What is this depth religion? Is it to be identified solely with what happens beneath the level of consciousness? If so, have we here, in final conclusion, not only a criticism of shallow intellectualism and presumptuous dogmatism, but a flight from reason, a dalliance with sheer obscurantism?

Thus alerted, I began to observe the frequent references to depth religion in contemporary Western literature, in various contexts, by different writers. Broadly speaking it is a reference largely associated with an interest in the character, significance, and extent of religious symbolism together with an interest in what the depth psychologists of our day have to say about this symbolism. A few examples, collected from various fields and thrown together without further comment for the moment, may serve to indicate this interest.

In the field of Christian theology we have Paul Tillich's description of modern man, frequently quoted and variously embroidered, as one who has "lost the dimension of depth." [18] There is also the remark of the Cambridge theologian, H. H. Farmer, that one of the problems confronting contemporary theology is the problem of "giving the unconscious depths their proper place." [19] Turning to students of religious symbolism, we find Professor Goodenough emphasizing how "deeply rooted" in the unconscious is this symbolism.[20] Professor Mircea Eliade similarly refers to what is "buried in the deepest strata of man's being" when he suggests that even modern man longs for the "new, regenerated life" symbolized by primitive and traditional rites of initiation.[21] For what is thus symbolized, Professor Eliade suggests, is a universal and persistent need. It pertains to the very nature of the human condition or situation. In the desacralized world of today this may not be immediately apparent. In the case of modern man there is no longer religious experience of this kind "fully and consciously assumed." Nevertheless we may learn, from the reports which come to us from psychologists, that the longing and need for this "regeneration," this "dying to live," persists. We also have hints of this continued "longing"—"man's eternal longing"— in some of the images and themes which occur in contemporary literature such as James Joyce's *Ulysses* and T. S. Eliot's *The Waste Land*.[22]

The imaginative activity and the dream experiences of modern man continue to be pervaded by religious symbols, figures, and themes. As some psychologists delight in repeating, the unconscious is religious. From one point of view it could be said that in the man of desacralized societies, religion has become "unconscious"; it lies buried in the deepest strata of his being.[23]

Thus religion still functions, as even "nonreligious men" may sometimes realize "in the depths of their being." [24] What is thus darkly hinted or conveyed in "secret spiritual messages" today may be better understood if construed in the light of what is overtly presented in primitive rites and myths. "Initiation lies at the core of any genuine human life." [25] Is Professor Eliade here teaching that modern man must not only search the depths but return to the depths?

Another writer, this time a sociologist, P. W. Martin, says explicitly that such a return is indeed indicated. From a wide, international experience of social service, in the service of

UNESCO and other agencies, he concludes that a return to the depths is urgent not only for man individually but for society. It is of interest that he too observes the significance of T. S. Eliot's *The Waste Land*. He combines this reference with reference to Toynbee and Jung in a book, *Experiment in Depth*, which proposes a rediscovery of "the creative reality behind religion." [26] He sees in contemporary depth psychology a "new instrument" enabling man to make this rediscovery. "The unconscious is the wellspring of life" and "the unconscious has insights going far beyond those of consciousness." [27] But Dr. Martin also sounds a warning which we must presently consider. The return to the depths, he says, must not be taken to mean the surrender of conscious control.

In a more recent but similar approach to the subject with similar purpose, this time by a practicing psychologist, Dr. Ira Progoff also urges a return to depths as vital to "authentic religious experience." [28] Depth psychology is here seen to provide "an urgently needed tool of survival for modern man." [29] Like Dr. Martin, Dr. Progoff combines this reference to modern psychology with a wider reference. In this the reference is to philosophy, biology, and medieval mysticism. He borrows from the "holistic philosophy" of the South African statesman-philosopher, Jan Christian Smuts. Smuts, it is said, "anticipated the conclusions that depth psychology would reach thirty years after Freud's original hypothesis." [30] They are, as Dr. Progoff sees them, conclusions which forbid any tendency to "break personality into segments." There must be no separation of "consciousness from the unconscious." The man we have to deal with is the whole man. Our approach to the subject must be "holistic." [31] This means that the word "depth" must not be taken too literally.

Dr. Progoff brings into the open what is implied by a good many writers: a narrow identification of "depth" with the unconscious, and hence some uneasy questions regarding "depth religion." But he leaves us with new questions as to just what may be meant by these terms.

The word depth . . . encompasses more than depths, it is heights as well. As an outcome of processes that take place in the depths of the psyche, a person may indeed reach the peaks of human experience. . . . In the special meaning of the word *depths* as it is used in depth psychology . . . *Depth is the dimension of wholeness of man* . . . not a level in the psyche literally and spatially . . . but a level in the human organism in principle . . . deeper down in the psyche in the sense that it is more fundamental than those mental contents that are in closer relation to surface consciousness and to sensory contact with the outside world. The depths contain what is implicit in the psyche, what is potential there. . . .[32]

Our final quotation refers us to the field of linguistic analysis. The criticism that religious statements do not make sense has led Professor Ramsey to reply that they do indeed make sense when it is realized that they refer in general to situations which have taken on "depth." [33] Without such depth, he remarks, no religion would be possible.[34] But his context makes it clear that he might very well say with Dr. Progoff that by "depth" he also means "height."

The objection may be raised that reference to the depths in discussions of religion is not so new as might appear. The whole, rich tradition of Christian mysticism—a tradition much richer than Dr. Suzuki allows when he compares it with Zen Buddhism [35]—points to "situations which have taken on depth," at least in the sense intended by Professor Ramsey, as the stumbling language of the mystics indicates. They, too, could say of the reality which they attested: "No concepts can reach it, no understanding can grasp it." [36] There is, however, this difference, that whereas in the West mystical experience has generally been regarded as reserved for the few, the return to the depths proposed by such writers as Dr. Progoff and Mr. Martin is intended, if not for the many, at least for the "not so few." [37] The relation to the unconscious depths emphasized by Professor Goodenough and Professor Eliade certainly refers to the many.

Or again it may be said that Schleiermacher more than a century ago anticipated much that is being said today when he invited the cultured despisers of religion to "listen to themselves before their own consciousness . . . lying directly on the bosom of the infinite world." [38] As Schleiermacher struggles with language, seeking to convey what this "descent into the inmost sanctuary" might mean, we might, in the light of our modern psychological science, conclude that he is really inviting his readers to listen, not to their consciousness, but to their unconscious (if that were possible) or at least to intimations which come from the unconscious. He speaks of an experience "as fleeting and transparent as the vapour which the dew breathes on blossom and fruit, . . . as bashful and tender as a maiden's kiss." [39] Nevertheless, for Schleiermacher, this "bashful" experience is still within the realm of conscious feeling. What his "cultured despisers" are invited to do is to "feel" the powers of nature as "their own." [40]

The modern psychologist, at least in thought or conception, has passed beyond the realm of conscious feeling. He is pointing, it would seem, to greater depths, more bewildering depths, than any suggested by Schleiermacher; he is pointing to the *un*-conscious; he is dealing with what is considered to begin in this realm of the unconscious. In this diagnosis he is joined today by some of the students of religious symbolism who see their symbols rooted in or bespeaking this same unconscious. It is largely the conjunction of these two accounts—what the psychologist has to say and what the historian of religion has to say—that leads us to speak of "depth religion." Together, it might be claimed, they have given us new insights, relevant to the whole study of religion. But they have also produced some new confusions and at the moment the confusions may be the more apparent. The need to resolve some of these confusions (if possible!) is also becoming apparent.

Questions certainly arise when it is suggested that a return to the depths is remedial or corrective, if this suggestion is joined with statements which virtually identify the depths with the unconscious. Nor are these questions silenced if identification is disclaimed in a way which still assigns to the unconscious a major role. A good deal depends, maybe, on what is seen to be remedied or corrected by a return to the depths. All that may be meant is that religious experience must catch up with religious profession and march along with it. Some of Toynbee's statements on the subject may be taken to imply no more than this as, for example, when he speaks of a recovery of religious vitality when religions "send their roots down to the subconscious depths." No objection may arise here especially if the view is taken that "beliefs are the codified expressions of experience." [41] Nor again need we anticipate objection on the view that response to divine revelation means an encounter between God and man "in the depths of man's being." Allegiance to creeds is frequently claimed on the ground that creeds should be accepted as maps which point the way to experience. The individual believer may not at first find meaning for his life in all the creedal statements to which he adheres. But give him time, or give the creeds time, and the creeds will "come to life." Experience will then catch up with profession and there will be the religion of the heart, which may be all that is meant when a "return to the depths" is counseled. But a good deal more than this is often implied.

What is often suggested is a correction, not of experience, but of beliefs themselves or statements of belief by a return to the depths. And here, indeed, we may rightly expect demur.

Such a correction is implied when religion is associated with an intuitive grasp of truth as distinguished from what may be attained by the discursive intellect. Or again it seems to be implied when theological systems and propositions are regarded as subject to revision in the light of a "depth understanding" or "immediate apprehension" of biblical truth. More broadly, there is the sweeping implication that "from the depths" we have both the first word and the last word: the first, initiatory word, the primordial utterance of faith, taking the form of a spontaneous, "deeply rooted," pregnant, poetic symbol, and the last word, too, as this same symbolic utterance is regarded as restraining or forbidding the disposition of the intellect towards too narrow definition. The poetry of faith, coming from the depths, rebukes the audacity of the presumptuous intellect when it claims too much for its systems, creeds, and propositions.

To a good many today, all this may sound salutary. It spells release from dogmatic intolerance. But what if this release is bought at too great a price? What if this same utterance from the depths, said to be established beyond all reasonable question, is also seen to exclude all reasonable question? Have we here a flight from reason? Or a suggestion that reason should abdicate? "Whatsoever things are true," wrote St. Paul, "think on these things." [42] Is there any longer a point in such thinking or room for it? Having dismissed from our twentieth-century ken the traditional portrait of man "the rational animal," must we now replace it by a portrait of man completely subject to the darkly irrational? Or is man able to use his wits only to prove that they are useless—or next to useless? In this proposed recourse to "the depths" for direction and correction are we on the verge of what Dr. Martin calls "the crassest and most elementary of errors"? [43]

The fact that this last remark comes from Dr. Martin, who is one of those who propose recourse to "the depths" is evidence that the issues we have indicated have not been brushed aside by some, at least, of those who recommend such recourse. Pursuing our questions, then, we may want, in particular, more explicit statement regarding the source of the correction which is said to come from the depths. We may also want to know more about what might be called the "timing" of it.

As to the source of "depth" correction, we are back with the question whether the "depths" are to be narrowly identified with the levels below consciousness, as is certainly suggested by some of the language used. There is more than a hint of the "oracular communication" from the unconscious (which Dr. Martin rejects) when "flashes of intuition," "deep apprehensions," and the like are too sharply distinguished from intellectual inquiry, argument, and statement. The issue which arises here is put succinctly by Dr. Farmer when he relates some aspects of the Christian doctrine of the Holy Spirit to present interest in "the depths." He is sensitive to the view which a good many are urging today: that the divine encounter with man should not be conceived "too exclusively in terms of the day-light area of fully personal, selfconscious awareness." He therefore allows for the work of the Holy Spirit "in the deeps of personality." But he points to what may follow if this is taken to mean a "straight identification of the working of the Spirit with movements in, and uprushes from the unconscious." We then have man at the mercy of his unconscious, controlled from below, no longer a responsible moral, intelligent being; "the self will uncritically subject itself to, and become submerged in, the processes of the unconscious." [44]

There may be the reply, as we have seen, that no narrow identification of "the depths" with the unconscious is conceived: "depth encompasses more than depths, it is height as well"; depth pertains to the wholeness of personality. But how far does such a reply take us? We may still want to know whether the conscious intellect has any share in determining this wholeness of personality. A step towards a reply is taken, perhaps, when it is affirmed that regard for the wholeness of personality means that there can be no sharp separation be-

tween the unconscious and the conscious. The contrary is
often assumed. It is often suggested that while the conscious
may be profoundly affected by traffic from the depths, there
is no cross traffic: the unconscious is left to go its own dark
way unaffected by any conclusion attained by the conscious
exercise of reason. But this is pure assumption. As Farmer
points out, we may equally well assume a "reciprocal interplay
between the two levels." [45] "We cannot exclude the possibility that (intellectual) argument may . . . penetrate to
deeper levels of the mind than the discursive intellect to which
it primarily appeals." [46]

Some psychologists today (including, I gather, Dr. Progoff)
would say that even the conception of "interplay" is inadequate. They question the propriety of speaking of *the* unconscious, as if it were a something or a somewhere. It better
betokens the human condition, they say, to think of this or
that man or woman behaving sometimes consciously, sometimes
unconsciously or sometimes both consciously and unconsciously.[47]

"Depth religion" might then be taken to mean some full
engagement of the total man in the quest for reality rather
than any clear-cut separation of what may be known intuitively
from what may be known intellectually. One may refer to the
model of Buddhist meditation—or, for that matter, the Quaker
model—where there is as much regard, if not more, for what
may be gathered by resort to silence as for speech and discussion. Much that is written about the "depths" betokens an
interest in the ways and methods presented by the oriental
religions. There is the thought here perhaps that whether or
not we are interested in *what* Hindus or Buddhists believe we
have a good deal to learn from *how* they come to believe it.
There is the suggestion that they have retained a communication with "the world invisible" which Western man has lost.
Western man, it is said, is altogether too pragmatic. He does

too much of his religious thinking with the "top of his mind." He needs to do more of it on his knees and in the silence. The eternal escapes him because he has allowed himself to be wrapped in time. He is intoxicated by his own small history. Criticisms to this effect are accompanied by descriptions which present a return to the depths in terms of a fully integrated employment of all that a man has, all that he is, in the quest for that wholeness of life which religion is said to signify.

Whether the human condition is presented in these terms of unified behavior, sometimes conscious, sometimes not, or whether it is presented in terms of "interplay" between the conscious and the unconscious, the rationalist who is critical of all this reference to the depths may still put uneasy questions. He may still consider that what is here implied is that "reason" is not to be trusted and he may ask: what else is there to trust?

It is not within our present province to resolve the argument between the advocates of "depth" and their critics. It is sufficient to observe that such argument exists and then to consider what it betokens in regard to religious attitudes in the West, dogmatic or relativist. Does the fact of this argument or the apparent ground for it mean a revival of that rationalism which is cousin to dogmatism and hence a resurgence of dogmatism itself? As account is taken of some of the questions aroused by the confused reference to the depths, the impression may be left that the effect of the growing interest in "depth religion" is the reverse of what was suggested at the close of our last chapter. Instead of something which may be seen to promote a growing tendency in the West towards relativism we have here something, it may be thought, which is having the opposite effect: a revival of all that distrust of obscurantism, oriental or otherwise, to which, in the past, the dogmatist has made appeal.

But a further view of the situation may yield the conclusion that the present hesitation about depth religion and any dogmatism thereby encouraged constitute no more than a passing phase. It is a situation which may be compared with what is happening in regard to the ecumenical movement. The revival of sectarian standpoints does not mean that the ecumenical movement has come to a halt. Much the same may be said about the growing interest in depth religion. For the time being there may be disturbing questions but they are not necessarily unanswerable. Arbitrary and indiscriminate use of the word "depth" may be confusing and some of the inferences drawn from the discoveries made by the depth psychologists may be wide of the mark, as are some of the inferences drawn from modern studies of religious symbolism. And a good many statements about this "depth" have still to be reconciled one with another. But that there is something here to be taken into account in any estimate of the religious situation, whether we call it "depth" or not, or whether all that is called depth belongs together, is, I think, apparent.

It may be observed that some of the questions raised are raised by the very writers who advocate return to the depths. And there are others who, like Dr. Farmer, are persuaded, whatever hesitations they may have, that the role of the unconscious in determining the religious life cannot be denied. Not only this; they are also persuaded that the unconscious may be regarded as, so to speak, "on the side of religion."

It might also be claimed that, whatever the theologians and others have to say about it, a good many in the West today appear to be *practicing* "depth religion"; they are doing what Mr. Martin and other advocates of a return to the depths say they ought to be doing. Various groups of earnest people (many, but not all of them, church people) are breaking away from the pressures of workaday life for special days devoted to the religious exercises described by the word "retreat." Many of the exercises follow a monastic pattern, with long periods for conducted meditation, the observance of a rule of silence during the period of retreat—a day, two days, three days—and elaborate precautions against interruption and distraction. Within the last twenty or thirty years there has been a remarkable increase in the number of centers and retreat houses designed and set apart for this purpose. In pattern and intention this Western retreat movement might well be compared with the movement which has led to the establishment in Buddhist Burma of some two hundred meditation centers for the laity. The pious retreatant, it might be objected, is not necessarily a relativist. Nevertheless it is arguable that those who have found silence golden are more disposed than others to find language inadequate when it comes to stating the faith they live by, and hence more disposed to relativism.

Whatever reasons may be given for it, the movement towards relativism is certainly evident in the West today, even if it goes no further than a growing aversion to dogmatism. And the rejection of dogmatism need not mean the rejection of reason. A recent book by Dr. Peter Munz on the problem of religious knowledge is a case in point.[48] Threading together a good deal that has been said by others on the subject of religious symbolism, Dr. Munz begins by emphasizing the priority and pregnant character of what he calls the symbol-picture [49] and ends by affirming that this portends a new kind of Christian theology which will exhibit the flexibility of interpretation which relativism implies. At the same time, while he leaves scant room, if any, for dogmatism, he leaves full room for that exercise of rational judgment which most theologians are concerned to maintain. There are gaps in his argument and some questionable assumptions which expose him to criticism from the philosophers, but, from the standpoint of the historian of religion, which is our present standpoint, his treatment of the subject is certainly of interest.[50] It is a treatment which indicates a movement in the direction of relativism in the world of Western religious opinion today. His analysis is also relevant to our inquiry because he concludes by drawing a pattern of Christian confessional community comparable with the pattern we have observed in the Buddhist, Muslim, and Jewish traditions. He says in effect that such a pattern must follow, once the priority of the pregnant symbol is acknowledged.

Concerned to elucidate the role which religious symbols ought to play in our thinking, Dr. Munz concludes that there would be no religious thinking, no theology, without them; they constitute the very starting point of religious thought, the grist for our theological mills. This conclusion follows from a distinction drawn between a "positive picture" of the world, confined to things in time and space, as presented by modern science,[51] and a "symbol picture" related to the religious quest which is "a search for eternity." [52] Emphasizing the spontaneity of this "symbol picture," [53] Dr. Munz says, in effect, that it is a picture which "comes from the depths." [54] For the symbol picture, which is "the picture of the world meaningfully related to us," [55] is the consequence of "feeling states" or "modes of existence" so opaque, so tenuous, vague, and fluid that we should not be aware of them at all except for this symbolic expression. Otherwise, they would be, at best, "*unconscious* feeling states." [56] Dr. Munz gives the story of Abraham on the point of sacrificing his first-born, Isaac, as an example of a symbol thus produced. He speaks of Abraham's "acting under an impulse to symbolise a feeling state." [57]

What is especially significant for our present discussion is the *priority* assigned to symbolic utterance:

The symbol picture . . . composed of . . . rites and myths . . . must be prior to all religious thought. [Symbols] precede religious theories. . . .

The common view is that both ritual and myth are men's response to religious beliefs. We think of religious duties as flowing from the dogmatic truths we accept. We think that the primary

datum is the belief in a religious theory, and that all religious behavior, all ritual and all myth, are derived from belief. We think
that myths are illustrations of the belief; and that rites are actions
which we expect, on the assumption that the belief is true, to yield
certain results.

I propose to argue the reverse. . . .[58]

It is here especially that Dr. Munz is stating explicitly what
a good many other scholars have been implying for some time.
He draws the broad conclusion to which their various analyses
of the religious situation point, the conclusion which puts first
the poetic, imaginative announcement of religious faith, and
second, and only second, that which pertains to more deliberate
and avowedly rational interpretation, a conclusion to which
scholarship has been moving ever since, if not before, Marett,
in *The Threshold of Religion*, wrote that "savage religion is
something not so much thought out as danced out." [59]

But to follow some accounts of this direction is, as we have
seen, to come to the uneasy conclusion that it means goodbye
to reason so far as the determination of religious life and
thought is concerned. Dr. Munz, however, avoids such a conclusion. The imaginative symbol picture, as he sees it, is food
for thought, not a substitute for thought. It enables us to
"detect" eternity in much the same way as the positive picture
has led some scientists to detect causality—neither causality nor
eternity being open to direct observation.[60] Reason then steps
in to round off the account, as choice is made between different
concepts of eternity.[61]

It is a principal part of Dr. Munz's purpose to find ground
for argument, real argument of a kind which all reasonable
men may be persuaded to consider, whatever their particular
religious affiliation: argument which is neither fancy-free nor
inhibited by allegiance to dogmas which some may reject.[62]
He finds this ground in the symbol picture. The relation which
he conceives between this symbol picture and theological

reflection is perhaps best indicated when he remarks that the various parts of the symbol picture are not to be accepted uncritically: "one might as well say that a *chair* ought to be accepted uncritically." What we have in the symbol picture are "facts about which explanatory or interpretive statements are to be made." [63] "The symbol is the subject-matter of religious thought." [64]

On this basis he proposes a "new theology." The theologian of tomorrow, as he conceives him, will no longer suppose that he can start from "revealed propositions" constituting first principles. Instead, the theologian will arrive at his propositions only at third remove, that is, when he comes to the description and interpretation of his symbol picture.[65] At this stage there will indeed be argument, real argument, and full exercise of the theologian's reasoning capacity. But *not* dogmatism. For argument based on such reference to symbolism will be shy of anything in the nature of final or rigid definition, since, as Dr. Munz again and again emphasizes, symbols are anything but precise. They are so pregnant that they allow for and even encourage variety of interpretation. And here, as I see it, we have an urge towards relativism and at the same time a conscious avoidance of any despite to reason.

At least there is scant room here for dogmatism, as becomes even more evident when Dr. Munz proceeds to describe the kind of religious community which expresses and maintains the theological approach which he outlines. It is a community existing "primarily for the cultivation of the symbol picture." [66] He names this community "catholic." It is catholic in the sense that it seeks to embrace the whole "meaning and richness" of the symbol. Or at least, it seeks to embrace "large parts" of this meaning. For partial appreciation is all that is possible in the very nature of the case; the richness of the pregnant symbol forbids anything more. And to cry halt to interpretation is not only against the nature of the symbol picture for which the community exists; it is against the interests of the community; it means sapping the community of its "emotional vitality." (This comes very near to what Rabbi Stern and Professor Cantwell Smith have said about the enervating consequences of rigid ideologies.) Expectation of further interpretation means diversity of view within the community, with intention "to leave as much as possible open." [67]

At the same time there is neither indifference to what may be believed nor any roam-where-you-will relativism. For there is the restraint which comes from reference to the accepted set of symbols which a particular "catholic" community "cultivates." Hence there is unity, the unity of confessional allegiance.

I say confessional allegiance although that is not Dr. Munz's own name for it. The name derives from my own description. But the name is appropriate, for it will be observed how nearly our broad-confessional form of community corresponds to what Dr. Munz here conceives, starting from the nature of the symbol picture, deducing from this nature the consequent shape of community. But it may be of interest to observe how closely the two accounts fit: how at least one philosopher saying what logically ought to be agrees with at least one historian saying what has come to be. This symbol-adhering community which Dr. Munz has described as catholic is indeed very near the broad-confessional type of community which we have observed to be so actually and widely prevalent—in Buddhist Asia, in Islam, in Judaism, and now, to some extent at least, in Christianity. It does not destroy the comparison to acknowledge that the Buddhist pattern does not correspond to the Christian in every respect any more than the Islamic or Judaic patterns conform to the Christian pattern in every respect. Nor is ground for comparison removed by the recognition that there have been and are notable deviations from broad confessionalism in Christianity. There is seldom in actuality any pure form of broad confessionalism nor, for that matter, of any other type of community. Again the accounts correspond. Dr. Munz also expects and allows for deviation.

Encouraged, then, by the support of at least one philosopher, may we go further and say that within the Christian tradition there is increasing disposition towards the attitudes and conceptions of this broad confessionalism? This, perhaps, is doubtful. Neither what has come to be nor the thought of what ought to be provides firm ground for prophecy. As to Christian attitudes, it still remains difficult to say whether Christians are becoming more dogmatic or more disposed to relativism. What can be observed is the continuance of that tension within Christianity which we observed in earlier Christian history. For there is, as we have seen, both a growing interest in depth religion which makes for relativism and a dogmatism which is the more resurgent because of this disposition to relativism.

Nevertheless, the disposition towards relativism is sufficiently prevalent and persistent to lead us to consider some effects of it which have a bearing on Christian attitudes to other religions. To discern what attitudes may be expected is to take a further step towards knowing what Christians may contribute towards those prospects of world community which depend on religious toleration.

First, then, we may see in the recognition of depth religion that which promotes the view that behind or beneath all the manifest diversity in religion there is something in the very nature of the religious response which is fundamentally unifying. There is response to a reality, or an aspect of reality, however it may be described or interpreted, which binds man to man. Advocates of "experiments in depth" definitely regard such experiments as contributing towards the sense of religious unity.

Seen in its wider aspect, the relationship in depth becomes the "beloved community," the Universal Church. . . . There is no chasm between old and young, rich and poor, man and woman, or between those of different nationality, race, class *or creed.*[68]

Thus, when Mr. Martin proposes a search of the scriptures as a part of his experiment, he adds that they may be Christian, Buddhist, Indian, or Chinese scriptures. "What is essential is that they shall be 'searched,'" for "the man of faith draws the religions of the world together. Varied as these religions are, behind them all is the same fire."[69] Dr. Progoff sees the quest for the depth as one "reaching beyond differences [to a] common spiritual experience."[70] And even a writer like Dr. Kraemer, impatient of all attempts to exaggerate intellectual affinities or "similarities," allows for affinity in the depths.[71]

Second, we have here an approach which may be seen to offer better prospects of overcoming one of the main obstacles in the way of religious toleration: the obstacle presented by intellectual, creedal, and confessional differences. These remain. There is no attempt, as in some earlier approaches, to disguise or ignore them. There is rather an attempt to get under them, as it were, and possibly beyond them. This is attempted whether intellectual statements are seen to be different or not. Since such statements cannot communicate the full richness of the depth symbols, they are not treated as of first importance. A question may be raised as to whether they are treated with sufficient respect. Of first importance or not, it may be said, intellectual differences or agreements influence religious attitudes and behavior more effectively than is here recognized. Be this as it may, the "depth approach" seems to mean the view that it does not greatly matter whether religious believers say the same thing or not. The older search for consensus of religious opinion or intellectual agreement is largely abandoned. Intellectual statement is allowed only a secondary role. Thus Dr. Progoff observes that the "individual realization" which he has in view has been achieved by different believers within the frameworks of different religious systems.

He concludes that doctrines themselves are not of primary importance.[72] Devout Hindus and Buddhists might say amen to this. In a word, we have here a relativism, nurtured in the West itself, which is closely akin to oriental relativism. How far it will be accepted in the West remains to be seen. Meanwhile what is apparent is a growing body of Western opinion sufficiently vocal and influential to spell new communication between West and East. But whether this means one world, one religion, as a good many suppose, is as will be observed in the next chapter, open to question.

CHAPTER VIII

Religion and World Community

RELIGION has always been associated with human hopes and fears. In the twentieth century these hopes and fears are very largely concentrated on what may happen in a world which is so closely drawn together that the prospect before mankind is often presented in terms of one world or no world at all. Such language may be rhetorical. But it refers to facts which prompt a new hope of world community as well as facts which may shatter such a hope. In this connection the question arises of what may be expected of "the forces of religion," so evidently resurgent today, in regard to world community. We may put the question passionately, as many do, exclaiming against the scandal of religious division in a world alerted to the peril of division. Or we may put the question more soberly, as I have tried to do in these chapters, none the less concerned but constrained by our very concern to seek an answer in the light of such modest science as we may claim.

In this final chapter I propose to gather together some of the conclusions which may be drawn from our survey by relating them to a widely held opinion: the opinion that one world means, or should mean, one religion. Three ways in which this one world religion may come to be have been conceived. We shall reject two of them, qualify the third, and conclude, in the light of our survey, that while there is small prospect of one world religion there is yet fair prospect of effective religious contribution to world community.

In our survey we have been largely concerned with religious attitudes, using the term "attitude" broadly to include prevailing states of mind which influence religious behavior. We have considered what Van der Leeuw might have called the "middle distance" of the landscape set before us. Thus it has not been a case of drawing straight conclusions from what Hindus or Muslims, as the case may be, may profess to believe. Nor has it been a case of disregarding the importance and effects of creeds and systems. We have allowed for them in the background along with much else. But what lies immediately behind the foreground depicted, of religious behavior, is the middle ground of attitudes or states of mind: attitudes affected by other things than religious doctrines and interpretations.

A main consideration has been how such attitudes, varying from one religious tradition to another, may affect attitudes to other religions and other believers. For some kind of coming together on the part of Hindus, Buddhists, Jews, Muslims, Christians, and others is generally conceived when there is talk of marshaling religious interest in support of world community, and this coming together may be seen to depend very largely on how such believers regard each other to begin with.

How believers may regard each other obviously depends very largely on what they believe. Here there are manifest differences which cannot be ignored. But a good deal may be seen to depend also on how such differences are regarded, or what importance is attached to them. Such regard may be seen, in turn, to depend on how the believer estimates his own statements of belief. This is very evident in the case of Hinduism where, in consequence of the view that all religious statements are only relatively true, there is a liberal toleration of intellectual diversity both within and beyond the Hindu community. Such a standpoint sharply challenges the opposite, more exclusive and intolerant attitudes presented by Western

Christendom where a quest for certainty has been joined with the conviction that grounds for certainty are known. Naming the one attitude "relativist" and the other "dogmatic," we have been largely concerned with what these two attitudes may signify, how they may vary, how they may arise, in what contexts and with what consequences.

A second consideration has been the way in which basic attitudes may be expressed and maintained by different forms and conceptions of religious community. At one extreme, community is gathered around a fully elaborated and explicit statement of faith. "You believe what I believe" is here a primary and exclusive condition of belonging to such community. At the other extreme there is the Hindu pattern with no such condition and no possibility of it, because no one interpretation of faith is sufficiently accepted, dominant, or central to provide such a condition.

What has become more and more evident in the course of our survey, however, is that neither of these two extremes represents the pattern of religious community which is most prevalent in the world today. Coming in between the pattern exemplified by the confessional churches in the West, with emphasis on doctrinal agreement, and the opposite Hindu pattern, with its tolerance of doctrinal diversity, we observed, in the case of Buddhism, a pattern which reflects something of both, yet differs from both. Like the first, it presents us with community gathered around a particular, unifying confession of faith. The Buddha is significantly named *the* light of the world. Reference to the Buddha character is common to all Buddhists despite varieties of interpretation and practice. Yet the Buddhist reiterates the Hindu neti neti which forbids dogmatic intolerance. At the same time the Buddhist's relativist attitude is restrained by his commitment to what the Buddha stands for.

The further we pursued our inquiries the more extensive we

found this third pattern of community to be. For, strange as it might seem at first, there is much in Islam, and again in Judaism, which invites comparison with what is found in the Buddhist world. In particular we may note the view that neither Muslim nor Jew is committed to a "set of ideas." In keeping with this view there is the claim that Muslims are less dogmatic and more tolerant of diversity than may be at first apparent. Their confession of faith, as in the case of the Jews, is maintained by a discussion of right practice rather than by a discussion of right doctrine.

Turning finally to the Christian tradition, we were led to ask whether Christians, any more than Muslims or Jews, were committed to a set of ideas. Have we not here also forms and conceptions of community which belong to our third pattern rather than to that exemplified by the pattern of the confessional church with its emphasis on doctrinal agreement? Christianity has, it is true, exhibited the dogmatism which arouses the criticism of oriental observers. But today there is similar criticism *within* the Christian tradition itself, together with the growth of relativist attitudes, reflected in, and encouraged by, the interest in "depth religion." Even within the confessional churches themselves we have the issue which is presented when it is asked whether, in the very nature of the case, the confession of the Christian faith can or should be wedded to subscription to some precise propositional statement. In this connection we may observe the significance of Dr. Munz's discussion of religious symbolism. Whether we can accept all that he says on the subject or not, his discussion points to new directions of thought which have a manifest bearing on prospects of religious cooperation. For what is here signified is ground for loyalty to one's own faith which is at one and the same time ground for tolerant respect of others.

In grouping certain forms of Christian community with Jewish, Muslim, and Buddhist forms we are not, of course, saying that these four religions are comparable in other respects. In important respects—perhaps more important than those we have here considered—they are, indeed, very different, each from the other. For example, insofar as the Christian conception of community includes the conception of "new being" in Christ, it might be held that it is different from any other.

Our comparison has sole reference to a pattern of confessional community which deviates from that presented by the confessional church with its emphasis on subscription to a particular propositional statement of faith. Along these lines we conclude that we have to allow for at least two types of confessional community. Instead, therefore, of a twofold classification with the patterns exemplified by Christianity and Hinduism set in sharp contrast, we end with a threefold classification. In view of the fact that the confession of faith is narrowly associated with subscription to a specific statement, the first type might be called subscriptionist or narrowly confessional. The second type might be named confessional or broadly confessional or (if the theory of Dr. Munz is accepted) symbol-confessional. The third type might be termed nonconfessional, for whatever approach to confessionalism there may be in this (Hindu) pattern, it is not emphasized as in the other two types as a determinant of community. Alternatively, the three types might be named in terms of the attitudes expressed: dogmatic, quasi-relativist, and relativist.

This threefold classification does not mean, however, that when one attitude is dominant in a particular tradition other attitudes are entirely abandoned, absent, or avoided. In fact, the reverse is more frequently the case. The dogmatist makes entry everywhere. So does the relativist. All that is claimed is that, taking the religious world by and large, the three patterns named are evident and conceptually distinct, if not always so in fact, with here a disposition in one direction and there a disposition in another direction.

From the standpoint of our discussion of religion and world community, however, what is of greater consequence than any question of classification is the conclusion that, however it may be classified or named, the most prevalent type of religious community in the world today is that which expresses and maintains an outlook which may be described as *tolerantly* confessional. The conclusion follows that the great majority of religious people are neither quite so close-minded nor so open-minded as might be the case if choice lay between the dogmatism encouraged by the one extreme and the roam-where-you-will relativism encouraged by the opposite extreme. This conclusion qualifies expectations in regard to world religions and world community in at least four respects.

In the first place, there is the geographical extent of the "in between" type of community. It exists not only in the West, but also in Buddhist Asia and in the Muslim countries in between. It is, in fact, world-wide. As such, it qualifies (to claim the least) any sharp distinction which may be drawn between East and West. It reduces, if it does not remove, one of the obstacles which may otherwise seem to be in the way of religious people coming together.

Second, there is the inter-faith aspect. The attitude thus indicated is seen to be shared by men of different faiths. Indeed, if it is allowed that even in Hinduism there are traces of confessional allegiance, then we have here something which is present in all five of the great religions which we have reviewed. In this respect, if in no other, adherents of different traditions may understand each other. As it is said that the saints of all religions recognize each other, so it may now be said that the men of pledged loyalty who are to be found in all the great religions may respect each other. Their own fealty should make them the more disposed to expect and appreciate such fealty in others. "I don't agree with Brown. But at least I know where he stands and I trust him the more for it." That is a frequent attitude, not only in politics but in religion.

Third, where an aversion to dogmatic exclusiveness and rigidity is found in company with a definite allegiance to particular confessional symbols there is better prospect of the forces of religion cooperating *effectively* in the interests of world community. For something more is required than a mere coming together on the part of religious people. There is, as we have observed, a twofold demand or requirement. There is the more vocal demand for religious toleration: in a day when world community seems so urgent, it is regarded by many as iniquitous that religions professing to promote harmony should add to the obstacles in the way by perpetuating religious divisions. "Let them bury their differences and come together! Let them set an example." So runs the familiar, one might say the popular, protest.

But there is a second demand. It may not be so widespread or so vocal, but it is perhaps more percipient. This is the demand for the strength of motivation which religion is seen to provide. For world community, it is said, there must be religious resolution. Such a view may arise from a sober analysis of the modern secular state. There is one thing which the state itself cannot produce, and that is the motivation essential for its social life. Some may not go quite so far: they may simply say that religious motivation cannot be ignored and that it is desirable, if not essential, to enlist it in the cause of world community. But here the difficulty arises that the strength of religious motivation which is sought is seen to be associated with the very differences which the first demand, the demand for religious toleration, often ignores. Depth of religious conviction more frequently keeps company with particular beliefs and practices which promote religious differences than with beliefs and practices which may be held in common with other believers.

All this being the case, it may be concluded that we cannot have it both ways; we cannot have tolerant religious attitudes promoting a coming together in the interests of world community and, at the same time, effective religious conviction; the two demands are incompatible.

In the symbol-confessional form of community, however, it appears that we may indeed have it both ways. We have the particularity which is seen to be dynamic, and all the more dynamic because in this case it is not wedded to a mere set of ideas. On the other hand, just because the particular reference goes beyond mere ideas to that which transcends them (the pregnant symbol, if you will), the presumptuous intolerance which forbids any coming together is excluded.[1] Thus for the Christian to know the love of God is indeed to confess the Christ, but it is also to respond to the love which is "broader than the measures of man's mind."[2]

Fourth, the fact that the most prevalent form and conception of community is a confessional form which refers to particular loyalties has a very definite bearing on the *kind* of coming together in the name of religion which may be anticipated in the cause of world community. Such particular loyalties may not stand in the way of religious cooperation. But they may very well stand in the way of any prospect of one all-inclusive world religion which is what a good many people regard as a first condition of world community.

This last point brings us to our discussion of the several ways in which it is conceived that such a unity may be achieved, a discussion which has to do with what may be regarded as probable rather than with what may be regarded as desirable. It has been suggested that "the whole trend of global life today is in the direction of a single world-religion."[3] Three ways of achieving this one religion have been conceived. Our question now is whether it is "practical politics" to think in these terms at all. Do the aspects of global *religious* life which we have observed in the course of our survey point to the probability of one world religion? And what of the three ways proposed? To what extent do they correspond to the facts of the situation as we have observed them? These are the questions in mind.

The three ways which we shall consider are (a) the way of displacement, (b) the way of synthesis, and (c) the way which Professor Hocking names "reconception."

According to the theory of displacement, one of the present great religions will become *the* world religion and all the rest will give place to it. Only so, it is argued, can there be any effective religious contribution to world peace. In favor of this conclusion, it may be held that this is, in fact, how the great majority of religious people see the situation. The prevalence of confessional forms and conceptions, emphasizing a particular allegiance, suggests as much. A good many Christians and a good many Muslims might certainly be expected to take this view. It is reflected in their continued missionary enterprise and it is considered by some to be confirmed by the success of that enterprise. Most Hindus and Buddhists would disclaim any thought of the kind, but it might be argued that they nevertheless propose a Hindu or Buddhist view which would at least displace any religious teaching which stands in the way of its acceptance. "Let all mankind accept our standpoint. Only so can there be peace."

The displacement theory can therefore be said to be in keeping with religious views and confessions. Whether it is also in keeping with the actualities of the situation is another question, a question posed strongly today by the resurgence of all the great religions. None of them shows any readiness to be displaced, and least of all, perhaps, the small but persistent Jewish minority. There is also the fact that religious views are frequently adjusted to these same realities. It is held by some Christians, indeed, that it is Christian duty as well as Christian policy to make such an adjustment. Christian thought and action in regard to the international situation, or any other, it is held, must be based on realistic appraisal; this means adjustment to religious pluralism, the pattern of many religions which

is likely to continue for many years to come.⁴ In the Muslim
world there has been similar acceptance of the situation. As
for Hindus and Buddhists, while they may claim to have a
universal message, the claim is most frequently accompanied
by the view that this same message means no displacement of
other faiths. As for the Jews, there are indeed some Jews today
who say that Jews are, and should be more, missionary minded.⁵
But this is not typical of Jewish opinion in general.

All in all, the prospect of any one religion displacing all
others, at least in the immediate tomorrow, is small. Contemporary developments are, in fact, in the opposite direction, for
not only do the great rivals remain firmly on the stage, exhibiting new energy and purpose, but they have been joined by a
spate of "new religions" to add to the complexity of the pat-
tern.⁶

The alternative conception of synthesis is the very opposite
of the idea that the various religions should give place to one,
for what is here conceived is that all religions should remain
on the stage, compare their lines, select from them, and produce one new religion, reflecting the best insights of all. Instead of any one religion being granted a final say, all will thus
contribute to the common say. Synthesis goes beyond syncretism with which it is often confused. Syncretism means a sink-
ing of differences. They are ignored and dismissed as relatively
unimportant. On such a showing different believers might profess adherence to one world religion while going very much
their own ways.

This, it might be said, is just what a good many people are
in fact doing today, especially in America. Provided a man is
"a Christian of some kind" or even no more than "religious,"
it is widely held that it does not matter much how he expresses
or practices his faith.

A step beyond syncretism is taken when it is suggested that
religious believers can agree to differ on many things because

the articles of faith on which they are already in agreement present "the real truth of the matter." Lord Herbert of Cherbury, in the seventeenth century, named five such tenets (or *notitiae communes*): that there is a Divine Being, that this Being is to be worshiped, that this worship means moral obedience, that this obedience will be rewarded while disobedience will be punished, that such reward and punishment follows, not only here and now, but in a future life.[7] Similar essays in reduction were in vogue at the beginning of the present century. But the tide of modern scholarship in the field of the history of religions has turned against any such reduction, and the majority of religious leaders are more than willing to swim with this tide. In the new emphasis of what is particular and special in each tradition, they find very acceptable grist for confessional mills. Much the same stand as that taken by a resurgent denominational dogmatism against ecumenical proposals for unity is here taken against syncretism by much the same people for much the same reason: syncretism and synthesis are seen as twin offspring of relativism.

One of the reasons for a certain suspicion of comparative studies in religion in some church circles is that syncretism is seen as the possible fruit of them, while the fruit of syncretism is seen to be, not one world religion, but a plurality of eccentric cults. Whatever the reasons and arguments may be, there is the fact that churchly zeal and pastoral concern with a good deal of support from the academies results in such strong opposition to the way of syncretism that it can scarcely be regarded as a "live option."

As for the arguments, most of them refer confusedly both to syncretism and synthesis. In reply, the distinction between the two may be urged, with the comment that what is here soberly proposed as a way towards one world religion is not an indiscriminate syncretism but the scrutiny, selection, winnowing, and judgment in the direction of new system which synthesis properly implies. Granted this point, however, it may still be objected, if the emphasis is on "practical politics," that it is not in this way that living religion comes to be. A group of learned pundits around a conference table may indeed devise some new creed acceptable to all of them. But will the common people hear them gladly?

It may nevertheless be claimed that religious history exhibits more in the direction of synthesis than is sometimes recognized. All the great religions have from time to time opened doors to beliefs and practices from other traditions. But here it may be replied that the name for what has happened in this way is not synthesis but "adaptation." In their new contexts the beliefs and practices thus imported have been differently conceived. Such "adaptation" may have stimulated what Professor Hocking calls "reconception." Which brings us to the third way proposed for the realization of one world religion.

What is proposed on the theory of reconception lies in between the view that one of the present great religions will displace all others and the view that all religions will be displaced by one new synthetic religion. There is to be neither the abandonment of traditional affirmations nor their continuance in their present form. Instead, in each of the great living religions there will be reconception in the light of a new occasion and a new challenge. The challenge includes the impact of other faiths. The new occasion includes the emergence of world community, for, as Professor Hocking sees it, world community is already in the making; modern man is "standing on the threshold of a new thing, civilization in the singular." [8] It is the *religious* community which "spins the web of a potential world society." [9] He points to what is happening in the modern secular state which may be seen to "depend for its vitality upon a motivation which it cannot by itself command." [10]

At the same time, man today is also standing on the threshold of a new day in the realm of religion, and this new day will come with the reconception which will result from the response to new challenge. It is a reconception which will take place in each tradition, with Christianity (Professor Hocking hopes) leading the way. It is important here to note what Professor Hocking means by what we might call the *process* of reconception (considered first apart from what may come of it). Something more is involved than the admission of new insights, and something more, too, than a reinterpretation of this or that traditional belief. There will be a reconception of each traditional faith considered as a whole. In each religion there will be the question: what do we really stand for? This will mean the rediscovery of what is essential. But it will also mean discerning, as not before, the full implications of the faith. There is here no suggestion that believers should come together at the expense of their convictions or by diluting their convictions. On the contrary, what Professor Hocking conceives is a greater depth of conviction as believers are challenged to distinguish between what is really vital (or essential) and what is not. The reconception contemplated takes place *within* each religion; it involves no abandonment of any religion, no stepping out of it, but its enlargement and development. What is suggested is that a religion, as a result of such reconception, will be not *less* itself but *more* itself; it will, so to speak, come to its true self as it is more responsive to that reality with which it has to do. It might indeed be said that Professor Hocking is so much at pains to demonstrate this line of development in the case of Christianity that other believers have some ground for the suspicion that what he really has in mind as the coming world religion is the Christian religion so amended and enlarged that others will be disposed to accept it.[11] As to what may come of such reconception, much depends on what may be seen to be really essential in each particular faith. It is here that questions begin to arise. Pro-

fessor Hocking believes that what will thus be found is a
"Way," to be found in all the great religions. Even at present
one "Only Way" may be discerned in the several ways "present
in all. . . . The several universal religions *are already fused
together, so to speak, at the top*," as may be concluded from
the fact that the mystics of all ways recognize each other.[12]
As there is growth towards what Professor Hocking calls
"maturity" in religion, growth stimulated by increasing interest in other faiths and consequent reconception, it may be
expected that what is now recognized or apprehended only
by the few will come to be realized by the many. In a world
which is becoming "one world" similar responses to similar
challenges and pressures in a mental environment affecting all
should make "toward simplicity and a care for stark veracity
beneath the indispensable poetry; and this can only make for
convergence of the several great religions on certain common
essentials." [13]

It is part of the strength of the theory of reconception that
it builds firmly on an analysis of the existing situation and an
assessment of probabilities. Syncretism or synthesis, as we have
seen, may be excluded as improbable. And there is at least
no immediate prospect of one of the present religions displacing all others. But reconception has been taking place all along
the line of the history of the great religions. All at one time or
another and in greater or lesser degree have borrowed from
other traditions, incorporating elements which have come
alongside, reconceiving them and making them their own.
Hinduism has been notably hospitable in this respect. Mahayana
Buddhism may be presented in terms of a renaissant Buddhism
quickened by a lively dialogue with a renaissant Hinduism
and also influenced, perhaps, by contact with Nestorian Christianity.[14] As for Christianity, no historian can disregard the
influence not only of Greek thought but of Asian thought.
Whether this "reconception" has been quite so much to the

good as Professor Hocking and others think, whether it has meant not only an enlargement of view and practice but a growth in the understanding of what is really essential in each tradition or a progressive response to a progressive revelation, all this, indeed, is subject for debate. But that reconception of this kind has in fact occurred in the past cannot be denied.

Nor can it be denied that there is new impetus towards such reconception today, new challenge, new invitation, as the great religions of the world are brought face to face with one another as never before. It is precisely an invitation to such reconception, an invitation expressly extended by some Hindu writers, to which Christians in India are exposed: as one Hindu writer puts it, they are not invited to cease to adore the Christ whom Hindus may also adore but only to abandon some of their interpretations and reinterpret the Christ in the light of some Hindu teachings which may be accepted as compatible with their essential loyalty to Christ.[15] Some Buddhists in commending their own teaching to the Christian world say much the same thing.[16] As for the Christian invitation, Dr. A. C. Bouquet, who begins his survey of other faiths by emphasizing his Christian allegiance, concludes by saying:

Just as Benjamin Whichcote, John Smith and others like them called themselves Christian Platonists at Cambridge in the seventeenth century, without one whit abating their Christian allegiance, so one conceives that at some time in the future it might not be improper for believers to exist who called themselves Christian Buddhists, or Christian Confucians, or even perhaps Christian Vedantists or Christian Moslems.[17]

Whether this can be taken to mean that Dr. Bouquet would also allow for "Buddhist Christians and Hindu Christians" is perhaps another question. But other writers would certainly do so. "Reconception," in short, is today very much in vogue. It must indeed be added that it is also, in some quarters—many quarters, perhaps—firmly opposed. Nevertheless, it is sufficiently in evidence to warrant the conclusion that a theory of reconception is in accord with what is actually happening.

The case for reconception is perhaps even stronger if we include not only a reconsideration of religious ideas but a reconsideration of religious attitudes, including attitudes towards differences in belief. Professor Hocking himself hints at this when he says that his one world religion will not mean the obliteration of all differences.

It is when we come to the conclusions which Professor Hocking draws from this process of reconception that questions arise. His view that the nearer each religion comes to what is really essential in its own particular tradition the nearer all will come to constituting one world religion depends very largely on his assumption of an underlying unity. Some of his phrases suggest no more than a revival of the older view which has been so much under fire: that differences in religious belief can be ignored; that what the great religions have in common is all that matters; that it is only where they agree that we come to essentials: all else is minor. But Professor Hocking's full statement points to something more than this. The agreement he has in mind is not on the surface. It is not yet fully realized or perceived. This will only come with "reconception." As we take into account some of his references to the poetic character of religious utterance we might conclude that what he has in view should be named "reapprehension" rather than "reconception."

Even so it remains questionable whether such reapprehension will mean a single world religion. Our own survey leads us to place greater emphasis on what is particular, special, and diversifying than Professor Hocking appears to do. If we are right in concluding that the more prevalent type of religious community is through and through confessional, this seems to point away from any prospect of one world religion rather than towards it.

We may indeed be strengthened in this conclusion by what Professor Hocking himself has to say about the future. For he here draws a distinction between what may be seen for the more immediate tomorrow and what may be glimpsed beyond it. "The *immediate* vista for the coming civilization is that of a continued coexistence of at least a few of the great faiths," he says.[18] He adds that it cannot be a merely passive coexistence. What is indicated is something more than a tolerant "believe and let believe" with each religion going its own separate way. The meeting of religions which is now taking place, the growing interest in the beliefs and practices of other traditions beside one's own, the exposure to new, stimulating challenges, the welcoming of this exposure, the new lines of communication, the consequent reconception, all this offers an immediate vista of a coming together, in the interests of world community, even if it does not mean *one* world religion.

This opinion, however, introduces a new question. *Is anything more required in the interests of world community than such a continued coexistence of the great faiths?*—coexistence on this pattern of reciprocal and welcomed challenge? And we may be led to inquire further whether such coexistence may not be preferable to any one world religion.

Before considering these questions, however, we may conclude that so far as the immediate vista is concerned (and it is this, after all, that more directly interests us, since the prospect of world community is already upon us) none of the three ways seems to promise the prospect of one world religion. All of them ignore aspects of the situation which count against such a possibility. The way of displacement ignores the persistence of rival religions and the revived respect for what is particular. The way of synthesis, to say the least, ignores the extent and strength of conservative opposition to anything of this kind. As for the way of reconception, there is the objection that it is a way for religious aristocrats, capable of the profundity which Professor Hocking assumes and himself exemplifies. Even if it is granted that our thinking in this connection must be with reference to religious leaders rather than with reference to the rank and file of believers, the objection remains. The wish is father to the thought when all religious leaders are credited with the disposition to return to the depths which Professor Hocking implies. Achievement of the goal of one world, one religion, within the immediate future by any of these three ways—displacement, synthesis, or reconception—must, then, be dismissed as improbable. This being the case, it is arguable that some of the very efforts being made today to achieve religious cooperation may, if they are narrowly associated with the conception of one universal religion, constitute an obstacle in the way of such cooperation. Those who make such a conception of religious unity the prior condition for world unity may defeat their own purpose. Fascinated by the thought of one world, one religion, they may ignore other more probable and conceivably even better ways of realizing their goals. They may fail to consider the possibility that, even if the immediate vista offers no more than the continued coexistence of the great faiths of mankind, such a coexistence may suffice to promote world community.

There may, of course, be reasons other than those prompted by regard for world community for aiming at the goal of one universal religion. Confessional loyalty may inspire such an aim. A good many Jews, Christians, and Muslims, for example, might say that in very loyalty to God this and nothing less— one universally accepted faith, all men everywhere offering the same worship to the One God—must be their ultimate aim.

But even when such an ultimate aim is conceived, a due regard for present possibilities may mean the consideration of a more proximate goal conceivably more attainable. Human plans and purposes, it may be argued, have to be adjusted to the realities of human situations. A case in point is Father Courtney Murray's recent argument [19] in regard to the religious situation in North America, an argument which is the more relevant to our discussion because Father Murray himself suggests that his conclusion may have a wider application: what may be done about the situation in America may, he suggests, be done about the situation in the world at large.

It can be taken for granted that Father Murray would prefer to have all Americans Catholic, all within the one household of faith. But the Americans he has to consider, the Americans of the United States, present a pattern of religious pluralism, or the coexistence of the different religious communities, with every indication that this pattern is likely to persist for the foreseeable future. His problem, as a good Catholic who is also a good citizen, is the problem of what may be done within the pattern of this persistent pluralism in the interests of North American community. He lays it down, to begin with, that on Catholic principles the pattern may be accepted even if it is not all that Catholics may desire and includes what they might disapprove. Quoting a statement by Pope Pius XII, Father Murray conceives that Catholics may "tolerate at times that which it is impossible to correct." [20] They may do so as the best, most realistic way of promoting the common good.

Father Murray himself is the more disposed to tolerate the North American pattern because he believes that good has indeed come out of it and further good may be achieved in and by its persistence. It has at least provided religious motivation, and like Professor Hocking, whom he quotes, Father Murray sees the state in need of such a motivation, a motivation which the state itself has no power to evoke.[21]

Furthermore, the North American experiment with this pattern, which comprises four major groups, Protestant, Catholic, Jewish, and secular, has proved that religious pluralism is compatible with political unity and stability. Whether the experiment will endure and progress depends, as Father Murray sees it, on two main conditions. It depends first on these four groups "conspiring" together in fruitful argument under the present "articles of peace" (not "articles of faith") to promote "American society—civil, just, free, peaceful, one." [22] It depends second on a return to the doctrine of Natural Law in which the Fathers of the Church believed as did the Fathers of the Republic.[23] In the past this belief provided the moral consensus requisite for the health of the American society.

Father Murray's immediate concern is local; his thought is focused on the problem presented to American Catholics by religious pluralism in America. But in an interesting aside, as it were, he cites a papal opinion which contemplates the continuance of religious pluralism on the international scene. It is here that he makes the suggestion that what has been found relatively good for America may be found relatively good for the world at large: "America offers . . . a pattern in miniature." [24] If this is so, then the larger world pattern will be a pattern similar to that conceived by Professor Hocking, a pattern of coexistent religions engaged in "enlarged dialogue."

Perhaps the time has come when we should endeavor to dissolve the structure of war that underlies the pluralistic society, and erect the more civilized structure of the dialogue. It would be no less sharply pluralistic; but . . . amid the pluralism a unity would be discernible—the unity of an orderly conversation.[25]

There is, however, this difference in Father Murray's view: the unity he contemplates is not an underlying unity but a unity "amid" the pluralism. The reason for this way of putting it appears if we take it, as I think Father Murray means us to take it, that the orderly conversation he has in mind will be based on a general respect for the doctrine of Natural Law which he advocates. As he interprets it the doctrine posits a "dynamic order of reason in man," in man *as man*, whether he be Protestant, Catholic, Jew, or Secularist, or Christian or

Hindu. As against Professor Hocking's underlying unity he emphasizes what may be called a coincident unity, or a ground of unity *alongside* grounds of difference.

What here concerns us, however, is not Father Murray's emphasis on Natural Law doctrine. This, indeed, is an important and relevant subject, one which is receiving new and increasing attention on the part of Protestants. The present stress on Natural Law may very well be one of the things most conducive to world order and peace. But what is more relevant to our present discussion is Father Murray's acceptance of religious pluralism, the possibilities in regard to political community which he sees in this pattern, and the suggestion that what has worked in America will work in the world at large. Such a conclusion may not be convincing to those unfamiliar with the American scene, nor, perhaps, to those who are familiar with no other. But to those who have come upon this scene after experience of very different conditions elsewhere as, for instance, in England or Burma, where one dominant faith has shaped the whole cultural outlook, the American scene, in all its challenging complexity, may indeed appear relevant. For here we have a diversity, a religious pluralism, which is even more extensive than Father Murray's reduction of it to four major groups might suggest. As to a sense of unity, national unity, that again may be more evident to those not nurtured here. We may shrug shoulders at a rather vociferous, one might even say a fanatical, zeal for "the American Way" but it is a significant zeal and a mounting zeal. On the part of a significant number it is a religious zeal.

One thing to be observed is that religious pluralism is not merely tolerated in America; it is valued and approved. By many people it is held to be not only compatible with good citizenship but conducive to it. Along with this valuation goes a similar and associated valuation of the so-called separation of church and state. I say *so-called* separation because this is

sometimes taken to mean the view that the state must go its
separate way, or rather that statesmen and public servants must
go their separate way, while citizens in general, in regard to
their civic or political conduct, are unaffected by any religious
motivation. Actually, this is far from being the case, in either
theory or practice, though some today might desire it.

Now, if we ask why religious pluralism and the "separation"
of church and state are valued and approved we may, if we
probe deeply enough, get an answer somewhat as follows: The
American Way of Life means freedom and, not least, freedom
in religion. Freedom in religion is essential to genuine religion
or sincere religious conviction. Coercion in religion is inimical
to such conviction. State control of religion, or state interference with religion, would amount to coercion, as would any
demand for uniformity in religious belief and practice.

I am not claiming that all Americans would answer in this
wise. But many of them, perhaps the majority, would certainly
do so, and among these many would go further and add: It is
not only in the interest of religion or of believers that there
should be this freedom; it is in the interest of the state, for
where there is effective religious motivation we can expect
good citizenship; and we can expect this only where there is
religious freedom.

Such a view is probably a majority view because a great part
of the religious life in America is after the pattern of what in
Britain is termed the "free church." The term "free church"
may be used to distinguish nonconformist or dissident forms
of religious community from "established" forms, approved,
supported and, in some cases, prescribed by the state. But the
term "free church" also points to a certain outlook or attitude
which is one of the things we have to allow for in any appraisal
of the religious situation in general. Throughout the religious
world there are those who emphasize freedom in religion as
one of the freedoms to be most prized by man. As they see it,

if there is to be what John Oman, one of the exponents of this view, called "honest religion," there must be freedom for the prophets, freedom of inquiry, freedom of interpretation. Religious faith, they would insist, cannot be dragooned. Some are even doubtful whether it can, or should, be tutored. Any kind of "indoctrination," to their mind, defeats its purpose if that purpose is the awakening of faith. Carried to extremes, such a view may not only accept diversity to the point of division as incidental to religious freedom, but as essential to it. Far from regarding religious division as a necessary evil, the price to be paid for freedom, they may value it as positively good since it promotes the criticism and challenge on which progress in intelligent faith is held to depend: competition makes for the health of religion. To the charge that it may also make for the breaking of religious community, they might reply that the only religious community they value is the community of *convinced* believers, the community of free men, free to believe. Such a view puts a premium on religious pluralism.

Over against such opinion, there is the view which places prior emphasis on ordered community, the maintenance of such community, the avoidance of schism and heresy, the need for tutelage and qualified instruction in the interests of informed faith, respect for preserved traditions and for established authority and appointed guides. In support of such opinion it may be claimed that where there is community of this kind there is, in fact, no absence of deep, genuine, and intelligent conviction, but rather the contrary. On such a view religious pluralism may be tolerated as the price to be paid for human infirmity. There is, in this case, anything but zeal for it. But it is accepted and the best is made of it.

In the religious world generally there is a tension between these two attitudes. What is familiar enough on the Christian scene is to be found elsewhere: for example, Zen Buddhism, with its respect for the Zen "master," its master-pupil relationship, its ordered monastic life, might be contrasted, in this respect, to Theravada Buddhism, with its emphasis on individual responsibility and its freer pattern of monastic life.

Now my point here is that the tension between these two views in the religious world corresponds to the tension between the two demands made of religion in the interests of world community: the demand for what religion can contribute in the way of effective motivation and the demand that the religions of the world should come together. And it is also relevant to observe that the same believers who reflect tension of interests in the religious world are themselves, as citizens, the spokesmen of these demands. John Churchman is also John Citizen and may be, too, John Statesman. In this respect the term, "forces of religion," which we have used to indicate the strength of a distinctive religious motivation, may be misleading, as may be our Western pattern of church organizations with their appointed spokesmen, a pattern only faintly reflected elsewhere. If a "force of religion" is conceived as a force with its own separate membership set against a "force of the world," differently recruited, with its own separate camp, we may fail to allow for the John Churchman-John Citizen who has a foot (or perhaps we should say a heart or a head) very much in both camps. As such he is perhaps more sensitive than a good many religious leaders to the demand which impinges upon all religions of a world which is on the threshold of civilization in the singular. He is both the spokesman of this demand and also, in part, its answer. This answer will reflect the value he sets on his freedom as John Churchman as well as any demand he may make as John Citizen that "religions should come together."

Those who conceive diversity to be in the interest of true religion may also be concerned to maintain a similar diversity in any coming pattern of world civilization. That this is indeed so is apparent from the fact that the resurgence of the great religions today is closely associated with the resolution to maintain local and distinctive cultures. The consequent diversity of culture may be conceived as in the best interests of world civilization. Granted that the peace of the world is a primary consideration, it is not the only consideration. What may also be in view is a welfare which goes beyond and depends upon something more than the maintenance or realization of world peace, a welfare which is seen to be partly dependent on variety. Belief in a coming world civilization does not necessarily signify belief in a drab uniformity. "Just because civilization is becoming one and world-wide, the localisms which preserve the world from monotony, and conserve those precious semi-solitudes in which alone thought and fine art and every creative impulse flourish, must be the more vigorously protected and prized." [26] I am not here concerned to examine the grounds for this argument. It is enough for our present purpose to observe that it exists. Further evidence of it may be found in the number of very deliberate efforts, from Quebec to South India, which are being made to revive and preserve local cultures. It follows from this view that diversity in religion, far from being regarded as opposed to the prospect of world civilization, may be regarded as contributing towards it. Whether it also follows that religious pluralism is similarly contributory depends on whether religious pluralism is identified with acrimonious division. Here the issue appears to depend on the spirit animating religious rivalry. There may, it is maintained, be rivalry or competition in the realm of religion, as in other realms, which, far from being detrimental to community, contributes to its enrichment and advance. In other words, much depends upon the attitudes taken towards religious differences, and towards those who affirm them.

All told, our survey points to the conclusion that such differences will persist. They are of a kind which makes the prospect of One World-One Religion a very remote prospect, to say the least. But the prospect of one world is not remote. Nor, it may be hoped, is the prospect of religious contribution towards such world community remote, despite continued differences. While a pattern of coexistence may or may not be all that is desirable, it seems to be all that can be expected.

Such a conclusion may be sobering. It falls short of the great expectations of those who saw in the comparative study of religions a study which would lead to one religion for one world. It may perhaps be held that in arriving at this conclusion I have forsaken the "depths" to which reference was made in my last chapter; the realities of the situation which have been considered in these final pages have been very much on the surface. Furthermore, it may be said that my whole account has been in terms of human response to that transcendent Reality with which religion has to do, rather than in the terms which might have been used if some attempt had been made to discuss the nature of such Reality. In other words, while creedal statements and systems of belief have not been ignored, they have remained in the background, not looming nearly so large in my presentation as they do in some other statements. The depths, it is true, have been explored far enough to make possible some account of what Dr. Munz calls the symbol picture. And it may be noted that it has not been a question of taking Dr. Munz's word for it, and his word alone, that there *is* such a symbol picture to be taken into account. In this regard Dr. Munz simply threads together what a good many others are saying, although they may not use his terms or accept all of his conclusions. They are sufficiently in agreement with him to confirm his statement, which we have made our own, that the pregnant character of the religious symbol accounts very largely for the diversity of interpretation, as also for the unity in diversity, which we have observed. But having said this much, we have not proceeded to discuss the different symbols any more than we have discussed, except incidentally, the various beliefs and systems of religious thought. In brief, there has been little or no attempt in these pages to explain religious differences in terms of *what* men and women believe. The emphasis has rather been on the way they may hold these different beliefs or on their attitudes in regard to what they believe and what others believe, dogmatic or otherwise.

Perhaps I have gone too far in this direction, for it can scarcely be denied that *what* men and women believe may profoundly affect their attitudes and their conceptions of community. Would Muslim history have been the same if Muslims had exchanged submission to the Divine Will for belief in Amita Buddha? Most historians and all Muslim historians would say no. If I have not emphasized this aspect of the situation sufficiently it has been partly because I have sought to stress other aspects which are not so generally recognized and partly because I can safely assume that other writers will see to it that the intellectual expressions of religious faith are not neglected. The disposition to present the religions of the world in terms of their intellectual statements and classify them accordingly is persistent. There is still too little regard for what I have earlier called the middle distance between religious ideas and religious conduct with room or time in between for the growth of attitudes to whatever may be believed, attitudes indeed partly affected by the nature of the beliefs which may be held but also influenced by other conditions. There is also still too little regard for the prior poetry of religion and the imaginative expressions of faith. And there is still need to take into fuller account all the many and various ways in which men and women may indicate the faith by which they live. One might say, perhaps, that religious faith is shy. It is not usually worn on the sleeve, and there is need to look for much more than is immediately apparent.

It might also be held that I should have tried to round off

my account by some attempt at interpretation even if this interpretation had been in terms, as it must necessarily have been, of my own Christian commitment. I say that it must necessarily have been in such terms in my own case for no one can claim impartiality when it comes to interpretation. Indeed, it is generally accepted today that, even if one's purpose is limited to description, there is no such thing as complete impartiality. Each observer can only see the scene with eyes which are very much his own; he himself contributes to what he sees and seeks to describe; and such equipment as he may bring to the task is equipment gathered in the main from his own tradition. Nevertheless there is point, as was said earlier, in *aiming* at some approach to impartiality. There is also point in maintaining the boundary between description and interpretation.[27] It is by observing these limits that the historian of religion can best make his contribution, even if it means an account which remains, as it were, without a roof. His study may not, in itself, "change the aspect of the world" [28] as earlier writers said it would. But it may perhaps help to clear the ground in a way which contributes towards world community if it is a study which is pursued "reverently, discreetly, advisedly, soberly; considering the causes for which it may be ordained." And for myself, I would complete the quotation and add: if it is pursued "in the fear of God."

Notes

1. Cf. Reinhold Niebuhr, *The Structure of Nations and Empires*, pp. 29, 33. "The United Nations is not, and cannot be, a constitutional world order." Dr. Niebuhr argues that such a possibility depends on "a measure of integration, which the world community lacks, and presumably will lack for decades to come." Cf. *ibid.*, p. 33: "All communities of mankind . . . are dependent on the one hand upon some internal force of cohesion and on the other hand upon the unifying power of a central authority."

After reading Dr. Niebuhr's book, I changed my original phrase, "prospects of world order," to "prospects of world community." As I now see it, an effective sense of world community may be a prior condition of world order. Whether Dr. Niebuhr himself would draw this conclusion from his analysis, however, I am not sure. He speaks of "the reciprocal relation between dominion and community" (p. 158). Associating dominion with order, we should perhaps allow a similar reciprocal relationship between world order and world community. As a more effective sense of community would promote world order, so also, it might be said, the establishment of world order would promote the sense of community. Nevertheless, there is ground for the view that the sense of community comes first. A similar priority was indicated by the Archbishop of Canterbury after his recent interview with Pope John when he remarked that the spirit of unity is precedent to any church union.

Apart from this issue, there is the consideration that the contribution of "the forces of religion" is better seen as primarily a contribution to the sense of community. This, again, however, may be qualified by the view that what religious teachers may relevantly contribute is a doctrine of natural law—if agreement could be reached on this subject—which might promote a system of international law conducive to world order and hence to world community. Dr. Niebuhr dismisses "the idea of unifying the world community, through world law" as "so illusory that it has intrigued only the most abstract idealists" (p. 262). A generally accepted doctrine of natural law, however, may be distinguished from a positive code of world law. Granted the possibility of such an agreed-upon doctrine, a system of world law might conceivably follow. While world law in itself or by itself would not unify the world, it would contribute to such unity.

The sequence which I conceive is: world community; world order (including, perhaps, world law); world peace. I see the contribution of religion at the first stage, world community, and hence speak of world religions and world community rather than of world religions and world peace.

I distinguish between world society and world community. World community, as I see it, means a more conscious emphasis of what is shared in common than does world society.

2. In the seventeenth century Lord Herbert of Cherbury in *De Veritate* (1624) maintained that all religions presented five principal tenets (or *notitiae communes*). Other writers, such as Christophe Meiners, may be cited as anticipating Max Müller's standpoint. But Joachim Wach (*The Comparative Study of Religions*, ed. Joseph M. Kitagawa, p. 3) was right, I think, in saying "that there can be little doubt that the *modern* comparative study of religions began with Max Müller, about a century ago." (Italics mine.)

Max Müller himself certainly believed that what he was proposing was a new study, so new that he doubted at first whether "the time had yet come for attempting to trace, after the model of the Science of Language, the definite outlines of the Science of Religion" (*Chips from a German Workshop* [October, 1867], p. xi).

Three years later, however, when he lectured on the subject at the Royal Institution, February 19, 1870, he was convinced that "a comparative study of religions should no longer be neglected or delayed. . . . A science of religion, based on a comparison of all, or, at all events, of the most important religions of mankind, is now only a question of time." (*The Science of Religion* [1872], First Lecture, pp. 10, 21.) In France Max Müller's contemporary, Émile Burnouf, expressed much the same view. (*La Science des Religions*, Preface [1870], refers to the previous publication of his chapters in the *Revue des Deux Mondes*.) See below, ch. II.

3. Max Müller, *Chips from a German Workshop, Vol. I, Essays on the Science of Religions* (2d ed., 1868), p. x: "The history of

religion . . . shows us throughout a succession of new combinations of the same radical elements." See also *The Science of Religion*, Fourth Lecture, p. 127: "A comparative study of the religions of the world will teach us . . . to be charitable both abroad and at home."

4. Paul David Devanandan, "Renascent Religions and Religion," in *The Ecumenical Era in Church and Society: a Symposium in Honor of John A. Mackay*, ed. Edward J. Jurji, pp. 149–50.

5. *Ibid.*, p. 166.

6. Few have affirmed the dynamic and cohesive power expected from religion more explicitly than the Muslim scholar, Ibn-Khaldun, in the fourteenth century: "To conquer, one must rely on the allegiance of a group animated with one corporate spirit and end. Such a union of hearts and wills can operate only through divine power and religious support." (Quoted by Will Durant, *The Reformation* [New York, Simon and Schuster, 1957], p. 693.)

7. William Ernest Hocking, *The Coming World Civilization*, p. 47. Dr. Hocking considers that twentieth-century experiments "expressly rejecting religion as a factor in political life" have shown that "with the clean excision of religion something *politically* essential has been lost." (*Ibid.*, pp. 5 ff.)

8. Edwin O. Reischauer and John K. Fairbank, *East Asia: The Great Tradition*, Vol. I of A History of East Asian Civilization (Houghton Mifflin Company, Boston), pp. 509–10.

9. Justin Martyr, *Apology* 1.14.

10. Stephen Neill, *Christian Faith and Other Faiths: the Christian Dialogue with Other Religions*, p. 18.

11. Cf. *The History of Religions*, ed. Mircea Eliade and Joseph M. Kitagawa, Preface by Jerald C. Brauer, p. 8: "Basic similarities are not stressed at the expense of peculiarities or differences. . . . The enterprise now seeks the basically religious by moving through individual historical experiences rather than by ignoring or moving around the peculiar or particular experiences." Cf. also Hendrik Kraemer, *Religion and the Christian Faith*, p. 73, for a further statement of the position he maintained in his earlier work, *The Christian Message in a Non-Christian World* (1938), ch. IV. Kraemer emphasizes that since "the different religions . . . are worlds in themselves, with their own centres, axes and structure," apparently similar statements, when related to their own, different contexts, may be seen as disguised dissimilarities. He

quotes W. E. Hocking's first postulate in regard to religious pluralism: "Religion *must* be particular" (*Living Religions and a World
Faith*) and John Dewey's "There is no such thing as religion in
the singular. There is only a multitude of religions" (*A Common
Faith*). He also cites Schleiermacher: "Religion ist wirklich nur in
Religionen" (Religion is real only in religions). As do others,
Kraemer finds in such acknowledgments of religious pluralism and
particularity, not withstanding qualifications made by their authors,
support for the conclusion that "Biblical thinking . . . is a type
wholly *sui generis,* distant from religious thinking in the usual
understanding of the word" (*Religion and the Christian Faith,*
p. 449).

Kraemer's position is of interest from the standpoint of our
present discussion not only because it reflects trends in modern
scholarship which emphasize religious differences but also because
his own work has had a very large influence on contemporary
Protestant attitudes to other religions: it has encouraged writers
who maintain what he himself calls "the particularly intractable
character of Christianity" (*ibid.,* p. 77).

12. Gershom G. Scholem, *Major Trends in Jewish Mysticism*
(rev. ed., New York, 1941), p. 6.

13. Max Müller, *Chips from a German Workshop,* I, xv.

14. Confessional church: The term may be taken in the first
place to refer to churches adhering to "confessions" of faith composed following the Reformation by Protestants, such as the Confession of Augsburg (1530) written by Melancthon and approved
by Martin Luther, and the Westminster Confession drawn up by
the Assembly of Divines (1643) and adopted by the (Presbyterian)
Church of Scotland (1689) as the statement of belief to which all
ministers of the church had to subscribe. Such "confessions" ex-
panded statements contained in creeds such as the Nicene creed
(approved at Chalcedon in 451 as the creed formulated at the
Council of Nicea in 325). The confessions also added articles
defining Protestant positions on such subjects as Justification by
Faith.

More broadly, any church or religious community adhering to
some particular symbol or symbols of faith may be described as
"confessional," i.e., confessing or maintaining a particular allegiance.

By "subscription" I mean adherence, without reservation or
qualification, to the literal meaning of some statement of belief as

distinguished from the broad "assent" to the Thirty-nine Articles which is all that is expected today in the Anglican Church.

On this view there may be "confession" without "subscription."

15. Cf. R. C. Zaehner, *The Concise Encyclopaedia of Living Faiths*, p. 16. He refers to Christians and their Marxian critics as "people . . . who take ideas as such with desperate seriousness. This has always been characteristic of the West."

16. Cf. Arnold Toynbee, *An Historian's Approach to Religion*, p. 127; cf. John Dillenberger, *Protestant Thought and Natural Science.*

17. Cf. D. S. Sarma, "The Nature and History of Hinduism" in *The Religion of the Hindus*, ed. Kenneth W. Morgan, p. 6: "There is . . . a great complexity of worship and belief within the Hindu fold. The greatest difficulty about the study of Hinduism, therefore, is that one is apt to miss the wood for the trees."

18. "Western dogmatic attitudes." I say "Western" rather than "Christian" here deliberately, with Marxian as well as Christian attitudes in mind. When a reference intended to include Judaism and Islam is made to "Western religions," however, it may be considered more accurate to speak of *Christian* dogmatic attitudes. Either description is open to question. See discussion in ch. VI.

19. T. R. V. Murti, *The Central Philosophy of Buddhism*, p. 340.

20. The "biblical" relativism here in mind is that indicated by Dr. Kraemer when he distinguishes between the biblical presentation and theological systems, saying that "the Bible in its direct, intense realism presents no theology." Biblical realism as the criterion of all theological thinking, he adds, "exposes all problems to an unexpected and revealing light" in a way which indicates that "the mystery of God's Essence" is "concealed" and "inaccessible." (*The Christian Message in a Non-Christian World*, pp. 65–73.) Is it the distinction here indicated between the biblical presentation and theological system which leads Dr. Kraemer to distinguish between the life weakening and the "life liberating" effects of "the drift towards relativity"? ("The Encounter between East and West in the civilization of our time," in *The Ecumenical Era in Church and Society*, ed. Edward J. Jurji, p. 99.)

Not all Christian writers would go as far as Kraemer in this respect but a good many today regard the biblical presentation as in general, essentially "poetic," as they also emphasize the limits of "theological" exposition. An example, taken at random, is Gustaf

Aulen's criticism of "the pretence of theology to speak of God in adequate terms" in "The Nature of the Affirmations of Faith" (*The Faith of the Christian Church*, trans. Eric H. Wahlstrom and G. Everett Arden; the Muhlenberg Press, 1948).

21. W. T. Stace, *Mysticism and Philosophy*, p. 6.

22. John Courtney Murray, S.J., *We Hold These Truths: Catholic Reflections on the American Proposition*, pp. 228, 229: "The Soviet State . . . is an *imperium*, a mode of rule, guided in its internal and external policy by a comprehensive systematic doctrine . . . an empire controlled by a dogma . . . the Soviet leaders act on the dogma."

Father Murray regards the view that communism is a legacy of Western history, a "Christian heresy," as a "pernicious fallacy popularized by Professor Toynbee" (*ibid.*, p. 226). My own statement may be taken to imply this view, and I think, indeed, that there is more to be said for it than Father Murray allows, as will be seen below in ch. VI. But in the present chapter I simply quote Father Murray's comment as a significant criticism of dogmatic rigidity, while at the same time I recognize that his criticism is specifically directed against dogmatic rigidity which supports claims to "the juridical omnipotence of government." He compares Marxian Communism with Jacobinism.

23. It may be held that even in Hinduism there is an element of confessional allegiance. In support of this claim, reference may be made to the *bhakti* tradition of devotion to Krishna. Or there may be reference to the opinion that all instructed Hindus regard their homage to a "chosen deity" as, in the final analysis, homage to Absolute Brahman. Even so it may be questioned whether this latter opinion is shared by all Hindus. And it is certainly not expected that all Hindus will be devotees of Krishna. Hinduism presents, it may be, confessional allegiances, in the plural, but nothing quite comparable with the central reference to the Buddha character presented by Buddhism.

24. In a parable ascribed to Shan-tao, one of the great teachers in the Pure Land sect, the Buddhist who trusts in Amita's vow to save all sentient beings is compared with a traveler pursued by wild beasts and bandits on his way to visit a friend in the far west. He comes to a great river. On the right side of the river great, scorching flames are roaring; on the left side great waves are raging, and there is only a thin white road. How dare he go for-

ward? But how dare he halt or turn back, with the wild beasts and bandits there behind him? He is full of alarm. Then he hears a voice from across the river: "Come! I will protect thee." He also hears another voice, from behind him: "Go! You will surely be saved." The voice crying "Come" is Amita's voice; the voice crying "Go" is the voice of Gautama (Sakyamuni, the teacher).

25. Franz Pfeiffer, *Meister Eckhart* (trans. C. de B. Evans); *Sermons and Collations* (London, John M. Watkins, 1924), p. 246.

26. G. K. A. Bell, ed., *Documents on Christian Unity: a Selection from the First and Second Series 1920-30* (Oxford University Press, 1955), VIII, 53, "The Reply of the Bishops of the Church of Sweden to the Conference of Bishops in the Anglican Communion, April 1922": "A concession of this right [to take part in Holy Communion] . . . presupposes . . . an essential agreement, proved by the confessional documents of the communion in question" (p. 74); "For us . . . decisive importance must be attached . . . to the question whether and how far the two communities agree in these ideas as to the content of that message of salvation . . . committed to both of them" (pp. 76, 77); "We do not feel justified in pretermitting to draw your attention to the very great importance that our Church attaches to the thorough instruction of the first communicants in the fundamentals of the Christian faith" (p. 82). The Swedish bishops had probably been informed that such instruction in the Anglican Church was sometimes not as "thorough" as might be expected from the Lutheran standpoint. They added circumspectly (p. 82), "Both churches may have something to learn from each other . . . with regard to the preparation for Confirmation" (the rite preceding admission to Holy Communion).

27. Peter Munz, *Problems of Religious Knowledge*, pp. 176 ff. See also the discussion of Munz in ch. VI, below.

28. E.g., Christopher Dawson, *The Historic Reality of Western Culture*, p. 71.

29. R. C. Zaehner, *The Concise Encyclopaedia of Living Faiths*, in his introduction, a recent and very forcible presentation of the East-West classification, in which Western religions are named "prophetic" and Eastern religions are named "mystical" or "immanentist," claims (p. 18) that his statement shows "how immense is the gulf between the two types of religion."

30. Even when there is due acknowledgment of such differences, as there is in Professor Zaehner's appraisal, the question may still

arise whether *sufficient* account is taken of them in any statement which ends by dividing the religious world into two with a wide gulf separating East from West. What constitutes "sufficient account" is no doubt in the long run a matter of individual judgment. But such judgment may depend on what is observed and what is selected as significant and relevant. Professor Zaehner emphasizes different attitudes towards religious beliefs, dogmatic and otherwise, as I do myself, besides differences in belief. But he attributes the different attitudes more narrowly to the nature of the beliefs which are maintained than I do in my own account, although I agree that we should not dismiss or minimize the effects of such intellectual differences as some are disposed to do.

As between Professor Zaehner's description and my own, I place greater emphasis on different forms and conceptions of community, I also place greater emphasis on differences *within* the Hindu pattern, and I distinguish more sharply between Hindu and Buddhist attitudes as well as among Jewish, Muslim, and Christian attitudes. Hence perhaps our different conclusions as to the "gulf" between East and West.

I am the more sensitive to this issue because I was myself at first disposed to see the situation in terms of a major dialogue between East and West. In other words, I was disposed to "follow the crowd," for there appears to be a general disposition on the part of serious students today to present the situation in such terms. As I proceeded in my inquiry, however, I became more and more convinced that a sharp line drawn between East and West may be misleading. The evidence points, especially in the changing world of today, as I see it, not to any one dialogue but to several dialogues, with the parties to such dialogues recruited, in each case or in several cases, on either side, from East and West.

Any attempt to see the situation as a whole runs the risk of oversimplification of what is, all told, a most complex pattern, and I am well aware that my own description is not immune from criticism in this respect.

CHAPTER II. *The "Science" of Religions*

1. Joachim Wach, *The Comparative Study of Religions*, ed. Joseph M. Kitagawa, p. 3 (italics mine).
2. See, for instance, Le Comte Goblet d'Alviella, *Introduction à*

l'histoire génerale des religions (Brussels, 1887), p. 2: "Je n'ai pas seulement à vous faire connaître l'histoire des religions, mais à vous la faire aimer."

The concluding paragraph of this lecture dealt with the subject of tolerance—tolerance which the study of the history of religions would promote. And what country had greater need of this lesson, asked Professor Goblet, than his own country, Belgium?

The lecture was an inaugural lecture, following Goblet's appointment as the first professor of the History of Religions at the University of Brussels. He observed at the time that the only other universities where this subject was taught were the Dutch universities, and the universities of Paris, Tubingen, and Geneva. In a footnote he added that the subject was also now being taught (1886) at Berlin, Marburg, Copenhagen, and Rome.

3. Friedrich Heiler, "The History of Religions as a Way to Unity of Religions," *Proceedings of the IXth International Congress for the History of Religions* (Tokyo, 1960), p. 21.

4. *Ibid.*, p. 22; cf. Max Müller, *Chips from a German Workshop*, "Opening Address Delivered by the President of the Aryan Section at the International Congress of Orientalists, 1874," IV, 371.

5. Max Müller, *Chips from a German Workshop*, "Essays on the Science of Religion," I, xix–xx.

6. Max Müller, *Lectures on the Science of Religion*, p. 106.

7. *Ibid.*, pp. 123, 127.

8. Emile Burnouf, *La Science des Religions*, 3d ed. (Paris, 1876), pp. 36, 37.

9. Max Müller, *Lectures on the Science of Religion*, p. 21.

10. Max Müller distinguished between what he termed theoretic theology concerned with the explanation of religion and comparative theology (another name for the new science of religion) concerned with the historical forms of religion, "dealing simply with the facts such as we find them" (*Lectures on the Science of Religion*, pp. 14, 47). Cf. Wach, *Comparative Study of Religions*, p. 3: "The term 'science of religion' (*Religionswissenschaft*) was used to denote the emancipation of the new discipline from the philosophy of religion and especially from theology." Cf. É. Burnouf, *La Science des Religions*, pp. 3 ff. "Toute science, celle des religions plus que les autres, veut un esprit libre et dégagé d'idées préconçues. . . . La science des religions n'a rien de commun avec la polémique religieuse."

11. Cf. Goblet d'Alviella, *Introduction à l'histoire génerale des religions*, p. 14: "À cet égard, j'ajouterais même volontiers que, pour faire l'histoire des religions, il faudrait se placer au point de vue positiviste, si cette phrase ne signifiait une adhésion formelle au systeme philosophique d'Auguste Comte, qui, lui aussi, a abordé l'hierographie avec une théorie préconçue." The whole of Goblet's inaugural lecture, in fact, dealt with various types of prejudgment inimical to the study of the history of religions. It is one of the most systematic and searching statements on the subject. Beginning with religious prejudices, he proceeded to discuss the prejudgments of "the adversaries of religious ideas," philosophical prejudgments, and even the prejudgments of specialists in the field of history of religions whose knowledge of a particular religion might be the cause of error (he cited Émile Burnouf's use of Hindu mythology as a case in point). He added a reference to the prejudgments of specialists engaged in a particular science, especially linguists and anthropologists. In brief, what he asked for, besides absence of prejudice, was a fully comprehensive view of the field.

12. Cf. Burnouf, *La Science des Religions*, p. 3.

13. Cf. Wach, *Comparative Study of Religions*, p. 14.

14. Max Müller, *Lectures on the Science of Religion*, p. 6.

15. *Ibid.*, p. 47.

16. *Ibid.*, p. 7.

17. *Ibid.*, p. 14.

18. Burnouf, *La Science des Religions*, pp. 3, 8, 13.

19. Max Müller, *Lectures on the Science of Religion*, p. 41; *Chips from a German Workshop*, I, 10.

20. Max Müller, *Chips from a German Workshop*, IV, 336.

21. *Ibid.*, p. 346.

22. Cf. A. C. Bouquet, *The Christian Faith and Non-Christian Religions*, p. 411: "Professor H. H. Farmer . . . is perhaps justifiably suspicious of a purely detached, objective study of religions of the world by any Christian. . . . Nevertheless, I do not think the discipline of making an objective study . . . is one which ought to be discarded. I consider it a good discipline for the mind of the would-be theologian. . . . After that he can go back to the non-Christian faiths and appraise them in the light of his Christian experience. But if he begins this appraisal before he has heard what they have to say for themselves he will run the danger of being unjust."

Dr. Bouquet has put his theory into practice. Having written a popular introduction to the subject (*Comparative Religion*), which he describes as "a plain tale, inspired by scientific method . . . an impartial treatise," he has more recently explored much the same ground from an avowedly Christian, interpretative standpoint in the book cited above.

Cf. Hendrik Kraemer, *World Cultures and World Religions: the Coming Dialogue*, p. 366. Dr. Kraemer's approach to the subject differs in several respects from that of Dr. Bouquet. But in this recently published book he draws a similar line between description and theological evaluation. Stating that he proposes to write a separate volume dealing with "the terms under which the dialogue between Christianity and the great living religions should take place," he adds that the structure of such a volume should be in four sections. In these four sections he proposes (*a*) an outline of the history and growth of each religion and culture, (*b*) "a phenomenological survey of the creative mobiles in such a religious/cultural whole," (*c*) a theological evaluation of each religion, and (*d*) a definition of the central points at issue between Christianity and the described religion.

In Kraemer's earlier treatment of the subject (*Religion and the Christian Faith*, pp. 35 ff.) the line between description and evaluation is not so clearly drawn, for it is here part of his purpose to show that the theologian is no more handicapped by initial prejudice than other observers. With reference to modern discussions, he concludes that the idea of scientific objectivity has to be replaced by an idea of impartiality which allows for the fact that "in the selecting and marshalling of facts we are partly led by our 'subjectivity.' " It is still more difficult to maintain the notion of objectivity, free from any elements of valuation and interpretation, when the notion of comprehension (*verstehen*) is introduced. He is therefore critical of Joachim Wach's "clear distinction" between the Science of Religion, concerned with description and comprehension, and the Philosophy of Religion, concerned with evaluation from "the standpoint of definite presuppositions." At the same time Kraemer allows that, while "to be unprejudiced is an unattainable goal," there is some point in aiming at this goal. He also leaves some ground for distinguishing between a scientific approach in which the aim is description and comprehension and an approach in which the aim of evaluation from a theological standpoint is clearly avowed and maintained.

It is arguable that something in the nature of a theological starting point is admissible in both approaches, though the aims may be different. Granted that no observer can claim to be free from prejudice, and that each cannot avoid approaching the subject from his own standpoint, it might then be claimed that such a standpoint is also a vantage point. The Christian or the Hindu, as the case may be, may observe what is not observed by others just because he is a Christian or a Hindu. We may then have complementary observations from different standpoints. On this showing, what is unavoidable is also desirable provided that the observers are on guard against their own prejudices and all of them are trying to observe the rules of the game.

23. Gerardus van der Leeuw, *Religion in Essence and Manifestation: a Study in Phenomenology*, tr. J. E. Turner, chs. 107–10.

24. *Ibid.*, p. 676.

25. *Ibid.*, pp. 684–88.

26. *Ibid.*, p. 677.

27. *Ibid.*, p. 673.

28. *Ibid.*, p. 674, footnote: "What I myself understand by the phenomenology of Religion is called by Hackmann 'The General Science of Religion.'"

29. Max Müller, *Chips from a German Workshop*, I, 50 ff. In a review of *Christ and Other Masters: an Historical Inquiry into Some of the Chief Parallelisms and Contrasts between Christianity and the Religious Systems of the Ancient World*, by Charles Hardwick (Cambridge, 1858), Max Müller criticizes Hardwick for his lack of "human, real, and hearty interest in his subject" (p. 53); his failure to express "any sympathy with the Pagan world" (p. 54). Max Müller suggests that such a sympathy is an antidote to the rationalistic pre-conceptions or prejudices which he attributes to Hardwick.

30. Erwin R. Goodenough, "Religionswissenschaft," in *A.C.L.S. Newsletter*, I (June, 1959, no. 6 [American Council of Learned Societies, New York]), 15: "It is possible that . . . science seems a threat to old formulations of religion precisely because it is a new formulation of man's relation to the tremendum, actually a totally new form of religion itself. . . . The emergence of this type of thinking . . . signifies the emergence of a new religion . . . the new religion of science. . . . Much of this spirit must become ours."

31. F. B. Jevons, *Evolution* (London, Methuen, 1900), p. 2: "The face of civilization has come to be illumined by hope."

32. Quoted in "The Somatic Mutation Hypothesis of Cancer," *British Medical Journal*, July 4, 1959, p. 18. Dr. Peyton Rous adds significantly that cancer research scientists should "be goaded by their ignorance,"—significantly, for the goad of ignorance also pertains to the spirit of science.

33. Cf. R. H. L. Slater, *God of the Living* (New York, Scribners, 1939), p. 43: "There is a third characteristic of the scientific spirit which is most important of all—the scientist's disciplined readiness to revise, and even abandon, cherished explanations when faced by hostile data or more adequate explanations. The word 'disciplined' is used advisedly. It is no easier for the 'natural man' in the science laboratory than it is for the 'natural man' anywhere else to forsake opinions to which he has grown accustomed. It is only by a loyal acceptance of the stern ethic of research, and by years of scientific training that he attains sufficient strength of mind to do so. Knowing the difficulty, he is suspicious of any influence which may weaken his intellectual integrity. Herein lies one of the possible grounds of misunderstanding and conflict between the scientific student and the religious teacher. 'The Church fears criticism, we invite it,' said one of my friends, a biologist. By his training the scientist is led to distrust dogmas carefully preserved through the ages. All that the Church teaches of loyalty and respect for its heritage may well seem to the zealous scientist a perilous influence likely to hinder the spirit of inquiry."

34. *An agreed-upon principle of verification?* A Muslim correspondent pointed out this issue when he wrote to me recently about his discussions with Christian theologians. The discussions were interesting, he said, but they left him asking: was there no possibility of some agreed-upon criterion? My correspondent may know the story of St. Francis at the court of the Sultan Melek-el-Kamel. (It has recently been told again by Fr. Giulio Basetti-Sani, O.F.M., *Mohammed et Saint François* [Ottawa, Commissariat de Terre-Sainte, 1959], pp. 163 ff.) Discussion being futile because there was no appeal to reason, while appeal to scripture raised the question, which scripture? Bible or Qu'rān?, St. Francis suggested ordeal by fire.

With our modern emphasis on religious experience it might seem that we are in a better situation. Ninian Smart, in *A Dialogue of Religions*, pp. 11–13, raises the same issue and goes some way to meet it. He allows that there may nowadays be some generally accepted reference to religious experience, but he adds that experience needs to be interpreted and this involves reflection and argument. But what are the rules of argument, whether for combat or agreement?

Another British author, John Wilson, writing both as a philosopher and as a teacher concerned to meet the questions put by young people today (*Language and Christian Belief* [London, Macmillan, 1958]), raises the issue with specific reference to the challenge of modern skepticism.

There is certainly a concern manifested by religious teachers of all faiths in regard to this universal challenge. Some may agree with Mr. Wilson that there is need for agreed-upon verification, though a good many are disposed to meet the challenge by preferring their own faith to others, persuaded that they are in better case than others. Nevertheless, this common pastoral concern may be one of the things making for religious cooperation, if not for argument. It might therefore be thought that I should have dealt with this issue in these pages by something more than passing reference. I was at first disposed to do so. But one argument against so doing was the fact that to deal with this issue at all adequately would mean another book, or, maybe, several books (such as Dr. Smart's).

35. Max Müller, *Chips from a German Workshop*, IV, 345.

36. Heiler, "The History of Religions as a Way to Unity of Religions," p. 9.

37. *Ibid.*, pp. 13 ff.

38. *Ibid.*, p. 9.

39. Max Müller, *Chips from a German Workshop*, I, xiv–xv.

40. Max Müller, *The Science of Religion*, p. 123.

41. R. R. Marett, *Threshold of Religion* (London, Methuen, 1909), p. xxxi.

42. R. J. Zwi Werblowsky, "Judaism, or the Religion of Israel," in *The Concise Encyclopaedia of Living Faiths*, ed. R. C. Zaehner, p. 24. Italics mine.

43. Cf. Émile Durkheim, *The Elementary Forms of the Religious Life*, tr. Joseph Ward Swain (Glencoe, The Free Press, 1947), pp. 3 ff.

44. Max Weber, *The Protestant Ethic and the Spirit of Capitalism*, tr. Talcott Parsons (London, George Allen and Unwin, 1930).

45. Hendrik Kraemer, *The Christian Message in a Non-Christian World*, p. 136.

46. Rudolf Otto, *Christianity and the Indian Religion of Grace.*

47. Wilfred Cantwell Smith, "Comparative Religion: Whither—and Why?" in *The History of Religions,* ed. Eliade and Kitagawa, p. 34: "The first and altogether fundamental step has been the gradual recognition of what was always true in principle, but was not always grasped: that the study of a religion is the study of persons. Of all branches of human inquiry, hardly any deals with an area so personal as this."

48. Ugo Bianchi, "Après Marbourg (Petit discours sur la méthode)," *Numen,* VIII (Fasc. 1, January, 1961) 65.

49. Cf. Wilfred Cantwell Smith, "Comparative Religion: Whither —and Why?", p. 51. Professor Smith refers only to dialogue between "representatives of diverse traditions." He notes experiments in this direction at McGill, Chicago, and Harvard universities. Since my association with the Center for the Study of World Religions at Harvard, where we have in residence scholars representative of different religions from various parts of the world, with consequent opportunity for the kind of dialogue "at the level of scholarship" which Professor Smith advocates, I have become persuaded that there is need to allow for the fact that scholars representing different religions may also, so to speak, represent different disciplines. Each may approach the subject in the terms of the related discipline, philology or sociology, as the case may be, which has most engaged his interest and influenced his studies. Thus we may have dialogue, for example, between a Hindu whose approach to the subject has been philological, and a Jew whose approach has been sociological.

Such dialogue may be the more rewarding because of the pooling of insights resulting from these different approaches. At the same time, the dialogue may be more difficult because of the added confusion of tongues, for scholars trained in one particular discipline are often insufficiently acquainted with the terms and distinctions pertinent to others. A good many specialists tend to go their own separate ways. To some extent this separation is overcome by conferences attended by scholars representative of different disciplines, such as the conferences arranged by the Society for the Scientific Study of Religions. But just as need is seen for something more than the occasional inter-faith conferences if there is to be sustained dialogue "at the level of scholarship" which Professor Smith proposes, so need may be seen for something more than occasional exchanges between scholars representative of different

disciplines. In our Harvard program we supplement the study of
the diverse religious traditions by a study of issues raised and insights promoted in such fields as the sociology of religion, the
psychology of religion, and the discussion of religious language
which is prompted by philosophical analysis. The specialists invited
to lead our seminars from time to time include not only those who
are specialists in some particular tradition but those who are specialists in some particular discipline. Hence the suggestion in my text,
as compared with Professor Smith's suggestion, refers to research
by scholars "representative not only of different Faiths but of
different disciplines."

CHAPTER III. *The Challenge of Hindu Relativism*

1. D. S. Sarma, "The Nature and History of Hinduism," in *The
Religion of the Hindus*, ed. Kenneth W. Morgan, p. 6.
2. Rig-Veda I.164: "Who saw that First when it was born? . . .
They call him Indra, Mitra, Varuna, Agni, and even the fleet-
winged celestial bird Garuda. The One Reality, the learned speak
of in many ways."
3. Paul David Devanandan, "Renascent Religions and Religion,"
in *The Ecumenical Era in Church and Society*, ed. Edward J. Jurji,
p. 166: "The Hindu population in our towns and villages is undoubtedly self-conscious, and to that extent strangely alive as
Hindus. This self-awareness is of recent origin. It became in-
creasingly noticeable as the nationalist struggle reached the point
when victory seemed to be around the corner, and the Moslem
minority raised the issue of . . . the partition of India on a religious
basis."
4. Rabindranath Tagore, *Gora* (New York, Macmillan, 1946),
p. 294: "I am a Hindu! A Hindu belongs to no party. The Hindus
are a nation. . . . Just as the ocean is not the same as its waves, so
Hindus are not the same as sects." Cf. *ibid.*, p. 104: "My mind is
in ecstasy with the deep and grand unity which I have discovered
running through all of India's various manifestations. . . . I am
one with all India."
5. Devanandan, "Renascent Religions and Religion," in *The Ecumenical Era*, ed. Jurji, p. 149.
6. This Hindu world outlook and missionary purpose is relatively new. While Hindu scriptures might speak of man in general,

Hindu teachers in the past seldom looked beyond India. Even as recently as twenty years ago, Professor Hocking and others could say that Hinduism was not a universal religion, conscious of a world-mission as were Buddhism, Christianity, and Islam. (W. E. Hocking, *Living Religions and a World Faith*, pp. 59 ff.) Today, however, Professor Ashby observes that "Hinduism is rapidly changing from its traditional provincialism, and claiming for itself a universal validity." (Philip H. Ashby, *The Conflict of Religions*, p. 169; cf. p. 180.)

In a recent symposium by Hindu writers intended for Western readers two of the contributors conclude their statement by making this very claim. "It is not too much to hope," says Dr. Sarma, "that the religion of the Hindus will soon be recognized by all as one of the great spiritualizing forces of the world, a force leading humanity to its goal." (Sarma, "The Nature and History of Hinduism," in *The Religion of the Hindus*, ed. Morgan, p. 47.) "Hinduism," says Dr. Chatterjee, "may with some justification be called a universal religion." (Satis Chandra Chatterjee, "Hindu Religious Thought," *ibid.*, p. 261.)

7. Sri Aurobindo, *Essays on the Gita: First Series* (2d ed., Calcutta, 1926), pp. 2–10.

8. The description of relativism (in general) as "life-weakening and life-liberating" is given in Kraemer's chapter "The Encounter between East and West in the Civilization of Our Time" in *The Ecumenical Era in Church and Society*, ed. Jurji, p. 92, where Kraemer also refers to relativism as "a paralyzing or . . . broadening factor." I infer from his account of Hindu relativism in his critique of Dr. Radhakrishnan's position that Kraemer places Hindu relativism in the "life-weakening" category. This critique is given in *Religion and the Christian Faith*, pp. 97 ff.

9. *Ibid.*, p. 111.

10. *Ibid.*, p. 112.

11. *Ibid.*, p. 110.

12. *Ibid.*, p. 129.

13. *Ibid.*, p. 101.

14. *Ibid.*, p. 104.

15. *Ibid.*, pp. 107 ff.

16. Cf. M. Hiriyanna, *The Essentials of Indian Philosophy*, p. 154. Elaborating his statement that Sankara's system is not to be described as "monism," Professor Hiriyanna states that Sankara's

identification of the individual self (jiva) with Brahman does not mean that the individual self is "lost in Brahman" but rather that the individual self has no being apart from Brahman (p. 158). Seen through the colored mirror of maya, the jiva may appear as entirely self-sufficient and *separate* from other selves and Brahman, and in this sense illusory, but only in this sense.

17. A. L. Basham, "Hinduism," in *The Concise Encyclopaedia of Living Faiths*, ed. R. C. Zaehner, p. 239.

18. Cf. Devanandan, "Renascent Religions and Religion," p. 168: "Hinduism is handicapped by the lack of a sacred writing that can claim to state in brief summary the main beliefs and practices characteristic of Hindu religion. The attempt is now being made to use the *Bhagavad Gita* for this purpose. Translations in Indian languages and simple expositions of the *Gita* teachings are being put out."

The primary Hindu scriptures, Vedas, (sruti, "that which was heard") are distinguished from "authoritative writings outside the Vedas" (smriti, "that which is remembered"). Dr. A. C. Bouquet observes that rigorist Hindus place the Bhagavad Gita in the second category. "I have been told that very strict Brahmin theologians will not accept it as canonical" (*Sacred Books of the World*, p. 228.) Hence, maybe, the incident reported by Rudolf Otto: "During a visit to Benares I met a young ascetic of Sankara's school. He conducted us to a hall where some men sat on the floor, eagerly reading the *Bhagavad Gita*. He looked contemptuously on them and remarked, 'We philosophers are above it.'" (*Christianity and the Indian Religion of Grace*, p. 22.)

On the other hand, I myself recall a comment to the opposite effect. It was made to me by a young clerk in a small town north of Delhi. When I asked him if he read the Bhagavad Gita, he shook his head. "No," he said, "that is above me. I cannot understand it." Dr. V. Raghavan in his "Introduction to Hindu Scriptures," in *The Religion of the Hindus*, ed. Morgan, while placing the Bhagavad Gita in the category of smriti, describes it as "regarded by many as the greatest of all the Hindu scriptures." This is probably today the general opinion, an opinion encouraged by Mahatma Gandhi's love and respect for the Gita.

19. Belief in karma is so taken for granted that a Hindu friend of mine once concluded an argument by saying, "You are going

against the *facts*." When I asked what facts, he replied, "The fact of karma for one thing."

20. S. Radhakrishnan, "The Hindu View," *The Wisdom of India* (*Wisdom* magazine, XXXIV [June, 1960], 24).

21. M. K. Gandhi in *Young India*, October 6, 1921; cf. C. F. Andrews, *Mahatma Gandhi's Ideas* (London, Allen and Unwin, 1929), pp. 35 ff.

22. Bhagavad Gita, XVIII. 58, 65. In this as in my other quotations from the Bhagavad Gita I have used the text and translation by Franklin Edgerton, *The Bhagavad Gita Translated and Interpreted* (Harvard Oriental Series), Cambridge, Harvard University Press, 1944. I have not, however, in this case, as in some other cases, quoted Edgerton's translation verbatim.

23. Otto, *Christianity and the Indian Religion of Grace*, p. 22.

24. Tukaram of Pandharpur (1608). The first quotation is from N. Macnicol, *Psalms of the Maratha Saints* (Calcutta, 1919), p. 66; the second from J. S. Hoyland, *An Indian Peasant Mystic* (London, 1932), pp. 19 ff. Cf. E. C. Dewick, *The Indwelling God*, p. 50: "With all his sense of God's nearness, Tukaram insists with unusual vehemence upon the *distinction* between man and God, as essential for true religion."

25. *One Hundred Poems of Kabir*, tr. Rabindranath Tagore, nos. l, lxix, quoted by A. L. Basham in *The Concise Encyclopaedia of Living Faiths*, ed. Zaehner, pp. 239, 240.

26. D. S. Sarma, in *The Religion of the Hindus*, ed. Morgan, p. 27.

27. R. N. Dandekar, "The Role of Man in Hinduism," *ibid.*, p. 145.

28. Rabindranath Tagore, *Gora* (New York, Macmillan, 1946).

29. Radhagovinda Rasak, "The Hindu Concept of the Natural World," in *The Religion of the Hindus*, ed. Morgan, p. 115.

30. D. S. Sarma, *ibid.*, p. 9.

31. V. Raghavan, *ibid.*, p. 275.

32. In further conversation, my friend spoke of Supreme Brahman *choosing* or *willing* to manifest Itself in this or that form of "personal" deity to this or that worshiper. It was, he insisted, mistaken to interpret the doctrine of "chosen deity" (*ishta-devatā*) in terms which suggest that the choice is made by the worshiper himself, as does D. S. Sarma (*The Religion of the Hindus*, ed. Morgan, p. 5). The worshiper might *imagine* that the choice was his

own. But he was really moved to make this choice by the operation
of the grace or power (maya) of Brahman. In short, my friend was
at pains to emphasize that he meant what he said when he said that
Supreme Brahman is God, *personal* God. At the same time he was
resolute against reference to Supreme Brahman as "He," as also
against anything which, to his mind, savored of anthropomorphism.
He suggested that a Christian might best understand the conception
of Supreme Brahman held today by scholars in the school of Sankara (like himself) in terms of the "Hidden God" or in Trinitarian
terms indicating a conception of divine suprapersonality. I have
frequently in the East, met with the same objection to "anthropomorphic" terms, an objection which may, I think, be misconstrued. As my friend emphasized, Hindu thought of the divine is
subject to the qualifying neti neti.

 33. M. Hiriyanna, *The Essentials of Indian Philosophy*, p. 21.

 34. Chandogya Upanishad, VI. 15. 3: "That which is the finest
essence—this whole world has that as its soul. That is Reality. That
is, Atman (Soul). That art thou, Svetaketa." (*The Thirteen Principal Upanishads*, tr. R. E. Hume [London: 1921], p. 249.)

 35. Brihadaranyaka Upanishad, I. 4. 10. (*Ibid.*, p. 83.)

 36. Chandogya Upanishad, VI. 2. 1, 2.

 37. Hiriyanna, *The Essentials of Indian Philosophy*, p. 20; cf.
Franklin Edgerton, *The Bhagavad Gita, or Son of the Blessed One*,
p. 13: "*Brahman.* The oldest meaning of this word seems to be
'sacred utterance.' . . . *Brahman*, the 'holy word,' came to mean
the mystic power inherent in the holy word."

 38. Rig-Veda X. 31. 7; cf. V. 29. 4; cf. Radhakrishnan, *Indian Philosophy*, pp. 99, 100, 166.

 39. Brihadaranyaka Upanishad, II. 4. 6: "This Brahmanhood, this
Kshatrahood, these worlds, these gods, these beings, everything here
is what this Soul is." Cf. Chandogya Upanishad, III. 14. 1; VII. 25. 2.
For an interesting discussion of the phrase "Brahman is all this,"
see Ninian Smart, *Reasons and Faiths*, pp. 36 ff. and footnotes.

 40. Svetasvatara Upanishad, IV. 4. 4.

 41. Brihadaranyaka Upanishad, III. 8. 9; cf. trans. by V. Raghavan, in *The Religion of the Hindus*, ed. Morgan, p. 321.

 42. Chandogya Upanishad, VII. 25. 1; Mundaka Upanishad, II.
2. 11.

 43. Katha Upanishad, IV. 1.

 44. Brihadaranyaka Upanishad, I. 4. 7; cf. Max Müller's trans.

(*Sacred Books of the East*, vol. I): "This Self is the footstep of everything."

45. Kena Upanishad, I. 3. 4; II. 11.
46. Brihadaranyaka Upanishad, III. 8. 1, 6–11.
47. *Ibid.*, III. 4. 2; cf. Kena Upanishad, I. 1–3.
48. Brihadaranyaka Upanishad, III. 4. 2.
49. Chandogya Upanishad, VI. 8. 4–7.
50. Brihadaranyaka Upanishad, II. 3. 6.
51. *Ibid.*, III. 6. 1.
52. *Ibid.*, II. 4. 14–15.
53. Cf. Hiriyanna, *The Essentials of Indian Philosophy*, pp. 19, 22, with reference to Aitareya Upanishad, III. 3: "The outcome of the identification therefore is that the ultimate reality, which may indifferently be termed either Brahman or ātman, is spiritual."
54. Chandogya Upanishad, VI. 2. 1–3; cf. Taitiriya Upanishad, II. 6: "He desired: 'Would that I were many. Let me procreate myself.' "
55. Brihadaranyaka Upanishad, I. 4. 17: "In the beginning this world was just Self (Ātman), one only. He wished: 'Would that I had a wife; then would I procreate. Would that I had wealth. . . .' So great indeed is desire. . . . Therefore even today when one is lonely one wishes: 'Would that I had a wife.' . . . He thinks that he is, assuredly, incomplete" (tr. by R. E. Hume, *The Thirteen Principal Upanishads*, pp. 85, 86). The motive ascribed is, perhaps, mixed. It includes desire for wealth and completion besides companionship. This mixture of motive, however, is, if anything, a further implication of "personality."
56. Isa Upanishad, 8.
57. Cf. Smart, *Reasons and Faiths*, pp. 37 ff.
58. Cf. Hiriyanna, *The Essentials of Indian Philosophy*, pp. 157 ff. "Salvation implies survival. The liberated *jīva* is not thus lost in Brahman" (p. 158). " 'That thou art' (Tat twam asi). It does not mean, as it is so often represented to do, that man and the qualified Brahman or God . . . are *as such* one. Such an attitude is as blasphemous, according to Advaita, as it is according to any religion or purely theistic doctrine" (p. 164).
59. Cf. D. S. Sarma, in *The Religion of the Hindus*, ed. Morgan, p. 11: "The heart of man hungers for a god of love, grace, and mercy. These sublime qualities may exist in the Supreme Spirit in some transcendent forms unknown to us but we can lay hold of

them only in their human forms. . . . Accordingly, Hinduism at its highest neither rejects theism nor accepts it." Cf. Satis Chandra Chatterjee's description of Sankara's system as "supertheistic": "Sankara's view is certainly not theism, but rather the perfection of the theistic faith" (*The Religion of the Hindus*, ed. Morgan, p. 25).

60. I Cor. 13:12; cf. II Cor. 3:18.

61. Mr. Hiriyanna, *The Essentials of Indian Philosophy*, p. 25.

62. Bhagavad Gita, IV. 6–8.

63. *Ibid.*, XVIII. 61.

64. Yajnavalkya Upanishad: *Māyā sā trividhā proktā satvarājasatāmasī,* quoted by Sri Jaya Chamarajendra Wadiyar Bahadur, maharajah of Mysore, *Dattrēya: The Way and the Goal* (London, 1957), p. 28. Cf. an interesting discussion of Sankara's system with reference to the "difficulty theory of maya" and "our knowledge of God" by K. Satchidananda Murty in *Revelation and Reason in Advaita Vedānta* (New York, Columbia University Press, 1959), pp. 247 ff.

65. Chandogya Upanishad, III. 13. 7.

66. Jaya Chamarajendra Wadiyar, *Dattrēya*, p. xiii.

67. *Ibid.*, p. 28.

68. *Ibid.*, p. 140, with reference to the Avadūta-Gīta.

69. Romans 8:16.

70. Brihadaranyaka Upanishad, III. 7. 15.

71. Bhagavata Purana. Cf. V. Raghavan in *The Religion of the Hindus*, ed. Morgan, pp. 363–64.

72. Bhagavata Purana, III. 11–13.

73. Cf. V. Raghavan in *The Religion of the Hindus*, ed. Morgan, p. 265.

74. Bhagavata Purana.

75. Bhagavad Gita, XVIII. 67.

76. Bhagavata Purana.

77. Katha Upanishad, I. 2. 23; cf. Svetasvatara Upanishad, VI. 21, and comment by Ninian Smart, *Reasons and Faiths*, p. 98, footnote on the "rudimentary doctrine of grace (prasada)" indicated in the Katha Upanishad.

78. S. Radhakrishnan, *Fellowship of the Spirit*, p. 5.

CHAPTER IV. *Buddhism: Confessional Relativism*

1. Cf. Philip H. Ashby, *The Conflict of Religions*, p. 180. Professor Ashby states that "Buddhism . . . has not developed a theory

in the matter (i.e., the view of other religions) which has differed to any appreciable degree from the traditional Indian or Hindu attitude." This perhaps is an overstatement. Granted that Buddhists have not "developed" any different "theory," Theravada Buddhists' attitude to religious speculation suggests indifference to other religious views rather than the interest evinced by Hindus. This indifference is implied by the teaching regarding "indeterminate questions." "The jungle, the desert, the puppet show, the writhing, the entanglement of speculation . . . conduce neither to wisdom nor to insight." (E.g. *Majjhima Nikaya* 1. 455.)

2. Addressing the Burmese Legislature (October 3, 1950) U Chan Htoon, now president of the World Buddhist Federation, said that one "main cause" for the bill pledging support for the Sixth Great Council was "the present world situation." Delegates from twenty-nine countries attending the World Buddhist Conference held in Ceylon in May, 1950, were, he said, convinced that "Buddhism is the only ideology which can give peace to the world." "I found there," he added, "that the western countries are longing for Buddhism now. . . . The peoples of the world are looking to Buddhism to save the world." (*The Light of the Dhamma*, Inaugural Number, The World Fellowship of Buddhists: Union of Burma Buddha Sasana Council, Rangoon, no date).

3. Zenryu Tsukamoto, "Buddhism in China and Korea," in *The Path of the Buddha*, ed. Kenneth W. Morgan, p. 183.

4. Typescript of Lecture by T'ai-hsü, "The Meaning of Buddhism for the Modern Mind," tr. F. R. Millican (Christian Literature Society, Shanghai, 1934).

5. U Thittila, "Principles of Buddhism" in *The Path of the Buddha*, ed. Morgan, p. 72.

6. U Shwe Zan Aung, *Journal of the Burma Research Society*, VIII, Part II, quoted by U Pe Maung Tin, *Buddhist Prayer* (Burma Christian Literature Society, Rangoon, 1960), p. 6.

7. In the third century B.C. the Buddhist emperor, Asoka, promoted a notable missionary enterprise. His son, Mahinda, introduced Buddhism to Ceylon and other Asokan missionaries visited Burma and Thailand. The Burmese tradition that Buddhism came to Burma even earlier, introduced by two *merchants* in the Buddha's own lifetime, points to the probability that Buddhist teaching, like Hindu teaching, was made known beyond India in these early centuries by Indian traders as well as by missionary monks.

8. "Animistic," pre-Buddhist beliefs and customs (such as *Nat*

worship in Burma) continued in Theravada countries, as did the existence of beliefs and customs inherited from Hindu traders and settlers. Shrines to Hindu deities are found in Buddhist temples. In some temples in Thailand scenes from the Hindu *Ramayana* are pictured on the walls. Mahayana teaching also challenged Theravada teaching, prevailing in northern Burma for a time, but for the last eight centuries in Burma and the last six or seven centuries in Thailand the dominating influence has been the Theravada teaching. In Ceylon, Buddhism has had a checkered history, disturbed by invasions from Hindu India and Christian Europe, and its resurgence there today is the more emphatic on this account.

9. U Thittila, in *The Path of the Buddha*, ed. Morgan, p. 71.

10. B. Ananda Maitreya Nayaka Thero, "Buddhism in Theravāda Countries," in *The Path of the Buddha*, ed. Morgan, p. 118.

Theravada opinion is reflected in the statement by the Burmese Minister for Home and Religious Affairs at the inaugural meeting of the Buddha Sasana Organization, 1951. Commenting on legislation promoting the reestablishment of Buddhist organizations in Burma, U Win observed: "Our religion has been in a neglected state for the past sixty years, since the overthrow of King Thibaw, Promoter of the Faith. The prosperity of Religion, as you are all aware, depends on the presence of a ruler who is genuinely inclined to promote it. . . . Now (that) . . . . the Government is duly elected by the people according to the (new) constitution it is inevitable that the Government becomes the Promoter of the Faith. . . . The Government wishes to see the unity of the Sanghas (the Monastic institutions)." The pattern of separation of Church and State familiar to Americans has led, I think, to erroneous conclusions regarding the association of resurgent Buddhism and neonationalism in southeast Asia. To suppose that Buddhist politicians are merely "using religion" for political ends is to ignore the outlook promoted by Buddhist history in this area.

11. E.g., Revelation 5: 1–10: "And I saw . . . a book . . . sealed with seven seals. . . . And I wept much that no one was found worthy to open the book . . . and I saw a Lamb . . . and he went and took the book . . . and the four living creatures and the twenty-four elders fell down before the Lamb . . . saying, 'Worthy art thou to take the book and to open its seals, for thou wast slain and by thy blood didst ransom men for God." Compare this with the description of the Mahayana scripture, The Perfection of Wis-

dom in 8,000 Lines, described as a book "sealed with seven seals," shown to a bodhisattva named "Ever-weeping" and the description of "Ever-weeping," slain himself in sacrifice, becoming thereby worthy of the Perfection of Wisdom. C.f. Edward Conze, "Buddhism: the Mahayana" in *The Concise Encyclopaedia of Living Faiths*, ed. R. C. Zaehner, pp. 296, 302, 303.

12. The fundamental neti neti of Buddhism is indicated by the Buddha's silence about nirvana, as recorded in the Pali canon. I do not suggest, therefore, that this neti neti was absent from the Theravada tradition. I suggest, however, that the Mahayana development meant a new emphasis of this neti neti and a consequent flexible relativism which in part explains the greater diversity in the Mahayana pattern.

13. Even in the T'ang period (618–907), "the Buddhist Age" in China, Taoism was accepted by the T'ang monarchs, Confucianism provided the guiding principles of government, and Muslims were active, as were Nestorian Christians and Manichaeans. The persecution of Buddhists by the Taoist emperor, Wu tsung, in 845 resulted in the destruction of over 4,000 monasteries and the expulsion of 260,000 priests and nuns.

14. In Japan today Buddhism coexists not only with Shinto, Confucianism, and Christianity, but with the "new religions." About twenty-seven "new religion" sects were organized after the Second World War. (Cf. William Woodard, "Japan's New Religions," *Japan Harvest*, V (Winter, 1957), 19–21; quoted by Joseph M. Kitagawa, *Religions of the East*, p. 22.

15. Th. Stcherbatsky, *The Conception of Buddhist Nirvāna* (Leningrad, 1927), p. 36.

16. Cf. Joseph M. Kitagawa, *Religions of the East*, pp. 31–34, 166 ff. Taking the conception of Church to mean the total unity of all Christians (p. 9) as distinguished from the conception of churches (local congregations), Professor Kitagawa cites "the Samgha universal" as an analogous conception in Buddhism (p. 34). He suggests that while the term Samgha was later used with particular reference to the monastic order as distinguished from the laity, the earlier reference embraced the whole Buddhist community, lay as well as clerical (p. 161). This is conceivable, though the evidence is meager. It is also arguable, as Professor Kitagawa suggests, that Samgha came to mean the monastic order in particular when the wandering monks began to reside in monasteries (vihara). We may

also agree that the expansion of Buddhism during the reign of Asoka encouraged the conception of a distinctive, total Buddhist community. This conception, of course, does not depend on whether the term Samgha refers narrowly to the monastic order or not. The more important question is the relation of the order to the laity, and I have argued elsewhere that the "gulf" between the monks and the laity in Theravada countries is not nearly so wide as is sometimes supposed. (Cf. *Paradox and Nirvana*, pp. 20 ff.) I agree with Professor Kitagawa that there is this conception of total community. I also suggest that Professor Kitagawa might find further support for his conclusions by considering the sense of community implied by such observances as the *Uposatha* sessions when the monks are required to acknowledge faults "giving scandal to laymen" (cf. Father Vincentius Sangermano, *The Burmese Empire* [London, 1895], p. 120), and also some possible implications of the layman's sense of obligation to the order.

The point I raise in my text in distinguishing between Church and churches has reference to the Mahayana history of the "sects." From what I can gather of the organization and outlook of the Shin sects in Japan, we have here a conception of community related to the maintenance of a "confessional" standpoint analagous to that of the confessional churches in Christendom. While not incompatible with the sense of "total Buddhist community," it qualifies it. I also question Stcherbatsky's use of the term "high Church" on the ground that it implies elements of the Catholic conception of the Body of Christ which are absent from the Buddhist conception.

17. It is sometimes remarked that while the conceptions of the dharmakaya and nirmanakaya are fairly easily understood, the conception of the samboghakaya (the subtle form of Buddha) is elusive. Perhaps we have here a situation comparable with that presented by the Christian doctrine of the Holy Trinity in regard to the nature and function of the Holy Spirit. While the conception of the Samboghakaya is not identical with that of the Holy Spirit, both refer to incessant and pervasive activity. Cf. E. Conze, in *Concise Encyclopaedia of Living Faiths*, p. 306; T. R. V. Murti, *The Central Philosophy of Buddhism*, p. 386; Lobsang Phuntsuh Lhalungpi, "Buddhism in Tibet," in *The Path of the Buddha*, ed. Morgan, pp. 280 ff.

18. In *The Path of the Buddha*, ed. Morgan, compare the remark

of the Theravada scholar, U Thittila, "Buddhism is not a religion . . . not a system of faith and worship" (p. 71) with the view of the Mahayana scholar, Zenryu Tsukamoto, that Buddhism's missionary progress in China was partly due to its new dress as a religion with "objects of worship" and "its own religious ceremonies" (p. 187).

19. *Kwan Yin's Saving Power: Some Remarkable Examples of Response to Appeal for Aid, Made to Kwan Yin by His Devotees . . . "He Who Hears the Voice of the World"* . . . , coll. trans., and ed. by (Miss) Pi-Cheng Lee (Shanghai, The Buddhist Book Store, 1931).

Passages from the Saddharma Pundarīka and the Sukāvatīvyuha are followed by twenty-one testimonies to Kwan Yin's saving power, giving the names of the contributors, including the former abbot of a Zen monastery. "To my personal knowledge," writes one contributor, "prayer by repeating the name of Kwan Yin Pusan . . . has cured eye diseases on many occasions." The editor adds a postscript affirming her opinion that "the dharani of the 'Great Compassion of Kwan Yin' is efficacious only with those who abstain from eating fresh meat."

Some Shin Buddhist teachers discourage petitions to Amita for specific benefits on the ground that this argues lack of faith in the compassionate Buddha. "After all," wrote Shinran, "in so far as we trust in the inconceivable power of His Vow (Amita's Vow) and in so far as we put our single trust in the inconceivable power of His Name and pronounce it, what more do we need to add from our side?" ("The Private Letters of Shinran Shonin," in *The Shinshu Seiten* [The Honpa Hongwonji Mission of Hawaii, 1955], p. 256.)

20. Some writers consider that Buddhism presents what are "virtually three separate religions . . . based on versions of the scriptures in Pali, Tibetan and Chinese" (e.g., Zenryu Tsukamoto, *The Path of the Buddha*, ed. Morgan, p. 182). In this chapter, partly for the sake of clearer emphasis on some of the points made, I have followed the view that "in modern times there are only two major schools of Buddhism . . . Theravāda and Mahāyāna," the third type, Tantrayana, being regarded as "not a separate school but . . . an added characteristic of the Mahāyāna Buddhism in Tibet" (Bhikkhu J. Kashyap, "Origin and Expansion of Buddhism," in *The Path of the Buddha*, ed. Morgan, p. 39).

21. U Thittila of Burma in his statement of Theravada principles (*The Path of the Buddha*, p. 95) shows sensitivity to this issue in his elaboration of the doctrine of *mettā*. Construing *mettā* to mean "*active* loving care for others," he says that "it is metta which in Buddhism is the basis of social progress." Several pamphlets published in Ceylon show interest in the same question, and I am informed that a Buddhist scholar at the University of Ceylon is preparing a systematic treatment of Buddhist social ethics.

22. E.g., Mrs. C. A. F. Rhys Davids, *Gotama, The Man* (London, 1928); *Sakya, or Buddhist Origins* (London, 1931), and other works. One of the most recent attempts to distinguish the Buddha's teaching from later interpretation and development is Professor A. J. Bahm's *Philosophy of the Buddha* (Harper and Brothers, New York, 1958), based largely on a critical examination of the Pali scriptures. Professor Bahm concludes that Gotama's Philosophy of the Middle Way consists in a single psychological principle: the principle that "happiness is to be found in accepting things as they are" (p. 19).

23. Christmas Humphreys, *Buddhism*, p. 71.

24. *Ibid.*, p. 74.

25. "It is only on the basis of the Buddhist world-view that a unified view of life can be worked out. Buddhism alone can re-establish the moral standards needed by mankind. . . . It asserts positively that there is in the universe no such thing as an independently existing individual thing . . . that there is an inescapable mutability in life." T'ai-hsü, "The Meaning of Buddhism for the Modern Mind." See Note 4.

26. Hajime Nakamura, "Unity and Diversity in Buddhism," in *The Path of the Buddha*, ed. Morgan, p. 380.

27. *Ibid.*, p. 373.

28. U Chan Htoon, Address to the Sixteenth Congress of the International Association for Religious Freedom, Chicago, U.S.A., August, 1958, p. 9. "*Ex cathedra* announcements are unknown, for the sole authority is the text of the Tipitaka."

29. Italics mine. The statement, as I have said, is made not by Mr. Humphreys but by his publishers. Besides this statement, there is the significance of the action taken by the Council of the London Society in promoting such a statement. No doubt a major reason for this was the need to answer Western inquiries. Even so, there is more than a hint here of the Western disposition towards confessionalism wrestling with a Buddhist hesitation in regard to such

definition, a wrestling evident in some of Mr. Humphrey's own statements (e.g., p. 15: "Buddhism, like any other form of relative truth, must vary").

30. U Chan Htoon, *Address to the Sixteenth Congress of the International Association for Religious Freedom,* p. 9.

31. H. Nakamura, "Unity and Diversity in Buddhism," in *The Path of the Buddha,* ed. Morgan, p. 391.

32. Phil. 2:2–8, "Be of the same mind . . . in lowliness of mind. . . . Have this mind in you which was also in Christ Jesus who . . . humbled himself."

33. The phrases quoted are from Right Reverend P. Bigandet, *The Life or Legend of Guadama, the Buddha of the Burmese,* 4th ed. (London, 1911, repr. from 2d ed., 1866), I, 62 ff. Bishop Bigandet describes the *shinbyu* procession as he observed it a hundred years ago: "When a young lad is to make his first entry into a house of the order, he is led thereto, riding on a richly caparisoned pony, or sitting in a fine palanquin carried on the shoulders of four or more men. He is allowed to use one or several gold umbrellas which are held opened over his head. During the triumphal march he is preceded by a long line of men and women, attired in their richest dresses, carrying a large quantity of presents destined for the use of the inmates of the *kiaong* (monastery). . . . This display of an ostentatious pomp is . . . an honor paid to the postulant . . . and on the part of the youth a last farewell to worldly vanities. He has no sooner descended from his splendid conveyance and crossed the threshold of the *kiaong* than . . . his head is instantly shaved; he is stripped of his fine secular dress, and habited in the plain and humble yellow garb . . . becoming his new position." (*Ibid.,* "Notice on the Buddhist Monks," pp. 263 ff.) According to this account the change of attire takes place at the monastery. At the *shinbyu* ceremonies which I observed during my own residence in Burma, however, the change of raiment ceremony took place at the boy's home, as described in my text. For a lively contemporary description of the *shinbyu* ceremony by a Burmese writer of today, see Mi Mi Khaing, *Burmese Family* (Bloomington, Indiana University Press, 1962).

34. W. C. B. Purser and K. W. Saunders, *Modern Buddhism in Burma* (Rangoon, 1914), pp. 99 ff.

35. H. Fielding Hall, *The Soul of a People,* 4th ed. (London, 1913), p. 18.

36. Bigandet, *The Life or Legend of Gaudama,* p. 315.

37. U Thittila, in *The Path of the Buddha*, ed. Morgan, p. 75.

38. D. S. Sarma, "The Nature and History of Hinduism," in *The Religion of the Hindus*, ed. Morgan, p. 11.

39. It is often here suggested that this ideal of active benevolence is altogether lacking in the Theravada tradition. When a Theravada scholar today claims that this is not so, when he affirms on Theravada principles "the ideal . . . of mutual service and practical brotherhood" (U Thittila, in *The Path of the Buddha*, ed. Morgan, p. 96) it may be argued that this is a new departure in Theravada teaching. Some may attribute it to the impact of modern pressures, others to the impact of Mahayana teaching as the two traditions are seen to be drawing together again today. But the Theravada teacher may justly reply that what he is saying today is what he has been entitled to say all along, whether he has said it before or not. He has been entitled to say it because there has been something more in his mind than Pali texts, analytic meditations, precepts and prohibitions, important as these may be; there has been the living thought of the Buddha himself, the never forgotten story of his ministry, a story which holds within itself the bodhisattva ideal.

40. In some texts the Buddha's compassion is presented as the fruit of his wisdom, e.g., Ashtasāhasrikā, XXII, 402–5. See trans. by Edward Conze, *Selected Sayings from the Perfection of Wisdom* (London, 1955), pp. 35 ff.: "He became endowed with that kind of wise insight which allows him to see all beings as on their way to their slaughter. Great compassion thereby takes hold of him. . . ." In other texts compassion precedes wisdom, e.g., *L'Abhidhamakosa de Vasubandhu*, tr. and annotated by Louis de La Vallée Poussin (Paris, P. Geuthner, 1923–25), II, 191: "The bodhisattvas seek for enlightenment . . . because they want to become capable of pulling others out of this flood of suffering." (I am indebted for these references to Dr. Clarence H. Hamilton.)

Taken together, these two examples may serve to indicate what is meant when the Buddha character is presented as a *symbol,* and, as such, as a reference which promotes unity while it allows for diversity of response and diversity of interpretation. Both texts reflect one of the distinctive features of the Buddha character symbol: the conjunction of compassion and wisdom. In this they are united, while diversity of response is exhibited in the precedence assigned to compassion in the one case and the precedence assigned to wisdom (enlightenment) in the other case.

A similar observation may be made in regard to the emphasis on compassion which is exhibited in the Mahayana presentation of the bodhisattva ideal in contrast to the emphasis on wisdom which may be discerned in the Theravada presentation of the arhat whose first aim appears to be his own enlightenment. Here, in this difference of emphasis, we have a diversity of response. But in both traditions the response may be seen as response to the same symbol inasmuch as in both traditions both virtues, compassion and wisdom, are nevertheless affirmed and held together as they are held together in the symbol of the Buddha character.

We might also observe what Buddhist history has done with this symbol of the Buddha character in much the same way as Merrill D. Peterson has recently observed what American history has done with the symbol of the Jefferson image. Here again, in both cases, there is a diversity of response. Yet in both cases the symbol may be observed to persist as that which makes for unity. In the American case, Mr. Peterson concludes by seeing the Jefferson symbol persisting in association with the American unifying concern for freedom. (Merrill D. Peterson, *The Jefferson Image in the American Mind* [New York, Oxford University Press, 1960], p. 457.)

41. *The Buddha-Carita of Asvaghosa,* tr. E. C. Cowell (Sacred Books of the East, Vol. XLIX, Oxford, 1894), p. 105.

42. *Ibid.,* p. 106.

43. H. Nakamura in *The Path of the Buddha,* ed. Morgan, p. 395.

44. Peter Munz, *Problems of Religious Knowledge,* pp. 176 ff.

45. Most of my quotations are from the translation by W. E. Soothill, *The Lotus of the Wonderful Law* (Oxford, 1930).

46. *Ibid.,* p. 113.

47. *Ibid.,* p. 128.

48. *Ibid.,* p. 157.

49. *Ibid.,* p. 178.

50. *Ibid.,* p. 68.

51. *Ibid.,* p. 71.

52. *Ibid.,* p. 145.

53. *Ibid.,* p. 119.

54. Majjhima-Nikaya, 1. 455.

55. The *Tannisho,* 10.

56. The doctrine of *anatta* is variously interpreted by Buddhists. According to the Theravada scholar, U Thittila, "it is this doctrine of anatta, no soul, for which Buddhism stands and on which Bud-

dhism differs from other religions." In keeping with this view, he emphasizes that the Buddha laid repeated stress on self-reliance. "Buddhism makes man stand on his own feet" (in *The Path of the Buddha*, ed. Morgan, pp. 76, 84). According to the Mahayana scholar, Professor Nakamura, however, the Buddha "did not deny the soul, but was silent concerning it. . . . It is quite wrong to think that there is no self at all according to Buddhism" (in *The Path of the Buddha*, ed. Morgan, p. 377). On the emphasis on individual autonomy, cf. N. Anesaki, "The Ethics of Buddhism," in *Hastings Dictionary of Religion and Ethics*, V, 448.

57. Soothill, *Lotus of the Wonderful Law*, p. 111.

58. *Ibid.*, p. 178.

59. *Ibid.*, pp. 180, 186.

60. *Ibid.*, p. 155. Tathagata, a name frequently given to the Buddha. Its original meaning is not known but in later usage it has been presented as composed of "tatha" (thus) and "agata" (come) or "gata" (gone), signifying (a) One who has come, and (b) one who has gone. In northern Buddhism each "manifest" Buddha (Gautama Sakyamuni, Amitabha, etc.) is conceived to be "one who has come" (Tathagata) from the realm of Thusness or Oneness, so that it can be said that "To trust in Amita but means/ To trust in all Buddhas" (The San-Amidabutsugewasan, quoted in The Shinsu Seiten (Hawai), p. 208. This, I think, supports the view that in northern Buddhism all the Buddhas named refer to one Buddha character.

If Tathagata is taken to mean "one who has gone" then the term might be translated (perhaps additionally rather than alternatively) as the Perfect One: One who has arrived (arrived at Truth), one who has followed the Path. Cf. E. Conze, *Buddhism: Its Essence and Development* (Bruno Cassirer, Oxford, 1951; Harper Torchbooks, New York, 1959), p. 36.

61. A. C. Bouquet, *The Christian Faith and Non-Christian Religions* (Harper and Brothers, New York, 1958), p. 8.

62. Myanaung U Tin, "Buddhism and Modern Creeds," *The Light of the Dharma*, Vol I, No. 1, Inaugural Number, The World Fellowship of Buddhists: Second Conference Issue (Union of Burma Buddha Sasana Council, Rangoon), pp. 15, 16.

63. I.e., the *Tannisho: a Book Deploring the Heterodoxies*. In the introductory paragraph, the writer says: "I cannot but deplore the fact that we are at variance in regard to true faith about which

we heard from our late Master. . . . Unless we are guided by the Good Teacher of the Way, how can we think of entering the gate of the Easy Path? Let us by no means throw into disorder the tenet of the Way of the Other-Power by interpreting things in our own light" (cf. the Shinsu Seiten, p. 263).

In the Muryujukyo, a Japanese translation of the Chinese version of the Sukhāvatīvyūha Sutra, a fundamental scripture of Pure Land Buddhism, the perfect character of the bodhisattvas is exhibited in their zeal for truth which leads them to subdue heresy. While they are "impartial," feeling no hatred, no one-sided love, they are also "like Brahma, because they are most superb in all good doctrines . . . like *Garuda* because they subdue all heretical views" (cf. Shinsu Seiten, pp. 48, 49.

CHAPTER V. *Islam: Confessional Practice*

1. E.g., Christopher Dawson, *The Historic Reality of Christian Culture*, p. 71: "The three great Western religions . . . Judaism, Christianity and Islam."

In one of the most recent surveys, *Religions of the East*, Professor Kitagawa includes Islam among "Religions of the East," but it may be noted that he begins his discussion of Islam by observing that Islam is "a spiritual cousin" of Judaism and Christianity.

2. The disposition to describe the Muslim faith as a Western faith exists on the part of Christians rather than on the part of Muslims. Hendrik Kraemer observes that the Egyptian scholar, Taka Hussain, who presents this view, is exceptional in this respect. "His thesis is: Egypt, including Islam, belongs to the West, not to the East. . . . This is a bold and far-reaching idea, particularly so because it is as well in the East as in the West the habit to reckon the Muslim world and Islam to the East. In the Muslim world itself this latter position is . . . the more spontaneously accepted because the whole history of the Muslim world is one of long-drawn-out antagonism to and struggle with the West." (*World Cultures and World Religions*, pp. 113–14.)

3. It may perhaps be observed that Dante nevertheless allowed that at least one Muslim deserved a better fate than hell. He placed Averroes in Limbo. But this may reflect a respect for Arab culture rather than a respect for Islam, a distinction in line with the distinction drawn by other Christians of Dante's time.

4. H. A. R. Gibb, *Mohammedanism: an Historical Survey*, 2d ed., p. 33.

5. Tor Andrae, *Mohammed the Man and His Faith*, tr. Theophil Menzel, p. 185.

6. Kenneth Cragg, *The Call of the Minaret*, pp. 94, 101.

7. Gibb, *Mohammedanism*, p. 11, and others emphasize Muslim criticism today of the term "Mohammedanism." Cf. Cragg, *Call of the Minaret*, p. 92; Wilfred Cantwell Smith, *Islam in Modern History*, p. 19, footnote 18: "The personality of Mohammed is essentially irrelevant."

Muslim sensitivity to this point is indicated by the following letter published in *Epiphany* (Oxford Mission to Calcutta), in 1932:

To the Editor of the Epiphany

Dear Sir,—The term "Islam" is a Causative Infinitive from the Root S.L.M. meaning Peace. The Quranic Diction "Islam" accordingly means "an entire Self-Resignation to the Supreme Will which alone is the way to attain 'peace' in every sphere of life. It is, just as the Quran says, that Eternal Religion which was preached by the numerous Messengers of God to different peoples of different lands in different ages.

In consonance with the teaching of the Quran we, Muslims, only regard our Holy Prophet as one of those Divine Messengers who themselves were none other than the true followers of "Islam." In short, they were all perfect and ideal "Muslims." The life-examples of all these great personages have always been tending and attracting the whole human race towards the aforesaid "Islam." (As for our Prophet's being, the last and greatest Ring of the Chain of Prophethood, I should like to discuss it in a separate letter to you.)

"Islam" is thus above all sorts of so-called "ities" and "isms." Yet you, as well as many of your co-religionists, are often ludicrously found to synonymise the term "Islam" with your own coined "Muhammadanism." This simply appears to be an outcome of your willful ignorance. If not, please explain the change in the next issue of your esteemed journal.

Yours faithfully,

Nesar Ahmed

Chittagong

8. A notable example of this understanding of the Muslim emphasis and of Christian concern for its maintenance is given in the contrast drawn between two Muslim apologists by Wilfred Cantwell Smith (*Islam in Modern History*, pp. 85 ff.), to which we refer later in this chapter. "A true Muslim, however, is not a man who believes in Islam . . . but one who believes in God . . . committed to the revelation through his Prophet." (*Ibid.*, p. 146.)

9. Cf. Qur'ān, Sura IV, 135 (tr. Arberry, *The Koran Interpreted*, I, 120): "O believers, believe in God and in His Messenger and the Book He has sent down on His Messenger and the Book which He sent down before."

In my quotations from the Qur'ān I have used Arberry's translation except in the cases of Sura LVII, 30, where I have preferred "Manifest and Hidden" to Arberry's translation (see note 22): Sura L, 15, where I have preferred the more familiar "closer to man than his own neck vein" to Arberry's translation (see note 23); and Sura IV, 51, where I have preferred "partners to God," noting Arberry's variant in note 24.

10. Cf. Sura II, 23 (tr. Arberry), I, 32: "And if you are in doubt concerning that We have sent down on Our servant." Other translations read: "that which we reveal unto Our slave." It is true that Muhammad has been greatly revered. In many a mosque the name of Muhammad appears to the left of the name of Allah. In the eleventh century A.D. Al-Ghazali wrote of "imitating God's Apostle in all his goings out and comings in" (James Robson, "Al-Ghazali and Sunna," *The Muslim World*, XLV [No. 4, October, 1955] 324–33). Popular piety has moved in the direction of ascribing to the Prophet a supernatural character which he himself denied, and Sufi mystics saw him not only as the chief of the saints but also as the exalted mediator. F. H. Hilliard has summarized this movement of veneration in *The Buddha, The Prophet and the Christ* (London, George Allen and Unwin, 1956), but he concedes that it is remarkable that "the doctrine of the person of the Prophet proceeded even as far as it did," in view of other aspects of Islamic thought (p. 158). Attention has also been called to the many biographies of Muhammad which have appeared in modern times. It is nevertheless true that Islamic orthodoxy is fundamentally resistant to any exaggerated emphasis of the Prophet's person and status. He is primarily the instrument of Revelation, the *man* Muhammad called by God.

11. Hendrik Kraemer, *The Christian Message in a Non-Christian World*, pp. 141 ff. Dr. Kraemer describes Islam as "taking God as God with awful seriousness." He refers to Al-Ghazali with respect.

12. John Crossley in "A Monthly Letter about Evangelism" (Department of Evangelism, Division of Studies, World Council of Churches, January, 1960) reports: "In Lagos about 20 Christians and Muslims are meeting once a quarter; at each meeting papers are read on a theological subject (e.g. Revelation, Salvation) one by a Christian and one by a Muslim."

13. Professor Ernst Benz, of Marburg University, in a lecture given at Harvard Divinity School, 1960.

14. 'Abd Allah' Inan, quoted by Wilfred Cantwell Smith, *Islam in Modern History*, p. 101, footnote; p. 106, footnote, who remarks that the legacy of antagonism born of fear, hatred, and bitterness in the Middle Ages "has gradually given way to mere misunderstanding and failure of appreciation. In recent times improvement has rather swiftly gathered momentum. Nonetheless, it will clearly be some time yet,—and will involve continued effort, before the estrangement is on any but a small scale transcended in friendly collaboration."

15. *City of Wrong: a Friday in Jerusalem* by M. Kamel Hussein, tr. Kenneth Cragg (London, Geoffrey Bles, 1959), is a very interesting study of human motives and conduct based on the story of the Crucifixion of Jesus. It has been welcomed as a sign of new Muslim interest in Christian thought. (Cf. Stephen Neill, *Christian Faith and Other Faiths*, p. 62.)

16. Muhammed 'Abduh, quoted by Emile Dermenghen, *Muhammed and the Islamic Tradition*, trans. Jean M. Watt (New York, Harper & Brothers [Men of Wisdom Series], 1958), p. 138.

17. E.g., Mayor Nathan Phillips of Toronto, himself a Jewish citizen, in a speech at the Temple Emanu-el, Montreal, recently emphasized the fact that Canada is a nation of minorities. This meant new opportunity, and also responsibility, for Jewish citizens.

18. Cf. R. C. Zaehner, *The Concise Encyclopaedia of Living Faiths*, p. 16.

19. H. A. R. Gibb, *Mohammedanism*, p. 17.

20. Sura XCVI, 1–4. Cf. Tor Andrae, *Mohammed: the Man and his faith*, p. 43, on the different accounts of Mohammed's Vision.

21. Sura II, 256 (the Throne verse) (Arberry, *The Koran Interpreted*, I, 65).

22. Sura LVII, 3. Arberry translates: "the Outward and the Inward" (*ibid.*, II, 258).

23. Sura L, 15. Cf. Arberry, *ibid.*, p. 234.

24. Sura IV, 51. (Arberry, *ibid.*, I, 108: "Whoso associates with God anything. . . .")

25. Sura XVII, 90–95 (Arberry, *ibid.*, I, 312): "They say, 'We will not believe thee . . . till thou goest up into heaven, and we will not believe thy going up till thou bringest down on us a book that we may read.'" Sura XXIX, 50–51 (Arberry, *ibid.*, II, 102): "They say, 'Why have signs not been sent down upon him from his Lord? . . . Is it not sufficient for them that We have sent down upon thee the Book that is recited to them? Surely in that is our mercy. . . .'"

"The Qur'an . . . is a miracle—yes, rather, THE MIRACLE" (Mohammed Abd Allah Draz, "The Origin of Islam" in *The Straight Path*, ed. Morgan, p. 16).

26. Mohammad Abd Allah Draz, *ibid.*, p. 36.

27. Cf. H. A. R. Gibb, "Islam," in *Concise Encyclopaedia of Living Faiths*, ed. Zaehner, p. 183.

28. Sura XVII, 16. Tr. Arberry, *The Koran Interpreted*, I, 303: "And every man—We have fastened to him his bird of omen upon his neck."

29. Cf. Laurence E. Browne, *The Prospects of Islam* (London, S.C.M. Press, 1944) p. 10.

30. Sura XCVI, 1. (Cf. Arberry, *The Koran Interpreted*, II, 345.)

31. Sir William Muir, *The Life of Mohammed*, ed. T. H. Weit, 2d ed. (Edinburgh, J. Grant, 1923), p. 118; quoted by Kitagawa, *Religions of the East*, p. 233.

32. H. A. R. Gibb, *Mohammedanism*, p. 84.

33. A *Hindu* friend of mine once roundly challenged a statement that Muslims were invariably intolerant. He had, he said, Muslim friends who were very tolerant. "They are *Sufi* Muslims," he added. Cf. L. E. Browne, *The Prospects of Islam*, p. 63.

34. Charles J. Adams, The Muslims and World Peace (typescript of paper prepared for conference convened by the Church Peace Union, 1959), p. 13.

35. Sura II, 186–89 (Arberry, *The Koran Interpreted*, I, 53–54).

36. Mahmond Shaltout, "Islamic Beliefs and Code of Laws," in *The Straight Path*, ed. Morgan, p. 89.

37. Syed Ameer Ali, *The Spirit of Islam*, new ed. (London, Christophers, 1922), pp. 170 ff.

38. Charles Gore, *Philosophy of the Good Life* (London, J. M. Dent [Everyman's Library], 1935), p. 97.

39. Sura IX, 5, 29. (Arberry, *The Koran Interpreted*, I, 207, 210, translates: "Slay the idolators. . . .")

40. E.g. Ameer Ali, *The Spirit of Islam*, p. 218: "Islam seized the sword in self-defense, and held it in self-defense as it will ever do"; cf. Ahmed A. Galwash, *The Religion of Islam* (Cairo, Al-Azhar Magazine, 1940), pp. 83 ff., who says that (a) Muslims at first were "driven to have recourse to arms" in self-defense; (b) much of the later fighting had little to do with religion. " 'There is no compulsion in religion' trumpets forth loudly the peaceful spirit of Islam." The true Muslim is called upon to wish for peace. "Even in fighting the *aim* was nothing but peace."

41. Sura IX, 10–14. (Arberry, *The Koran Interpreted*, I, 208.)

42. Galwash, *The Religion of Islam*, pp. 86 ff. "The measure to be taken for the removal of evil is not positive non-resistance . . . but on the contrary the most effective methods ought to be used for the extirpation of evil. The means suited to particular cases are to be employed, whether they be harsh or mild."

43. Wilfred Cantwell Smith, *Modern Islam in India*, pp. 254 ff.

44. Quoted by W. C. Smith, *ibid.*, pp. 150 ff.

45. H. Kraemer, *The Christian Message in a Non-Christian World*, p. 356.

46. Cf. Mohammad Rasjidi, "Unity and Diversity in Islam," in *The Straight Path*, ed. K. W. Morgan, p. 408.

47. Cf. G. Bergsträsser's *Grundzüge des Islamischen Rechts* ed. Joseph Schacht, p. 7: The Sharia is "the epitome of the true Islamic spirit, the most decisive expression of Islamic thought, the essential kernel of Islam." Quoted by H. A. R. Gibb, *Mohammedanism*, p. 84.

48. Wilfred Cantwell Smith, *Islam in Modern History*, p. 20.

49. *Ibid.*, p. 41.

50. *Ibid.*, p. 33.

51. *Ibid.*, p. 127.

52. *Ibid.*, pp. 128, 134.

53. *Ibid.*, p. 133.

54. *Ibid.*, p. 134.

55. Cf. note 8, *supra.*

CHAPTER VI. *Jewish and Christian Confessions*

1. Louis Finkelstein, *The Beliefs and Practices of Judaism*, p. 10.

2. *Ibid.*, p. 11.

3. Deut. 5:33. Cf. R. J. Zwi Werblowsky, "Judaism, or the Religion of Israel" in *The Concise Encyclopaedia of Living Faiths*, ed. R. C. Zaehner, on the significance of the Hebrew word *mitsvah:* "good deed" or "religious act," literally "commandment."

4. Deut. 6:20–24.

5. Quoted by Zwi Werblowsky, "Judaism, or the Religion of Israel," in *Concise Encyclopaedia of Living Faiths*, ed. Zaehner, p. 40, from *Selected Poems of Jehudah Halevi*, tr. Nina Salaman (Philadelphia, 1946). Cf. Martin Buber, *Two Types of Faith*, p. 34: "Judaism in its way of faith itself subsequently turned aside to dogmatically 'believing that,' until its Credo in the Middle Ages reached a form not less rigid than that of the Christian Church— *except that its formulae were never set in the centre*" (italics mine). It is significant that Buber adds this qualifying phrase ("except that its formulae . . ."), a qualification of a qualification, since his reference to the "turning aside" to dogmatism is written in qualification of what he says in general of the Jewish way of faith. I am grateful to Professor Krister Stendahl for drawing my attention to the fact that Buber's distinction between two types of faith is relevant to the distinction I have drawn in my text between different "confessional" ways, as also Buber's presentation of the Jewish way of faith.

6. Leo Baeck, *The Essence of Judaism*, p. 10.

7. Deut. 6:4.

8. Ellis Rivkin, "Modern Trends in Judaism," in *Modern Trends in World Religions*, ed. Joseph M. Kitagawa, p. 90.

9. Robert Gordis, "The Implications of Judaic Ethics for International Relations" (a paper read at a conference convened by the Church Peace Union at Princeton, 1959).

10. Harry Joshua Stern, *Martyrdom and Miracle* (New York, Bloch Publishing Company, 1950), p. 159.

11. *Ibid.* Cf. Leo Baeck, *The Essence of Judaism*, pp. 77–80.

12. Stern, *Martyrdom and Miracle*, p. 118.

13. *Ibid.*, p. 119.

14. Judah Goldin, *The Living Talmud: the Wisdom of the Fathers*, p. 21.

15. *Ibid.*

16. Perhaps I should emphasize that I am not suggesting that *all* Jews share the attitude presented in these pages; still less that my few quotations from contemporary writers and brief reference to the Talmud support anything in the nature of a general description of Judaism. Nor do I suggest that *all* Buddhists or *all* Muslims share a similar attitude, nor, again, that there is no difference among the Jewish, Buddhist, and Muslim attitudes here considered. I am not attempting any general comparison. My argument is rather that if we have due regard for differences *within* the major traditions and see the study of religions as the study of *people*, we may observe, as among *some* Jews, *some* Buddhists, and *some* Muslims, attitudes presenting a "family resemblance."

17. II Tim. 1:13, 14.

18. Arnold Toynbee, *An Historian's Approach to Religion*, p. 127.

19. *Ibid.*, p. 121.

20. *Ibid.*, p. 127.

21. Cf. John Dillenberger, *Protestant Thought and Natural Science*, pp. 51 ff. His acute analysis of Protestant scholasticism is very relevant to my argument: that in taking account of the impact of Greek thought on Christian attitudes we have to allow for "the subtle influence of form upon content." Observing "the early humanist association with the kind of Aristotelianism exemplified in Melanchthon," Dr. Dillenberger links the consequent "tendency to express truth through precise definition" with the literal interpretation of the Bible and he raises the question whether such literalism was in keeping with what the Reformers intended by a return to the Bible. The Bible was still supposed to come first, with metaphysics subservient, but did the Bible really come first when it was read and interpreted as a Greek metaphysician might read and interpret it? Dr. Dillenberger notes (p. 111) how "the defense of a literal Scripture began to crumble in England in the middle of the seventeenth century" when the authority of Aristotle waned. His analysis points to the continued tension between Greek and biblical attitudes to which I refer.

22. Cf. H. E. W. Turner, *The Pattern of Christian Truth* (London, A. R. Mowbray, 1954), pp. 26 ff. "First among the fixed elements in the Christian tradition are the religious facts themselves . . . the fact of Christ as the Historical Redeemer. . . . The Church's grasp on the religious facts was prior to any attempt to work them into a coherent whole."

23. Rom. 10:9.

24. Phil. 2:11.

25. *Letters of the Younger Pliny.* X. xcvi.

26. Ignatius, *Epistle to the Smyrnaeans.* VIII. On this and kindred passages in Ignatius' writings with reference to his conception of the church and its unity see the interesting discussion by Virginia Corwin, *St. Ignatius and Christianity in Antioch* (New Haven, Yale University Press, 1960), pp. 192 ff., 247 ff.

27. I Cor. 2: 9 ff.

28. Toynbee, *An Historian's Approach to Religion*, p. 119.

29. A. C. Bouquet, *The Christian Faith and Non-Christian Religions*, p. 424. Dr. Bouquet's statement is the more significant because he emphasizes that he writes as a Christian clergyman, engaged in pastoral duty as an ordained minister of the Anglican Church, and, as such, one who "earnestly desires . . . to speak in the way that the Church to which I belong would have me speak" (p. 14).

30. S. Radhakrishnan, *Fellowship of the Spirit*, p. 5.

31. Cf. R. C. Zaehner, *The Concise Encyclopaedia of Living Faiths*, p. 16. Professor Zaehner observes that Marxist hostility to the idea of God is understandable in a Western world which "takes ideas as such with desperate seriousness." European civilization, since the rise of Christianity, "has been dominated by beliefs passionately held."

32. Cited in the *Catholic Encyclopaedia*, "Church," quoted by Walter Marshall Horton, *Christian Theology: an Ecumenical Approach*, p. 230.

33. William Nicholls, *Ecumenism and Catholicity* (London, (S.C.M. Press, London, 1952), p. 15; cf. p. 112, where Mr. Nicholls argues for a position between rigid confessionalism with the "heretical" claim that "we alone know how to confess" the faith, and the abandonment of any kind of confessionalism. To abandon confessionalism altogether, he says, tends towards "a theological rela-

tivism which is even worse," for such relativism "fails to take revelation seriously" and means a "radical corruption of Churchmanship."

At the Third Assembly of the World Council of Churches held in New Delhi, India, in 1961, a further step in the direction of doctrinal confession was taken. The Council is now said to represent a fellowship of Churches which confess the Lord Jesus Christ as God and Saviour according to the Scriptures and therefore seek to fulfill together their common calling to the glory of one God, Father, Son, and Holy Spirit. This amended description reflects not only adherence to Trinitarian doctrine but adherence to the Bible, while it allows for some degree of flexibility of interpretation in both respects. It is of interest to observe that the amendment was made at the same Council which welcomed as new members representatives of the Russian and other Eastern Orthodox churches as well as representatives of two Pentecostal churches. With reference to the latter an Anglican writer remarks, (a) that "the Pentecostal Churches are . . . the most rapidly growing Churches in the world" and (b) that "it is important to understand that, by and large, the Pentecostal Churches are creedally orthodox." (Canon Max Warren, *C.M.S. News-Letter*, London, Church Missionary Society, No. 254, November, 1962).

34. Nicholls, *Ecumenism and Catholicism*, p. 112.

35. I am indebted to Father Gustav Weigel, S.J., for information, in response to my inquiry, with reference to Bettenson's statement (in *Documents of the Christian Church*, p. 374) that the Tridentine Confession is "recited publicly by all bishops and beneficed clergy. It is the symbol imposed to this day on all converts to Roman Catholicism."

Father Weigel informs me that the Tridentine confession of faith is no longer required to be recited by converts to Catholicism. It is not used in the liturgy at all, and never has been. "However, it is demanded of all who go into orders and of all who will teach theology. In Catholic schools of theology the whole faculty will recite the confession in public at the beginning of every school year."

He adds that the exact status of the confession is not clear, according to Catholic theologians, although none of them would deny the orthodoxy of the statement.

36. Declaration on behalf of the Eastern Orthodox Church read

by the Metropolitan of Thyateira at the World Conference of Faith and Order, August 18, 1927, cited by G. K. A. Bell, *Documents on Christian Unity: a Selection from the First and Second Series 1920–30*, p. 184.

37. W. M. Horton, *Christian Theology: an Ecumenical Approach*, p. 64.

38. Bell, *Documents on Christian Unity*, pp. 46, 47; Report of a Joint Conference, May, 1922, of Anglican and Free Church Theologians.

39. Zaehner, ed., *The Concise Encyclopaedia of Living Faiths*, p. 16.

40. Robert McAfee Brown, *The Spirit of Protestantism*, pp. 216 ff.

41. Granted that there is also today an increasing regard for the "nontheological factors" which tend to promote ecclesiastical divisions, this same regard also promotes, in some quarters, a counter insistence on the demand for doctrinal statement. And there is general agreement that at least some minimal statement of doctrine is required as a basis of Christian community. It was, for example, the particular concern of one of the sections (of which I was a member) at the recent Oberlin (U.S.A.) Conference on Faith and Order to discuss such a minimal statement.

42. W. Nicholls, *Ecumenism and Catholicity*, p. 112. The term "relativism" is variously used by Christian writers, as indeed by others—so variously that a writer may be critical of relativism while himself expressing a standpoint which others might associate with relativism. Jacques Maritain, for example, while critical of intolerance and fanaticism, condemns "the error of the theorists who make relativism, ignorance, and doubt a necessary condition for mutual tolerance." But when he states what he himself regards as the necessary condition of mutual tolerance, he states a position which others might identify with relativism: "The more [a man] grasps truth, through science, philosophy, or faith, the more he feels what immensity remains to be grasped within this very truth. The more he knows God, either by reason or by faith, the more he understands that our concepts attain (through analogy) but do not circumscribe Him. . . . The more strong and deep faith becomes, the more man kneels down, not before his own alleged ignorance of truth, but before the inscrutable mystery of divine truth. . . ." (*On the Use of Philosophy* [Princeton, Princeton Uni-

versity Press, 1961], pp. 22 ff.) Such a statement recalls Toynbee's frequent approval of Symmachus' phrase, "The heart of so great a mystery . . . ," and Toynbee's comment that "Hinduism lives to speak for Symmachus today." But the position which Toynbee thus presents is the position I have described in these pages as one variant of relativism, as Toynbee himself (if I rightly understand him) would describe it. (Cf. Toynbee, *An Historian's Approach to Religion*, pp. 127 ff., 297 ff.)

43. Albert William Levi, *Philosophy in the Modern World* (Bloomington, Indiana University Press, 1959), p. 4.

44. *Ibid.*

45. *Westcott House Chronicle* (Cambridge, England), 1960.

CHAPTER VII. *"Depth Religion" and Western Dogmatism*

1. Cf. R. H. L. Slater, "Christian Attitudes to Other Religions," *Canadian Journal of Theology*, II (No. 4, October, 1956). In this article a comparison of Dr. Kraemer and Dr. Toynbee was accompanied by the comment that it is illuminating to consider not just the views and conclusions expressed by these two writers, but the way in which they arrived at these conclusions. I described depth religion as follows: "In particular we may observe the very general recognition of what we may term *depth religion*. By this term is meant the whole realm of reference which is indicated when a distinction is made between the language of faith and the language of theological or philosophical explanation; between the connotation of such terms as 'theo-centric' and 'theological'; between religions considered as systems of belief and religions considered and studied as total systems of life and faith most variously expressed. Both the Biblical realists and their liberal opponents make this same recognition, though in different ways." I added that the science of comparative religion today pointed in a similar direction, passing "beyond the language of intellectual interpretation to the poetic language of faith, to depth religion."

2. Kraemer's more recent book, *Religion and the Christian Faith*, is frequently regarded, by both his disciples and his critics, as essentially a repetition of the standpoint maintained in *The Christian Message*—no more—and, as such, a continuation of his attack on the liberal attitude to other religions. Dr. A. C. Bouquet, for example, who describes Kraemer as "the ablest and most learned

opponent of the more liberal attitude," says that in this second book Kraemer "renews his attack" on the liberal position (*The Christian Faith and Non-Christian Religions*, p. 398). With respect to some of his conclusions as to what other religions *teach*, Kraemer is open to this criticism. But Kraemer himself very definitely affirms his intention of qualifying the position maintained in his earlier book as he now concentrates on "the human religious consciousness, manifest in the many religions" and says that here there is evidence of a universal "drama between God and man" (*Religion and the Christian Faith*, pp. 6 ff.). He might, I think, say that the significance of what he has to say in this direction has not been sufficiently studied or appreciated either by his friends or by his critics.

In a brief criticism of H. H. Farmer, for whom he has considerable praise, Kraemer chides Farmer for "speaking so systematically about Christianity." It is a criticism which exhibits what is fundamental in Kraemer's own approach and it concludes significantly with the claim that recognition of the drama of the encounter of God and man, "silent, unconscious or conscious," "would deepen and mould differently the whole treatment of types of religion." (*Ibid.*, p. 220.)

In his recent book, *World Cultures and World Religions*, Kraemer writes of a coming dialogue with other religions in which Christians must be prepared to learn. But he still sees other religions as presenting a formidable challenge to a position which Christians must affirm without compromise and he is still critical of any presentation of the situation which, to his mind, would obscure the gravity of this challenge.

3. Arnold Toynbee, *A Study of History*, III (London, Oxford University Press, 1934), 235 ff.

4. Toynbee, *An Historian's Approach to Religion*, p. 122.

5. *Ibid.*, pp. 122, 123.

6. *Ibid.*, pp. 124 ff.

7. Kraemer, *Religion and the Christian Faith*, p. 145.

8. *Ibid.*, p. 440.

9. *Ibid.*, p. 245.

10. *Ibid.*, p. 299.

11. *Ibid.*, p. 220.

12. *Ibid.*, p. 257.

13. *Ibid.*, p. 333. Cf. p. 323. Wilhelm M. L. de Wette, a biblical

scholar who wrote in the first decades of the nineteenth century, appears to have been the first to use the word *ahnung* in the sense which Kraemer uses it. " 'Ahnung' meant a premonition, a presentiment, a discernment of the order of God prior to its conceptual expression" (John Dillenberger, *Protestant Thought and Natural Science,* p. 202).

14. Kraemer, *The Christian Message,* p. 136.

15. In his various writings (e.g., in the conclusion of *An Historian's Approach to Religion,* pp. 253, 299) Toynbee frequently recalls the statement of the pagan, Q. Aurelius Symmachus, in controversy with Saint Ambrose: "The heart of so great a mystery cannot ever be reached by following one road only."

16. Observing that Mahayana Buddhism and Christianity have "two intuitions in common . . . they both accept Suffering as an opportunity for acting on the promptings of Love and Pity," Toynbee speaks, in the same book, of the "Christian-Mahayanian way of life" (pp. 89, 90).

17. Kraemer, "The Encounter between East and West in the Civilization of Our Time," in *The Ecumenical Era in Church and Society,* ed. Edward J. Jurji, p. 99.

18. Paul Tillich, article in the *Saturday Evening Post,* June 14, 1958, quoted by Ira Progoff, *Depth Psychology and Modern Man,* p. 26. Cf. Tillich, *The Shaking of the Foundations* (New York, Charles Scribner's Sons, 1948), pp. 52 ff. Cf. also Joachim Wach, *The Comparative Study of Religions,* p. 42: "Man must experience himself and see himself in his relationship to Ultimate Reality in the *depth dimension* of this relationship." (Italics mine.)

19. H. H. Farmer, *Revelation and Religion,* p. 71.

20. Erwin R. Goodenough, *Towards a More Mature Faith* (New York, Prentice-Hall, 1955), p. 55. Cf. p. 51: "Our most important thinking is done by those parts of the mind of which we are not aware."

21. Mircea Eliade, *Birth and Rebirth,* pp. 128 ff.

22. *Ibid.,* pp. 134–35.

23. *Ibid.,* p. 128.

24. *Ibid.,* p. 135.

25. *Ibid.*

26. *Experiment in Depth,* pp. 264, 5 ff. Dr. Martin, a sociologist, threads together T. S. Eliot's theme of "timeless moments," Toynbee's theme of "withdrawal and return," and Jung's depth psychology, to suggest a breakthrough to "a different realm of being:

where the truth experienced is a deeper truth; where the love experienced is a deeper love; where the creative process is not a theory of what may be going on in the Universe, but an immediate experienced reality; where personality is not the scattered fragmentary ego-consciousness we know, but a living in depth, the direct discovery of the 'different spiritual dimension'" (p. 260).

27. *Ibid.*, p. 67.

28. Ira Progoff, *Depth Psychology and Modern Man*, pp. 265, 25 ff.

29. *Ibid.*, p. 277.

30. *Ibid.*, p. 101.

31. *Ibid.*, pp. 4 ff., 100 ff.

32. *Ibid.*, pp. 7, 8.

33. Ian T. Ramsey, *Religious Language*, pp. 20, 72. Cf. "situations which are perceptual with a difference" (p. 38).

34. *Ibid.*, p. 15.

35. D. T. Suzuki, *Mysticism: Christian and Buddhist.*

36. *Ibid.*, p. 70.

37. P. W. Martin, for example, describes "Jung, Eliot and Toynbee . . . men who have sought new vision in the depths" as "the spearpoints of a possibly creative minority" (*Experiment in Depth*, p. 15).

38. Friedrich Schleiermacher, *On Religion: Speeches to Its Cultured Despisers*, tr. John Oman (New York, Harper Torchbooks, 1959), pp. 41, 43.

39. *Ibid.*, p. 43.

40. *Ibid.*

41. S. Radhakrishnan, *Fellowship of the Spirit*, p. 9. Dr. Radhakrishnan describes religion as "life experienced in its depth" (p. 6).

42. Phil. 4:8.

43. Martin, *Experiment in Depth*, p. 67.

44. H. H. Farmer, *Revelation and Religion*, pp. 67 ff.

45. *Ibid.*, pp. 72, 73.

46. *Ibid.*, p. 15.

47. Progoff, *Depth Psychology and Modern Man*, p. 8.

48. Peter Munz, *Problems of Religious Knowledge.*

49. *Ibid.*, pp. 50 ff. Dr. Munz relates the symbol to what he describes as a "feeling state" and here, so to speak, he calls a halt. "The symbol picture is an end in itself" (p. 63). He questions the

widely accepted view that "the symbol *stands for* something that is symbolised." Hence, too, he rejects Professor Eliade's view that symbols are "hierophanies," i.e., visible signs or manifestations of transcendental facts (pp. 100, 101).

50. I was at first disposed to refer to Dr. Munz's statement as one which offers a philosophical explanation of the universal tendency towards a *qualified* relativism which I have traced in these chapters. Some, indeed, may accept it as such. But I am not attempting, in these pages, any such evaluation of the various writings which are here quoted. Keeping within the realm of description, I am content to refer to Dr. Munz's treatment of symbolism simply as one that exhibits sensitivity to issues raised by this subject which may affect religious attitudes relevant to prospects of world community.

51. Munz, *Problems of Religious Knowledge*, pp. 45 ff: "The positive picture of the world . . . drawn when one makes use of none but empirically verifiable observation . . . the picture . . . inferred from natural observation . . . observing what happens in space and time."

52. *Ibid.*, pp. 22, 50 ff.

53. *Ibid.*, p. 72 (for example).

54. *Ibid.*, pp. 50 ff. I find it hard to follow Dr. Munz's presentation of the relation of the symbol to "feeling states" ("the way in which one is . . . the mode of one's existence . . . the way in which we feel ourselves to be"). But in so far as he does relate symbols to these feeling states (cf. p. 56), while at the same time emphasizing "the tenuous—almost ghostly" character of such feeling states (p. 51), of which "we are aware . . . only aware when they are symbolized," he may be said to be referring us to the depths defined in much the same sense as the term "depth" is used by some of the other writers we have noted. We may also note his statement that symbols amount to something more than "an emotional projection" (p. 56).

55. *Ibid.*, pp. 54 ff.

56. *Ibid.*, p. 65.

57. *Ibid.*, pp. 237 ff.

58. *Ibid.*, p. 65.

59. R. R. Marett, *Threshold of Religion* (London, Methuen, 1914), p. xxxi.

60. Munz, *Problems of Religious Knowledge*, p. 131.

61. *Ibid.*, pp. 190 ff.

62. *Ibid.*, pp. 10, 174 ff.

63. *Ibid.*, p. 126; cf. p. 181 ("a symbol is a thing . . . something like a chair"); pp. 118 ff., 125.

64. *Ibid.*, p. 118.

65. *Ibid.*, pp. 125 ff.

66. *Ibid.*, pp. 176 ff.

67. *Ibid.*, p. 178.

68. Martin, *Experiment in Depth*, p. 224.

69. *Ibid.*, p. 232.

70. Progoff, *Depth Psychology and Modern Man*, p. 17.

71. Dr. Kraemer allows for such affinity when he emphasizes the biblical approach "exclusively concerned with . . . what happens in the depths between God . . . and man" (*Religion and the Christian Faith*, p. 299) and points to the universal "religious consciousness as the place of dialectic encounter with God" (*ibid.*, p. 8).

72. Progoff, *Depth Psychology and Modern Man*, pp. 263 ff.

CHAPTER VIII. *Religion and World Community*

1. Even if we accept Dr. Munz's view that the symbol should *not* be regarded as standing for something which is beyond the symbol itself (transcends it), the symbol, in Dr. Munz's account, may be regarded as transcending ideas and propositional statements. The symbol transcends doctrinal statements in a way which makes for tolerant relativism because of the pregnant character and flexibility of the symbol.

2. F. W. Faber, Hymn 499, *English Hymnal.*

3. A. C. Bouquet, *The Christian Faith and Non-Christian Religions*, p. 365.

4. With reference to W. E. Hocking, cf. Father John Courtney Murray's argument (citing Pope Pius XII) in *We Hold These Truths: Catholic Reflections on the American Proposition*, pp. 61 ff.

5. Leo Baeck in *The Essence of Judaism* pp. 69 ff.) affirms, not only that "Judaism has never abandoned its claim to be the world religion," but that "Christianity and Mohammedanism . . . are world religions insofar as they are derived from Judaism." It was, he says, Judaism which "produced . . . the idea of mission . . .

Judaism was the first religion to organize missions" (pp. 77, 78). Referring to the covenant which God made through Noah with all mankind as earlier than the covenant between God and the patriarchs, Dr. Baeck adds that various factors have made it "possible for the ignorant and easy for the malicious to deny the universal character of Judaism" (p. 71). The "so-called national particularism" of the Jewish religion has been misconstrued. But, rightly interpreted, it is compatible with the conception of mission which is implicit in the idea of election. Dr. Baeck quotes the promise to Abraham in Genesis 12:3 ("In thee shall all the families of the earth be blessed") and claims that "the pious tradition" has always presented Abraham as "the father of salvation to all men." He concludes, however, that the consciousness of mission in Judaism "does not mean that the belief of all men will be uniform" (p. 80). In spite of his insistence on the missionary character of Judaism, Dr. Baeck's statement is more in keeping with Professor Hocking's idea of reconception than with the idea of displacement. The same may be said with regard to the comparable statement by Dr. Rivkin that the meaning which may be discerned in the "manifestations of Judaism" inspires the faith that the truth thus made known will ultimately "prevail for all minkind." (See *Modern Trends in World Religions*, ed. Kitagawa, pp. 92, 93.) In similar vein Dr. Leon Roth, professor of philosophy at the University of Jerusalem for thirty years, refers to the Jewish virtue ("which some may call a vice") of world-mindedness: "Judaism can no more rid itself of its vision of the corporate unity of all men than of its story of all men's one ancestry and all things' one creator. . . . Jews have been said to have too close a sense of community. But they have never failed too to keep a watchful heart alive to the call of *inter*community" (*Judaism, a Portrait* [New York, The Viking Press, 1961], pp. 212, 213).

6. One of the most remarkable features of religious life in Japan in the last thirty years has been the phenomenon of "new religions." According to a survey made in 1957, twenty-seven new religious groups were organized in Japan after the Second World War under such names as Great-Wisdom Society, To-Tie-God-with-Man Teaching, World Messianic Teaching, Thinking of Parents Society, Pray-Teaching-True System, Ancient Gods' Way-System, and Perfect-Liberty Association. (See William Woodward, "Japan's New Religions," *Japan Harvest* [Tokyo], V, Winter, 1957. The

term "new religion" is also used with reference to sects organized before the Second World War, including the flourishing Tenrikyo religion (Religion of Heavenly Wisdom), dating from the middle of the nineteenth century, which affirms belief in a Creator-God. It is also used to refer to what were known as the Shinto sects in prewar days, as also to some splinter Buddhist groups. Some estimates refer to well over a hundred such "new religions." (See Raymond Hammer, *Japan's Religious Ferment* [London and New York, Oxford University Press, 1962], p. 136.)

7. Cf. Meynck H. Carré, ed., *De Veritate by Edward, Lord Herbert of Cherbury*, quoted by Horton Davies, *Worship and Theology in England* (Princeton, Princeton University Press, 1961), p. 95 and footnote.

8. W. E. Hocking, *The Coming World Civilization*, p. 51. In his Hibbert Lectures, *Living Religions and a World Faith*, Professor Hocking sees new occasion for reconception in the new meeting of religions which is taking place today (pp. 190 ff.). He refers to "a new era of broadening" in which each religion tends to "extend its base" and comprise what is regarded as valid in other traditions. Such broadening of interest, he observes, involves "deepening," for we are stimulated in this way to understand our own religion better. By this better understanding or reconception he means a better appreciation of what pertains to the "essence" of our religion or "the generating principle of religious life and of each particular form of it." While the reference in my chapter is mainly to his more recent book, *The Coming World Civilization*, since it is here that he relates his theory of reconception more particularly to prospects of world community, this thought is not absent from his earlier statement.

9. Hocking, *The Coming World Civilization*, p. 47.

10. *Ibid.*, p. 6. Referring to modern attempts to found secular states which reject religion, Professor Hocking argues that such experiments have shown that with "the clean excision of religion something *politically* essential has been lost" (p. 6). He refers to "faltering in fields in which the state is expected to act," such as those of law and order, education, and social care. We are finding, he says, that "the state by itself can do none of these things"; "the state alone cannot civilize" (p. 15).

11. *Ibid.*, p. 162: "Indeed, in so far as the world faith for the arriving civilization must be a mature faith, finding its way to a

natural union of the natural and the supernatural, it is possible to say that this religion under whatever name will necessarily be in substance Christian." In ch. IV, Professor Hocking discusses the qualifications of Christianity, in the light of its history and essential character, to "take a certain leadership" in promoting universal religion. Much that he says recalls the earlier views of Max Müller that Christianity is specially qualified, e.g., "religion, and *especially* the Christian religion, is committed to the thesis that the will of God is to be done in this world" (p. 122; italics mine). It is true that Professor Hocking may seem at times to reduce Christianity to a version of "natural religion," as when he says that "the faith of the Christian is continuous with the nature faith by which all men live" (p. 113). Perhaps his view is summarized in the statement which follows, a statement which is emphasized: the Christian faith "is the making-fully-explicit of this universal faith," a view comparable with that of the Anglican theologian, Frederick Denison Maurice. "I often think," writes Professor Hocking in his earlier book, *Living Religions and a World Faith* (p. 187), "of what C. F. Andrews said on one occasion in answer to a crudely direct question of mine—whether he had been engaged in trying to convert Indians to Christianity. . . . 'I always assume,' he said, 'that they *are* Christians.' "

12. Hocking, *The Coming World Civilization*, p. 149.

13. *Ibid.*, p. 161.

14. Dr. Conze revives the discussion of the possible influence of Christianity on Buddhist Mahayana thought in his treatment of Mahayana Buddhism in the *Concise Encyclopaedia of Living Faiths,* ed. R. C. Zaehner, p. 296.

15. Swami Ranganathananda, *The Christ We Adore* (The Ramakrishna Mission Institute of Culture, Calcutta n.d.), Transaction 14. The Swami writes that he "views with hope the future of Indian Christianity" as he sees the possibility of Indian culture ("the spirit of India") liberating Christians from what is "tribal" and "dogmatic." "It is our earnest hope that the Christian message passing through Christian experience will bear in its look a new charm and form of tolerance, and gentleness, peace and fellowship, capturing thus the Master's spirit in full."

16. E.g., U Chan Htoon, speech in support of the Union of Burma, "Buddha Sasana Council Act," October 3, 1950, quoted in *The Light of the Dhamma,* I, 33: "People may profess any

religion they like, but if their moral conduct is such as is in conformity with the principles of Buddha's Teachings . . . then there will be everlasting peace in the world. That was our belief. It does not mean that one must profess Buddhism to conform to Buddhist principles. A man of any creed can live according to these principles. As a matter of fact the Buddhist code of moral conduct does not transgress the tenets of any other religion."

17. See above, ch. VI, note 29; A. C. Bouquet, *The Christian Faith and Non-Christian Religions*, p. 424.

18. Hocking, *The Coming World Civilization*, p. 154 (italics mine).

19. John Courtney Murray, S.J., *We Hold These Truths*.

20. *Ibid.*, p. 61.

21. *Ibid.*, p. 212.

22. *Ibid.*, pp. 22 ff. Father Murray describes the four groups—Protestant, Catholic, Jewish, secularist—as constituting four "conspiracies" in the original Latin sense of the word conspiracy ("unison, concord, unanimity in opinion and feeling," "a breathing together").

23. *Ibid.*, pp. 30 ff.

24. *Ibid.*, p. 75.

25. *Ibid.*, p. 24.

26. W. H. Hocking, *The Coming World Civilization*, p. 151.

27. See above, ch. II, note 22.

28. Max Müller, *Chips from a German Workshop*, I, xx.

Selected Bibliography

(WORKS AVAILABLE IN ENGLISH)

I. SCRIPTURES

GENERAL

Ballou, Robert O. The Bible of the World. New York, Viking, 1939.

Bouquet, A. C. Sacred Books of the World. London, Penguin Books, 1954.

Braden, Charles S. The Scriptures of Mankind. New York, Macmillan, 1952.

Browne, Lewis. The World's Great Scriptures. New York, Macmillan, 1946.

Max Müller, Friedrich, ed. The Sacred Books of the East. 50 vols. Oxford, Clarendon Press, 1879–1910.

HINDUISM

Edgerton, Franklin. The Bhagavad Gita, tr. and interpreted, in Harvard Oriental Series, ed. W. E. Clark. Vols. 38, 39. Cambridge, Harvard University Press, 1944.

Hume, R. A., tr. Thirteen Principal Upanishads. London, Oxford University Press, 1921.

Lin Yutang, ed. The Wisdom of China and India. New York, Random House, 1942.

MacNichol, Nichol, ed. Hindu Scripture. London, J. M. Dent, 1938.

Max Müller, Friedrich. The Sacred Books of the East. Hinduism, 21 vols. Oxford, Clarendon Press, 1879–1910.

Radhakrishnan, S. The Bhagavadgita. London, Allen and Unwin, 1948.

———, and Charles A. Moore, ed. A Source Book of Indian Philosophy. Princeton, Princeton University Press, 1957.

Renou, Louis, ed. Hinduism. New York, Braziller, 1961.

BUDDHISM

Burtt, E. A., ed. The Teachings of the Compassionate Buddha. New York, New American Library, 1955.

Conze, Edward, ed. Buddhist Texts through the Ages. London, Faber, 1954.

Gard, Richard. Buddhism. New York, Braziller, 1961.

Hamilton, Clarence H., ed. Buddhism: a Religion of Infinite Compassion. New York, Liberal Arts Press, 1952.

Max Müller, Friedrich, ed. The Sacred Books of the East. Buddhism, 19 vols. Oxford, Clarendon Press.

Warren, Henry Clarke, ed. Buddhism in Translations. Cambridge, Harvard University Press, 1953.

Yamamoto, Kosho, *et al.* The Shin-shu Seiten: the Holy Scriptures of Shinshu. Honolulu, the Honpa Hongwanji Mission of Hawaii, 1955.

ISLAM

Arberry, A. J. The Koran Interpreted. 2 vols. London, Allen and Unwin, 1955.

Pickthall, M. Marmaduke. The Meaning of the Glorious Koran. New York, Alfred A. Knopf, 1930; New American Library, 1953.

Rodwell, J. M., tr. The Koran. London, J. M. Dent, 1915.

Williams, John Alden. Islam. New York, Braziller, 1961.

JUDAISM

The Bible. Old Testament (see under CHRISTIANITY).

Cohen, Abram. Everyman's Talmud. London, J. M. Dent, 1937.

Goldin, Judah. The Living Talmud: the Wisdom of the Fathers and Its Classical Commentaries. Chicago, and New York, University of Chicago Press and New American Library of World Literature, 1957.

CHRISTIANITY

The Bible. Revised Standard Version. New York, Nelson.

The New English Bible. Oxford University Press, Cambridge University Press.

II. ENCYCLOPAEDIAS

Catholic Encyclopaedia. 17 vols. New York, Appleton, 1907–22.

Ferm, Vergilius. Encyclopaedia of Religion. New York, Philosophical Library, 1945.

Hastings, James, ed. Encyclopaedia of Religion and Ethics. 13 vols. New York, Scribner's, 1913–22.

Jewish Encyclopaedia. 12 vols. New York and London, Funk and Wagnalls, 1901–6.

Malalasekera, G. P. Encyclopaedia of Buddhism. Colombo, Government of Ceylon, 1961.

Matthews, Shailer, and G. B. Smith. Dictionary of Religion and Ethics. New York, Macmillan, 1921.

Zaehner, R. C., ed. The Concise Encyclopaedia of Living Faiths. Hawthornden, 1960.

III. SUPPLEMENTARY READING

Abrecht, Paul. The Churches and Rapid Social Change. New York, Doubleday, 1961.

Andrae, Tor. Mohammed: the Man and His Faith. London, Allen and Unwin, 1936.

Andrews, C. F. Mahatma Gandhi's Ideas. New York, Macmillan, 1930.

Ashby, Philip H. The Conflict of Religions. New York, Scribner's, 1955.

Aurobindo, Sri. Essays on the Gita. Calcutta, Arya Publishing House, 1928.

—— The Life Divine. 2 vols. 2d ed. Calcutta, Arya Publishing House, 1943–44.

Baeck, Leo. The Essence of Judaism, ed. Irving Howe. New York, Schocken Books, 1948. Rev. ed. based on trans. by Victor Grubenwieser and Leonard Pearl (London, Macmillan, 1936).

Basham, A. L. The Wonder that Was India. London, Sidgwick and Jackson, 1954.

—— "Hinduism," in Concise Encyclopaedia of Living Faiths, ed. R. C. Zaehner. New York, Hawthornden, 1960.

Bell, G. K. A., ed. Documents on Christian Unity: a Selection from the First and Second Series, 1920–30. London, Oxford, 1955.

Bendix, Reinhard. Max Weber: an Intellectual Portrait. New York, Doubleday, 1960.

Bouquet, A. C. The Christian Faith and Non-Christian Religions. New York, Harper, 1958.

—— Comparative Religion. London, Penguin, 1942.

Brown, Robert McAfee. The Spirit of Protestantism. New York, Oxford, 1961.

Browne, Laurence E. The Prospects of Islam. London, S.C.M. Press, 1944.

Buber, Martin. Two Types of Faith, tr. Norman P. Goldhawk. New York, Macmillan, 1951, and Harper Torchbook, 1961.

Burnouf, Emile. La Science des religions. 3d ed. Paris, Maisonneuve et Cie, 1876.

Cragg, K. The Call of the Minaret. New York, Oxford University Press, 1956.

Dasgupta, Surendranath. A History of Indian Philosophy. 5 vols. Cambridge, Cambridge University Press, 1933–55.

D'Arcy, M. C. Catholicism. London, Clonmore, 1955.

Dawson, Christopher. The Historic Reality of Western Culture. New York, Harper, 1960.

de Vries, Egbert. Man in Rapid Social Change. New York, Doubleday (for World Council of Churches), 1961.

Devanandan, Paul David. "Renascent Religions and Religion," in The Ecumenical Era in Church and Society, ed. Edward J. Jurji.

Dewick, E. C. The Indwelling God. Oxford, Oxford University Press, 1938.

Dillenberger, John. Protestant Thought and Natural Science. New York, Doubleday, 1960.

——, and C. Welch. Protestant Christianity. New York, Scribner's, 1955.

Duméry, Henry. Phénoménologie et Religion. Paris, Presses Universitaires de France, 1958.

Edgerton, Franklin. The Bhagavad Gita or Song of the Blessed One. Chicago, Open Court, 1925.

Eliade, Mircea. The Sacred and the Profane: the Nature of Religion, tr. Willard R. Trask. New York, Harcourt, Brace, 1957.

—— Yoga: Immortality and Freedom, tr. Willard R. Trask. New York, Pantheon, 1958.

—— Birth and Rebirth, tr. Willard R. Trask. New York, Harper, 1958.

—— The Myth of the Eternal Return, tr. Willard R. Trask. New York, Pantheon Books, 1954. Reprint under title Cosmos and History: the Myth of the Eternal Return. New York, Harper Torchbook, 1959.

—— Myths, Dreams and Mysteries: the Encounter between Contemporary Faiths and Archaic Realities, tr. Philip Mairet. New York, Harper, 1960.

——, and J. M. Kitagawa, ed. The History of Religions. Chicago, University of Chicago Press, 1959.

Epstein, Isidore. The Faith of Judaism: an Interpretation for Our Times. London, Soncino, 1954.

Farmer, H. H. Revelation and Religion: Studies in the Theological Interpretation of Religious Types. London, Nisbet, 1954.

Farquhar, J. N. Modern Religious Movements in India. London, Macmillan, 1929.

Finkelstein, Louis. The Beliefs and Practices of Judaism. New York, Devin-Adair, 1941.

——, ed. The Jews: Their History, Culture and Religion. New York, Harper, 1950.

Gibb, H. A. R. Mohammedanism. 2d ed. London, Oxford, 1953; New York, New American Library, 1955.

—— Modern Trends in Islam. Oxford, Oxford University Press, 1947.

—— "Islam," in Concise Encyclopaedia of Living Faiths, ed. R. C. Zaehner.

Goodenough, Erwin R. Towards a Mature Faith. New York, Prentice Hall, 1955; reprint, Yale University Press, 1960.

—— "Religionswissenschaft," in ACLS Newsletter, Vol. I, Number 6. New York, American Council of Learned Societies, 1959.

Heiler, Friedrich. "The History of Religions as a Way to Unity of Religions," in Proceedings of the IXth International Congress for the History of Religions. Tokyo, 1960.

Herberg, Will. Protestant, Catholic and Jew. New York, Doubleday, 1955.

Hiriyanna, M. The Essentials of Indian Philosophy. London, Allen and Unwin, 1949.

—— Popular Essays in Indian Philosophy. Mysore, Karyalaya, 1952.

Hiriyanna, M. The Quest after Perfection. Mysore, Karyalaya, 1952.

Hocking, William Ernest. Living Religions and a World Faith. London, Allen and Unwin, 1940.

—— The Coming World Civilization. New York, Harper, 1956.

Horton, Walter Marshall. Christian Theology: an Ecumenical Approach. New York, Harper, 1955.

Hume, Robert E. The World's Living Religions. Rev. ed. New York, Scribner's, 1959.

Humphreys, Christmas. Buddhism. London, Penguin, 1951.

Hutchison, John A., and James A. Martin. Ways of Faith. 2d ed. New York, Ronald Press, 1953.

Jaeger, Werner. Early Christianity and Greek Paideia. Cambridge, Harvard University Press, 1961.

James, E. O. Comparative Religion: an Introductory and Historical Survey. London, Methuen, 1938; New York, Barnes and Noble, 1961.

Jurji, Edward J., ed. The Ecumenical Era in Church and Society. New York, Macmillan, 1959.

Kitagawa, Joseph M., ed. Modern Trends in World Religions. La Salle, Open Court, 1959.

—— Religions of the East. Philadelphia, Westminster, 1960.

——, and Mircea Eliade, eds. The History of Religions. Chicago, University of Chicago Press, 1959.

Kohn, Hans. The Age of Nationalism. New York, Harper, 1962.

Kraemer, Hendrik. The Christian Message in a Non-Christian World. Grand Rapids, Kregel, 1938.

—— Religion and the Christian Faith. London, Lutterworth, 1956.

—— "The Encounter between East and West in the Civilization of our Time," in The Ecumenical Era in Church and Society, ed. Edward J. Jurji.

—— World Cultures and World Religions. Philadelphia, Westminster, 1960.

Kubler, George. The Shape of Time: Remarks on the History of Things. New Haven, Yale University Press, 1962.

Littell, Franklin Hamlin. From State Church to Pluralism: a Protestant Interpretation of Religion in American History. New York, Doubleday, 1962.

MacNichol, Nichol. The Living Religions of the Indian People. Calcutta, Y.M.C.A., 1934.

Malalasekera, G. P., and K. N. Jayatilleke. Buddhism and the Race Question. Paris, UNESCO, 1958.

Martin, James Alfred, Jr., *see* Hutchison, John A.

Martin, P. W. Experiment in Depth. London and New York, Routledge and Kegan Paul and Pantheon Books, Inc., 1955.

Martindale, C. C. The Faith of the Roman Church. London, Methuen, 1927.

May, Rollo, ed. Symbolism in Religion and Literature. New York, Braziller, 1961.

Moore, George Foot. Judaism in the First Centuries of the Christian Era. 3 vols. Cambridge, Harvard University Press, 1927–30.

Morgan, Kenneth W., ed. The Religion of the Hindus. New York, Ronald Press, 1953.

———, ed. The Path of the Buddha: Buddhism Interpreted by Buddhists. New York, Ronald Press, 1956.

———, ed. Islam—the Straight Path: Islam Interpreted by Muslims. New York, Ronald Press, 1958.

Max Müller, Friedrich. Chips from a German Workshop. Vol. I, 2d ed. London, Longmans, Green, 1868.

——— Chips from a German Workshop. Vol. IV. London, Longmans, Green, 1875.

——— Lectures on the Science of Religion. New York, Scribner's, 1872.

Munz, Peter. Problems of Religious Knowledge. London, S.C.M. Press, 1959.

Murray, John Courtney, S.J. We Hold These Truths: Catholic Reflections on the American Proposition. New York, Sheed and Ward, 1960.

Murti, T. R. V. The Central Philosophy of Buddhism. London, Allen and Unwin, 1955.

Nakamura, Hajime. Ways of Eastern Thinking, compiled by Japanese National Commission for UNESCO. Tokyo, Printing Bureau, Japanese Government, 1960.

Neill, Stephen. Christian Faith and Other Faiths. London, Oxford, 1961.

———, *see also* Rouse, R.

Niebuhr, H. Richard. Christ and Culture. New York, Harper, 1951.

Niebuhr, Reinhold. The Structure of Nations. New York, Scribner's, 1959.

Northrop, F. S. C. The Meeting of East and West. New York, Macmillan, 1946; paperback ed., 1960.

Otto, Rudolph. Christianity and the Indian Religion of Grace. Madras, Christian Literature Society of India, 1929.

—— Mysticism, East and West. New York, Macmillan, 1932; Meridian Books, 1957.

Pratt, J. B. The Pilgrimage of Buddhism. New York, 1928.

Progoff, Ira. Depth Psychology and Modern Man. New York, Julian Press, 1959.

Radhakrishnan, S. Indian Philosophy. London, Allen and Unwin, 1923.

—— East and West in Religion. London, Allen and Unwin, 1954.

—— The Hindu View of Life. London, Allen and Unwin, 1957.

—— Fellowship of the Spirit. Cambridge, Center for the Study of World Religions, 1960.

Ramsey, Ian T. Religious Language. London, S.C.M. Press, 1957.

Robinson, Richard H. "Buddhism in China and Japan," in Concise Encyclopaedia of Living Faiths, ed. R. C. Zaehner.

Rouse, R., and S. C. Neill. A History of the Ecumenical Movement, London, S.P.C.K., 1954.

Scholem, Gershom G. Major Trends in Jewish Mysticism. 3d ed. London, Thames and Hudson, 1956.

Slater, Robert Lawson. Paradox and Nirvana. Chicago, Chicago University Press, 1951.

—— "Modern Trends in Theravada Buddhism," in Modern Trends in World Religions, ed. J. M. Kitagawa.

Smart, Ninian. A Dialogue of Religions. London, S.C.M. Press, 1960.

—— Reasons and Faiths. London, Routledge and Kegan Paul, 1958.

Smith, Wilfred Cantwell. Islam in Modern History. Princeton, Princeton University Press, 1957.

—— Modern Islam in India, Lahore, Minerva, 1943.

—— "Comparative Religion: Whither and Why?" in The History of Religions, ed. M. Eliade and J. M. Kitagawa. Chicago, Chicago University Press, 1959.

Stace, W. T. Mysticism and Philosophy. Philadelphia, Lippincott, 1960.

Suzuki, D. T. Mysticism: Christian and Buddhist. New York, Harper, 1957.

Thomas, Edward J. The History of Buddhist Thought. New York, Knopf, 1933.

—— The Life of Buddha as Legend and History. 3d ed. London, Routledge and Kegan Paul, 1949.

Toynbee, Arnold. An Historian's Approach to Religion. London, Oxford University Press, 1956.

—— Christianity among the Religions of the World. New York, Scribner's, 1957.

Turner, H. E. W. The Pattern of Christian Truth: a Study in the Relation between Orthodoxy and Heresy in the Early Church. London, Mowbray, 1954.

Van der Leeuw, Gerardus. Religion in Essence and Manifestation: a Study in Phenomenology, tr. J. E. Turner. London, Allen and Unwin, 1938; New York, Harper Torchbook, 1963.

Wach, Joachim. The Comparative Study of Religions, ed. Joseph M. Kitagawa. New York, Columbia University Press, 1958.

—— Types of Religious Experience. Chicago, University of Chicago Press, 1951.

Weber, Max. The Religion of India: the Sociology of Hinduism and Buddhism. Glencoe, Free Press, 1958.

Welch, C., see Dillenberger, John.

Werblowski, R. J. Zwi. "Judaism, or the Religion of Israel," in Concise Encyclopaedia of Living Faiths, ed. R. C. Zaehner.

Zaehner, R. C. At Sundry Times. London, Faber, 1958.

—— "Introduction," in Concise Encyclopaedia of Living Faiths, ed. Zaehner.

Index